VARIETIES OF
SOCIAL EXPLANATION

VARIETIES OF SOCIAL EXPLANATION

An Introduction to the Philosophy of Social Science

DANIEL LITTLE
Colgate University

Westview Press
BOULDER • SAN FRANCISCO • OXFORD

Copyright © 1991 by Westview Press, Inc.

Published in 1991 in the United States of America by Westview Press, Inc., 5500 Central Avenue, Boulder, Colorado 80301, and in the United Kingdom by Westview Press, 36 Lonsdale Road, Summertown, Oxford OX2 7EW

Library of Congress Cataloging-in-Publication Data
Little, Daniel.
   Varieties of social explanation: an introduction to the
   philosophy of social science / Daniel Little.
      p. cm.
   ISBN 0-8133-0565-9.—ISBN 0-8133-0566-7 (pbk.)
   1. Social sciences—Methodology.   2. Social sciences—Philosophy.
I. Title.
H61.L58   1991
300′.1—dc20   90-43602
                                                                                          CIP

Printed and bound in the United States of America

The paper used in this publication meets the requirements
of the American National Standard for Permanence of Paper
for Printed Library Materials Z39.48-1984.

10   9   8   7   6   5   4

CONTENTS

PART II
VARIATIONS AND ELABORATIONS

EXAMPLES

FIGURES

ACKNOWLEDGMENTS

Friends and colleagues have provided useful criticism and stimulation at each stage. Colgate colleagues Jerome Balmuth, Maude Clark, and Jeffrey Poland encouraged me in the early phases of composition. Extensive comments received from Kenneth Winkler and Owen Flanagan in the later stages were an indispensable help in my final revisions. CFIA colleague Robert Powell offered valuable criticisms of some of the more formal material in the book. Spencer Carr's careful and detailed reading of the manuscript redefined my conception of what a good editor can do for a book. And students in courses in the philosophy of social science at Colgate University and Wellesley College allowed me to calibrate my expectations and gave me a better appreciation of the issues.

I am grateful for research support from several institutions as I composed this book. A research grant from the National Science Foundation program in the history and philosophy of science supported work on the first version of the manuscript. Funds provided by Colgate University's Research Council and Humanities Development Fund supported travel to conferences and research costs throughout. Research supported by the Social Science Research Council/MacArthur Foundation program in international peace and security has also found its way into this volume. And the Center for International Affairs at Harvard University provided a stimulating environment in which to complete the final version of the book. Joan W. Sherman meticulously copyedited the manuscript.

Daniel Little

1

INTRODUCTION

The social sciences today are witnessing a period of robust activity. Political scientists are deepening our understanding of the processes of cooperation and competition among nations, anthropologists are developing new tools for understanding the phenomena of culture—our own as well as that of others, historians are shedding new empirical and explanatory light on the past, and so on among the human sciences. Yet for the student of the social sciences—and perhaps for the practitioners themselves—one of the results of this growth is a sense of methodological cacophony. The issues and methods that are fundamental for one science are unknown to another; complex, many-sided disputes in one field are seen as arcane and pointless in another. Important questions arise. In what sense are the human sciences *scientific*? In what ways do they share empirical methods and explanatory paradigms? Is it possible to identify a coherent framework of assumptions about method, evidence, and explanation that underlies the practice of diverse social sciences?

In the strict sense the answer to this last question is no. There is virtually nothing in common between, for example, the thick descriptions of Balinese practices offered by Clifford Geertz and the causal analysis of English demographic change offered by Roger Schofield. However, in a looser sense there is room for some confidence that a degree of unification may exist— not around a single unified method of social inquiry but around a cluster of explanatory models and empirical methods employed in a wide range of social sciences today. Many social sciences offer causal explanations of social phenomena, for example; therefore it is important to clarify the main elements of the notion of social causation. Many social sciences premise their explanations on assumptions concerning the nature of human *agency*— both rational choice explanations and hermeneutic interpretations. Structural and functional explanations likewise play a role in a variety of social sciences, and issues concerning the microfoundations of macrophenomena crop up again and again in political science, economics, and sociology.

So there is a cluster of topics in the theory of explanation that together permit us to understand a wide range of social science research programs. The aim of this book is to examine the logical features of many of these topics. The level of detail is important. I have tried to avoid highly technical issues in order to make the discussion accessible to a wide audience. At

1

the same time I have striven for philosophical adequacy—to provide an account of these issues that is sufficiently nuanced to avoid traditional pitfalls and to shed light on current social science practice.

This book is organized around a large number of concrete examples of current social-scientific research. It contains discussion of social science explanations drawn from anthropology, geography, demography, political science, economics, and sociology; it also discusses social phenomena ranging from Asian peasant societies to patterns of residential segregation in industrialized societies. I have taken this approach because I believe that the philosophy of social science must work in close proximity to the actual problems of research and explanation in particular areas of social science, and it must formulate its questions in a way that permits different answers in different cases. Before we can make significant progress on the most general issues, it is necessary to develop a much more detailed conception of the actual models, explanations, debates, methods, etc., in contemporary social science. And we will need to develop a deeper recognition of the important degree of diversity found among these examples. I will therefore approach the general problems of the philosophy of social science from below, through examination of particular examples of social-scientific explanation. Close study of some of this diverse material will indicate that there is no single unified social science but rather a plurality of "sciences" making use of different explanatory paradigms and different conceptual systems and motivated by different research goals. Instead of a unity of science, a plurality of sciences will emerge.

In this view of the philosophy of social science, philosophers stand on the boundary between empirical research and purely philosophical analysis. Their aim is both to deepen our philosophical understanding of the social sciences through careful consideration of concrete research and theorizing and to provide the basis for progress in the area of science under consideration through careful analysis and development of the central theoretical ideas. Philosophers can learn about the logical structure and variety of social sciences only by considering specific examples in detail—thereby contributing to a more comprehensive theory of science that is genuinely applicable to social science. But at the same time philosophers can contribute to ongoing theoretical controversies in specific areas of research by clarifying the issues, by offering the results of other areas of philosophy (for example, rational choice and collective choice theory), by suggesting alternative ways of characterizing the theoretical issues, etc.[1]

PLAN OF THE BOOK

The chapters that follow are organized into three parts. Part I introduces three important ideas about the character of social explanation: that it requires identifying causes, that it flows from analysis of the decisionmaking of rational agents, and that it requires interpretation of culturally specific norms, values, and worldviews. These three ideas underlie much current social explanation, and they provide the basis for many of the debates that arise in the philosophy of social science.

Part II turns to elaborations and combinations of these basic models of explanation. Functional and structural explanations are sometimes thought to be distinctive types of explanation, but Chapter 5 argues that each depends on causal explanation of social phenomena. Materialist explanation (Marxism and related theories) is sometimes believed to be an autonomous form of explanation as well, but Chapter 6 suggests that this model of analysis actually depends on both rational choice and causal explanations. Economic anthropology, discussed in Chapter 7, attempts to explain features of social behavior and organization of premodern societies on the basis of rational choice models; much of the debate in this field follows from the contrast between rational choice and interpretive explanations described in Part I. And statistical explanations, common in many areas of social science, are sometimes held to be more rigorous than other forms of explanation. Chapter 8 presents the central ideas of statistical explanation and concludes that it is in fact a form of causal explanation.

Part III turns to several general problems in the philosophy of social science that arise throughout the first two parts. Chapter 9 considers the topic of methodological individualism, Chapter 10 turns to the topic of cultural relativism, and Chapter 11 concludes with a discussion of the doctrine of naturalism as a methodology for social science.

Each chapter contains a number of examples of social science explanation. These examples are chosen to illustrate various aspects of such explanation and to give the reader a more concrete understanding of social science research. They have been separated from the text so that the reader can refer to them more conveniently.

SCIENTIFIC EXPLANATION

The main topic of this book is the nature of social explanation. But we need to pose one question before we can proceed to the details: What is a scientific explanation? Let us refer to the event or pattern to be explained as the *explanandum;* the circumstances that are believed to explain the event may be referred to as the *explanans*. (See Figure 1.1.) What is the relation between explanans and explanandum in a good explanation?

The topic of scientific explanation encompasses several different questions. What is the purpose of a scientific explanation? What is the logical form of an explanation? What are the pragmatic requirements of explanation? What are the criteria of adequacy of an explanation? And what role do general laws play in scientific explanations?

Explanans

Explanandum

Fig. 1.1   Logic of explanation

"Why" questions

Explanation usually involves an answer to a question. Why did the American Civil War occur? Why are two-party democracies more common than multiple-party democracies? Why is collectivized agriculture inefficient? How does the state within a capitalist democracy manage to contain class conflict? These questions may be divided into several different categories. Some may be paraphrased as "why-necessary" questions, and others may be described as "how-possible" questions. Consider the "why-necessary" question. Here the problem is to show that an event, regularity, or process is necessary or predictable in the circumstances—that is, to identify the initial conditions and causal processes that determined that the explanandum occurred. Here we are attempting to identify the sufficient conditions that produced the explanandum. This description is overly deterministic, however; in many cases the most that we can say is that the circumstances described in the explanans *increased the probability* of the occurrence of the explanandum.

Answers to "why" questions commonly take the form of causal explanations—explanations in which we identify the cause of a given outcome. But there are other possibilities as well for a "why" question may provoke explanation based on an agent's motivations. Why did the Watergate cover-up occur? Because the president wanted to conceal knowledge of the break-in from the public before the election. Here, then, the "why" question is answered through a hypothesis about the agent's motives. And a "why" question may invite functional explanation as well. Why do bats make squeaky noises? Because they use echolocation to identify and capture their prey. In this case the question is answered by reference to the function that the squeaky noise capacity plays in the bat's physiology.

The other central type of explanation-seeking questions is the "how-possible" question. Generally these concern the behavior of complex systems—complicated artifacts, neural networks, social organizations, economic institutions. We note a capacity of the system—say, the ability of a frog to perceive a fast-moving fly and catch it with a quick flick of the tongue—and then we attempt to produce an account of the internal workings of the system that give rise to this capacity. A market economy has the capacity to produce inputs in approximately the proportions needed for the next production period, and we may ask how this is possible—that is, what are the economic mechanisms that induce steel, rubber, and plastic manufacturers to produce just the right amounts to supply the needs of the automobile industry?

"How-possible" questions are related to the demand for functional explanations of parts of systems. In this case we need to provide a description of a functioning system in which various subsystems perform functions that contribute to the performance capacity that the larger system is known to have. These are in fact a species of causal explanation; we are attempting to discover the causal properties of the subsystems in order to say how these systems contribute to the capacity of the larger system.

The covering-law model

What is the logical structure of a scientific explanation? We may begin with a common view, the covering-law model, based on the idea that a given event or regularity can be subsumed under one or more general laws. The central idea is that we understand a phenomenon or regularity once we see how it derives from deeper regularities of nature. In other words, the event or regularity is not accidental but rather derives from some more basic general law regulating the phenomenon. The covering-law model thus takes its lead from this question: Why was the phenomenon to be explained *necessary* in the circumstances?

This insight has been extensively developed in the form of the *deductive-nomological* (D-N) model of explanation (Figure 1.2). According to this approach an explanation is a deductive argument. Its premises include one or more testable general laws and one or more testable statements of fact; its conclusion is a statement of the fact or regularity to be explained. Carl Hempel's classic article "The Function of General Laws in History" (1942) provides a standard statement of the D-N model of explanation. "The explanation of the occurrence of an event of some specific kind E at a certain place and time consists . . . in indicating the causes or determining factors of E. . . . Thus, the scientific explanation of the event in question consists of (1) a set of statements asserting the occurrence of certain events $C_1, C_2, \ldots, C_n$ at certain times and places, (2) a set of universal hypotheses, such that (a) the statements of both groups are reasonably well confirmed by empirical evidence, (b) from the two groups of statements the sentence asserting the occurrence of event E can be logically deduced" (Hempel 1965:232).

The covering-law model of explanation draws attention to two important characteristics of scientific explanation. First, it provides a logical framework to use in describing explanations: as deductive arguments from general premises and boundary conditions to the explanandum. Second, it places emphasis on the centrality of general laws, laws of nature, lawlike generalizations, etc., in scientific explanation. It thus tries to explain the event in question by showing why it was necessary in the circumstances.

Not all scientific explanations depend on universal generalizations, of course. Some scientific laws are statistical rather than universal. The D-N model has been adapted to cover explanations involving these sorts of laws. The *inductive-statistical* (I-S) model describes a statistical explanation as consisting of one or more statistical generalizations, one or more statements of particular fact, and an inductive argument to the explanandum (Figure

L_i (one or more universal laws)
C_i (one or more statements of background circumstances)
—————   (deductively entails)
E   (statement of the fact or regularity to be explained)

Fig. 1.2   The deductive-nomological model of explanation

L_i (one or more statistical laws)
C_i (one or more statements of background circumstances)
========   (makes very likely)
E   (statement of the fact or regularity to be explained)

Fig. 1.3   Probabilistic explanation

1.3). In this case the form of the argument is different; instead of a deductive argument in which the truth of the premises guarantees the truth of the conclusion (represented by '_____' in the D-N argument), the I-S argument transmits only inductive or probabilistic support to the explanandum (represented by '======'). That is, it is perfectly possible for the premises to be true and yet the conclusion false. It was noted above that the D-N model interprets scientific explanation of a phenomenon as showing why the phenomenon was necessary in the circumstances. In spite of the formal parallel between the D-N model and the I-S model, they are sharply distinguished because a statistical explanation of an event does not show why it was necessary but rather why it was probable.

Even this account is not sufficient, however. Wesley Salmon shows that many statistical explanations of an event do not even lead to the conclusion that the event was *probable* in the circumstances—only that it was *more* probable in light of the circumstances than it would have been absent those circumstances. Salmon develops his own account of "statistical-relevance" explanations to explicate this feature of probabilistic explanation (Salmon 1984:36 ff.). Suppose, once again, that we are interested in explaining the occurrence of E in circumstances C and we know various conditional probabilities concerning the occurrence of such events. In particular, we know the probability of E occurring in a population A ($P(E|A)$) and the probability of E occurring in the subset population satisfying circumstances C ($P(E|A.C)$). If we find that $P(E|A) \neq P(E|A.C)$, then C is statistically relevant to the occurrence of E (Salmon 1984:32–33); therefore we explain the occurrence of E on the basis of the presence of C. (We will consider this model again in Chapter 2.)

These represent the main structures that have been offered to represent the logic of scientific explanation. But an adequate account of scientific explanation requires a more substantive discussion. In subsequent chapters we will consider a range of types of explanation—rational choice explanation, causal explanation, structural and functional explanation, and materialist explanation—in substantially greater detail.

Empirical versus theoretical explanation

Social scientists commonly distinguish between empirical and theoretical explanation. The distinction is not well drawn since theoretical explanations, if they are any good, must be empirically supportable. But the contrast is a genuine one that we can characterize more adequately in terms of the distinction between inductive and deductive explanation. An inductive explanation of an event involves subsuming the event under some previously established empirical regularity; a deductive explanation involves deriving a description of the event from a theoretical hypothesis about the processes that brought it about. Suppose we want to know why Bangladesh has a high infant mortality rate. We may seek to explain this circumstance by noting that the nation has a low per capita income (below $200) and that countries with low per capita income almost always have high infant mortality. (As we will discuss in Chapter 8, there is a high negative correlation between infant mortality and per capita income.) In this example we have explained a feature of Bangladesh (high infant mortality) by discovering another feature (low per capita income) with which that feature is usually associated (based on cross-country comparisons).

An important explanatory strategy in science is to attempt to explain a particular phenomenon or regularity on the basis of a *theory* of the underlying structures or mechanisms that produce the explanandum. Theories postulate unobservable mechanisms and structures; for example, physicists explain high-temperature superconductors through a theory of the properties of the exotic ceramics that display this characteristic. Ideally a theory of the underlying mechanisms should permit the derivation of the characteristics of the complex structure; ideally it should also be possible to derive the chemical properties of an atom from its quantum mechanical description.

Consider a typical deductive explanation in social science—a theoretical explanation based on a hypothesis about underlying social mechanisms. Suppose we are interested in the fact that low-level government employees tended to support violent attacks on the state in colonial Vietnam, in contrast to both their better-paid superiors and the less-well-paid, unskilled workers in the city. Why was this particular segment of society stimulated to violent protest? We may try to explain this circumstance in terms of the theory of relative deprivation. This is a theory of individual political motivation that focuses attention on the gap between what an individual expects from life and what he or she is in fact able to achieve. Ted Robert Gurr formulates this theory in terms of the "discrepancy between . . . value expectations and value capabilities" (Gurr 1968:37). Employing this theory we consider the case before us and find that low-level government employees have formed their expectations through comparison with their more privileged colleagues, whereas their incomes are tied to the same economic forces that govern unskilled labor. So when the cost of unskilled labor falls, incomes of low-level government employees fall as well. Finally, we determine that the current economic environment has created a downward pressure on unskilled wages. We now deductively derive a conclusion about the political behavior of low-level government employees: They will be more militant than either high-level government employees or unskilled workers because the expectations of these latter groups match their incomes. Here, then, we have a theoretical explanation of the militancy of low-level government workers.

Both inductive and theoretical approaches to social explanation must confront a particular difficulty. In the case of inductive explanation, we must ask whether the discovery of a more general empirical regularity embracing the event to be explained is in fact explanatory. Have we arrived at an adequate explanation of Bangladesh's infant mortality rate when we discover the regular relationship between income and infant mortality? It will be argued in Chapter 8 that we need to take a further step and hypothesize the mechanism that connects these variables. In this instance the hypothesis is not difficult to construct: Poor countries and poor families have fewer resources to devote to infant health care, with the predictable result that infants die more frequently. Inductive explanations generally appear to be of intermediate explanatory value. They further our explanatory quest by identifying some of the variables that appear relevant to the event in question. But they should be supplemented by further efforts to provide a theoretical explanation of the empirical regularities that they stipulate.

Turn now to the problems confronting deductive explanation. The central task here is to provide empirical support for the explanatory hypothesis and its application to the particular case. This involves two sorts of investigation: examination of the theory itself in a variety of circumstances and examination of the application of the theory in this particular case. In the relative deprivation case above, then, we must confront several questions. Is it in general true that militant political behavior results from a circumstance of relative deprivation? Further investigation will probably show that the theory describes one of a large number of mechanisms of political motivation: There are instances where individuals' behavior conforms to the theory and other instances where it does not. This does not invalidate the theory, unless the theorist has made rash claims of generality for the theory, but it does mean that we must use care in applying the theory. We must also examine the application of the theory to the particular case. Is there direct evidence showing that low-level government workers define their expectations in terms of the life-styles of high-level government workers? Is there direct evidence showing that their incomes were under stress during the critical period? And is there direct evidence supporting the hypothesis that their militancy was stimulated by this gap between expectation and capability?

Theoretical explanations are essential in social science. At the same time, however, it is important to emphasize the need for careful empirical evaluation of these theoretical hypotheses. What, then, is the function of theoretical analysis in social science? It is to provide the social scientist with an understanding of many of the processes within different social systems—the workings of rational choice, the logic of a market system, the causal influence of norms and values on social behavior, the role of ethnic and religious identity in behavior, and so forth. Social scientists must confront the range of phenomena that constitute their domain with a sensitivity to the diversity of social processes *and* a well-stocked tool box filled with the findings of various parts of social theory.[2]

Nonexplanatory social science

The examples that will be considered in this book have one thing in common: They all represent an attempt to *explain* social phenomena. It should be noted, however, that explanation is not always the chief goal of scientific research. For example, a common goal of some social research is simply to determine the facts concerning a given social feature. What were the chief characteristics of the Chinese population in the early Qing? Are labor unions effective at increasing safety standards in industry? Was there an industrial revolution? Does U.S. foreign policy ever make use of food as a weapon? In each of these cases, the investigator is primarily concerned with determining an answer to a factual question, one which can only be answered on the basis of extensive analysis and factual inquiry. Clearly, then, there is substantial variety in the forms that social inquiry may take; with its focus on *explanation*, this book will therefore concentrate on this key aspect of social research.

NOTES

1. This approach parallels that taken by much recent work in the philosophy of psychology. Fodor's work (1980) is a particularly clear example of this stance on the relation between philosophy and an empirical discipline.

2. Stinchcombe (1978) and Merton (1967) express this view of the role of theory in social explanation.

SUGGESTIONS FOR FURTHER READING

Achinstein, Peter. 1983. *The Nature of Explanation*.
Braybrooke, David. 1987. *Philosophy of Social Science*.
Elster, Jon. 1983. *Explaining Technical Change*.
Glymour, Clark. 1980. *Theory and Evidence*.
Hempel, Carl. 1966. *Philosophy of Natural Science*.
Miller, Richard W. 1987. *Fact and Method*.
Newton-Smith, W. H. 1981. *The Rationality of Science*.
Rosenberg, Alexander. 1988. *Philosophy of Social Science*.

PART I
MODELS OF
EXPLANATION

The following three chapters introduce several central models of social explanation: causal, rational-intentional, and interpretive. These models may be regarded as foundational; they represent the main alternative models of explanation in the social sciences. For a variety of reasons, these approaches are often thought to be in opposition to one another. It is sometimes held that causal explanations are inappropriate in social science because they presume a form of determinism that is not found among social phenomena. Rational choice explanation is sometimes construed as different in kind from causal explanation, and interpretive analysis is sometimes viewed as inconsistent with both rational choice and causal accounts.

It will be argued in this part, however, that such views are mistaken. Causal analysis is legitimate in social science, but it depends upon identifying social mechanisms that work through the actions of individuals. Social causation therefore relies on facts about human agency, which both rational choice theory and interpretive social science aim to identify. It will be held, then, that rational choice theory and (to a lesser extent) interpretive social science provide accounts of the distinctive causal mechanisms that underlie social causation.

2
CAUSAL ANALYSIS

Social scientists are often interested in establishing causal relations among social phenomena—for example, the fact that rising grain prices cause peasant unrest or that changes in technology cause changes in ideology. Moreover social scientists make different sorts of causal claims: singular causal judgments ("the assassination of Archduke Franz Ferdinand caused the outbreak of World War I"), generic causal relations ("famine causes social disorder"), causal relevance claims ("the level of commercialization influences the rate of urbanization"), probabilistic causal claims ("arms races increase the likelihood of war"), etc. Further, a wide variety of factors function as either cause or effect in social analysis: individual actions, collective actions, social structures, state activity, forms of organization, systems of norms and values, cultural modes of representation, social relations, and geographic and ecological features of an environment. (Why, for example, are bandits more common on the periphery of a traditional society than in the core? Because the rugged terrain of peripheral regions makes bandit eradication more difficult.)

The variety of causal claims and variables in social science might suggest that it is impossible to provide a coherent analysis of social causation. But this is unjustified. In fact the central ideas that underlie these various causal claims are fairly simple. This chapter will provide an account of causal explanation within which the variants mentioned above may be understood. And it will emerge that a broad range of social explanations essentially depend on causal reasoning, with certain qualifications. First, the causal assertions that are put forward within social science usually do not depend upon simple generalizations across social properties, that is, they rarely rely on a simple inductive generalization. Second, these claims typically *do* depend on an analysis of the specific causal mechanisms that connect cause and effect. Third, the mechanisms that social causal explanations postulate generally involve reference to the beliefs and wants, powers and constraints that characterize the individuals whose actions influence the social phenomenon.

THE MEANING OF CAUSAL CLAIMS

What does it mean to say that condition **C** is a cause of outcome **E**? The intuitive notion is that the former is involved in bringing about the latter, given the laws that govern the behavior of the entities and processes that constitute **C** and **E**. The social scientist or historian seeks to identify some of the conditions that *produced* the explanandum or that conferred upon it some of its distinctive features. The goal is to discover the conditions existing prior to the event that, given the law-governed regularities among phenomena of this sort, were sufficient to produce this event. There are three central ideas commonly involved in causal reasoning: the idea of a causal mechanism connecting cause and effect, the idea of a correlation between two or more variables, and the idea that one event is a necessary or sufficient condition for another.

In the following, then, I will discuss three causal theses. There is the causal mechanism (CM) thesis:

> CM C is a cause of E $=_{df}$ there is a series of events C_i leading from C to E, and the transition from each C_i to C_{i+1} is governed by one or more laws L_i.

This definition is intended to capture the idea of a law-governed causal mechanism. Contrast CM with the inductive regularity (IR) thesis:

> IR C is a cause of E $=_{df}$ there is a regular association between C-type events and E-type events.

This thesis embodies the inductive model of causation: A statement of causal relation merely summarizes a regularity joining events of type **C** and events of type **E**. Consider, finally, the necessary and sufficient condition (NSC) thesis:

> NSC C is a cause of E $=_{df}$ C is a necessary and/or sufficient condition for the occurrence of E.

This thesis invokes the idea that causes are necessary conditions for the occurrence of their effects and that some set of conditions is sufficient for the occurrence of **E**.

What are the relations among these conceptions of causation? I will hold that the causal mechanism view is the most fundamental. The fact of a correlation between types of events is evidence of one or more causal mechanisms connecting their appearance. This may be a direct causal mechanism—C directly produces E—or it may be indirect—C and E are both the result of a mechanism deriving from some third condition A. Likewise, the fact that **C** is either a necessary or sufficient condition for **E** is the result of a causal mechanism linking **C** and **E**, and a central task of a causal explanation is to discern that causal mechanism and the laws on which it depends.

MECHANISMS AND CAUSAL LAWS

What is a causal mechanism?

I contend that the central idea in causal explanation is that of a causal mechanism leading from **C** to **E**, so let us begin with that notion. A bolt is left loose on an automobile wheel; after being driven several hundred miles the wheel works loose and falls off. The cause of the accident was the loose bolt, but to establish this finding we must reconstruct the events that conveyed the state of the car from its loose-bolt state to its missing-wheel state. The account might go along these lines: The vibration of the moving wheel caused the loose bolt to fall off completely. This left the wheel less securely attached, leading to increased vibration. The increased vibration caused the remaining bolts to loosen and detach. Once the bolts were completely gone the wheel was released and the accident occurred. Here we have a relatively simple causal story that involves a number of steps, and at each step our task is to show how the state of the system at that point, in the conditions then current, leads to the new state of the system.

Thesis CM above offers a generalization of this mode of explanation. It refers to a series of events connecting **C** and **E**. This series of events C_i constitutes the causal mechanism linking **C** to **E**, and the laws that govern transitions among the events C_i are the causal laws determining the causal relation between **C** and **E**. (In the simplest case the event chain may be very short—e.g., the impact of the hammer produces the smashing of the walnut.) In this account events are causally related if and only if there are causal laws that lead from cause to effect (involving, most likely, a host of other events as well). And we can demonstrate their causal relatedness by uncovering the causal mechanism that connects them.

A causal mechanism, then, is a series of events governed by lawlike regularities that lead from the explanans to the explanandum. Such a chain may be represented as follows: Given the properties of **C** and the laws that govern such events, C_1 occurred; given the properties of C_1 and the relevant laws, C_2 occurred; . . . and given the properties of C_n and the relevant laws, **E** occurred. Once we have described the causal mechanism linking **C** to **E**, moreover, we have demonstrated how the occurrence of **C** brought about the occurrence of **E**.

Are there causal mechanisms underlying social phenomena? This question turns in part on the availability of lawlike regularities underlying social phenomena, which will be discussed shortly. Consider a brief example. Suppose it is held that the extension of trolley lines into the outlying districts of a major city caused the quality of public schools in the city to deteriorate. And suppose the mechanism advanced is as follows. Cheap, efficient transportation made outlying districts accessible to jobs in the city. Middle-class workers could then afford to live in the outlying districts that previously were the enclaves of the rich. Over a period of years, an exodus of middle-class workers from the city to the suburbs occurred. One effect of this movement was the emergence of a greater stratification between city and suburb; prior to suburbanization there was substantial economic mixing in residence, but after suburbanization the poor were concentrated in the city and the middle class in the suburbs. Middle-class people, however, have greater political power than poor people; so as the middle class left the central city, public resources and amenities followed. The resources committed to education in the city fell, with an attendant decline in the quality of public school education in the city.

This story depends on a series of social events: the creation of a new transportation technology, the uncoordinated decisions by large numbers of middle-class people to change their residence, a drop in the effective political demands of the remaining urban population, and a decline in educational quality. Each link in this causal chain is underwritten by a fairly simple theory of individual economic and political behavior, a theory that depends on individuals making rational decisions within the context of a given environment of choice. The story assumes that workers will seek the residences that offer the highest level of comfort consistent with their budget constraints, that they will make demands on local government to expend resources on their interests, and that effective political demand depends a great deal on class. These regularities of human behavior, when applied to the sequence of opportunities described in the story above, led to the changes stipulated. In other words this story describes the mechanism connecting the new trolley system to the degrading of the central city school system.

This example illustrates an important point about causal reasoning in connection with social phenomena: The mechanisms that link cause and effect are typically grounded in the meaningful, intentional behavior of individuals. These mechanisms include the features of rational choice, the operation of norms and values in agents' decisionmaking, the effects of symbolic structures on individuals' behavior, the ways in which social and economic structures constrain individual choice, and so on. This point follows from the circumstance that distinguishes social science from natural science: Social phenomena are constituted by individuals whose behavior is the result of their rational decisionmaking and nonrational psychological processes that sometimes are at work. (Chapter 3 will provide an extensive discussion of the role of rational choice theory in social explanation.)

What sorts of things have causal properties that affect social phenomena? The answers that may be gleaned from actual social explanations are manifold: actions of individuals and groups; features of individual character and motive structure; properties of social structures, institutions, and organizations; moral and ideological properties of groups and communities; new technological opportunities; new cultural developments (e.g., religious systems); characteristics of the natural environment; and more. In each case, however, it is plain how the revelant factor acquires its causal powers through the actions and beliefs of the individuals who embody it.

Consider an example of an explanation that depends on an argument about the mechanisms that mediate social causation (Example 2.1). Kuhn's

---

Example 2.1 Causes of the Taiping rebellion

There was a pronounced and permanent shift in the balance of power between the Chinese central government and local elites during the mid-nineteenth century. Why did this occur? Philip Kuhn attributes at least part of the explanation to the challenges presented to the Chinese political system by the Taiping rebellion. (a) Elites managed to wrestle control of local militarization from the state bureaucracy and create effective local militias. Prior to the 1840s the state had by and large avoided the use of large local militias to repress banditry and rebellion; after the 1840s it was no longer capable of repressing social disorder without recourse to local militias. (b) Local elites then effectively managed these organizations against the Taipings. "As the social crisis of mid-century propelled China toward civil war, the pace of local militarization quickened. As economic crises and exploitation drove the poor outside the established order, as scarcity sharpened the conflict among ethnic and linguistic groups, both heterodox and orthodox leadership became increasingly concerned with military organization" (105). (c) Elites managed this because the Qing regime was administratively overextended and because Qing military arrangements were not well designed to control rebellions that increased in scope rapidly. (d) This local militarization ultimately led to a permanent weakening of the center and an increase of local power and autonomy.

Data: historical data on local militia organization in China and the course of the Taiping rebellion

Explanatory model: analysis of local politics and the institutions of the centralized Chinese administration as a basis for explaining the shift in the balance of power between local and national political centers

Source: Philip Kuhn, *Rebellion and Its Enemies in Late Imperial China: Militarization and Social Structure, 1796–1864* (1980)

---

analysis in Example 2.1 asserts two causal connections: from administrative weakness to the creation of local militias and from the creation of local militias to a further weakening of the political power of the imperial center. Statements (a) and (b) are both factual claims, to be established on the basis of appropriate historical research. But (c) is a claim about the causes of (a) and (b), and (d) is a claim about (a)'s causal consequences. Statement (c) represents a "how-possible" question (described in Chapter 1); Kuhn identifies the features of the late Qing administrative system that made it possible for local elites to accomplish what they had not been able to do earlier in the nineteenth century—create local militias that gave them the power to resist political imperatives from the center. And (d) represents an analysis of the consequences of establishing effective local military organizations: a permanent shift in the balance of power between the state and local elites. The strength of the argument in each case, moreover, turns on the plausibility of the mechanisms through which these changes occurred as specified in Kuhn's historical narrative.

What is a lawlike regularity?

This account of causal mechanisms is based on the idea of a lawlike regularity. Causal relations, then, derive from the laws that govern the behavior of the entities involved. Carl Hempel provides an influential account of causal explanation along these lines in the following passage: *"Causal explanation* is a special type of deductive nomological explanation; for a certain event or set of events can be said to have caused a specified 'effect' only if there are general laws connecting the former with the latter in such a way that, given a description of the antecedent events, the occurrence of the effect can be deduced with the help of the laws" (Hempel 1965:300–301).

A lawlike regularity is a statement of a governing regularity among events, one that stems from the properties or powers of a range of entities and that accounts for the behavior and interactions of these entities. This description, it should be noted, goes beyond interpreting regularities as regular conjunctions of factors; it asserts that they derive from the causal powers of the entities involved. Consider the law of universal gravitation, according to which all material objects attract each other in proportion to their masses and in inverse proportion to the square of the distance separating them. This is one of the causal laws that govern the movements of the planets around the sun. The fact that they move in elliptical orbits around the sun is the causal consequence of this law (conjoined with appropriate boundary conditions).

Causal laws may be either deterministic or probabilistic. The law of gravitation is a good example of a deterministic law. All objects, without exception, are governed by this law. (They are subject to other forces as well, of course, so their behavior is not the unique effect of gravitational attraction.) An example of a probabilistic law is Mendel's law of inheritance. If both parents have one-half of a recessive gene—say, blue eyes—then the probability of their offspring having the recessive trait is 25 percent. When the offspring turns up with the trait, we may say that it is the result of the probabilistic law of inheritance of recessive traits; the cause of the outcome is the circumstance that both parents had one-half of the recessive trait.

Are there causal laws among social phenomena? The view that I will defend here is that there are regularities underlying social phenomena that may properly be called "causal," and these regularities reflect facts about *individual* agency. First, the fact that agents are (often and in many circumstances) prudent and calculating about their interests produces a set of regularities encapsulated by rational choice theory—microeconomics, game theory, social choice theory. And second, the fact that human beings conform to a loose set of psychological laws permits us to draw cause-effect relations between a given social environment and a pattern of individual behavior.

Social causation, then, depends on regularities that derive from the properties of individual agents: their intentionality, their rationality, and various features of individual motivational psychology. This finding has several implications. It follows that social regularities are substantially weaker and more exception-laden than those that underlie natural causation. As a result claims about social causation are more tentative and probabilistic than claims about natural causation. In Chapter 3 I will turn to a discussion of rational choice theory; it is regularities of the sort described there that ultimately provide the ground for causal relations among social phenomena.

It also follows that there are no processes of *social* causation that are autonomous from regularities of individual action. If we assert that economic crisis causes political instability, this is a causal judgment about social factors. But to support this judgment it is necessary to have some hypothesis about how economic crises lead individuals to act in ways that bring about political instability. (This requirement amounts to the idea that social explanations require microfoundations, a topic discussed in Chapter 9.) When Marx claims, for example, that the institutions of a market economy cause economic crises of overproduction, his argument proceeds through the effects on individual behavior that are produced by those economic institutions and the aggregate effects that individual actions have on the stability of economic institutions over time. This line of reasoning depends on assumptions about what representative economic players do in given circumstances. And these assumptions in turn embody the theory of individual rationality. Institutions and other aspects of social organization acquire their causal powers through their effects on the actions and intentions of the individuals involved in them—and *only* from those effects. So to affirm that an institution has causal powers with respect to other social entities, it is necessary to consider how typical agents would be led to behave in a way that secures this effect. To say that rumors of bank insolvency are sufficient to produce a run on the bank is to say that, given typical human concerns about financial security and the range of choices available to the typical depositor, it is likely that rumors will lead large numbers of accountholders to withdraw their funds.

THE INDUCTIVE-REGULARITY CRITERION

Let us turn now to the inductive side of causal reasoning (expressed by IR above). Chapter 8 will provide a more extensive discussion of statistical reasoning in social science; in this section we will consider only the basics of inductive reasoning about discrete variables. These are properties that have only a limited number of states—e.g., religious affiliation, marital status, occupation, high-, middle-, and low-income status, etc. This restriction limits us to analysis of causal relations among discrete types of events, individuals, and properties; consideration of correlations among continuous variables must await discussion in Chapter 8. The general idea expressed by IR is the Humean notion that causal relations consist only in patterns of regular association between variables, classes of events, and the like. According to this notion, a pair of variables, C and E, are causally related if and only if there is a regularity conjoining events of type C and events of type E. To say that inflation causes civil unrest, in this interpretation, is

Performance on mathematics test

Parental income	>90	80–90	70–80	<70
<10,000	.1	1	25	74
10,000–20,000	.1	3	30	67
20,000–30,000	.7	10	35	54
30,000–50,000	5.0	30	40	25
>50,000	5.0	32	43	20

Fig. 2.1   Hypothetical income–mathematical performance data

to say that there is a regular association between periods of inflation and subsequent periods of civil unrest.

The idea of an association between discrete variables E and C can be expressed in terms of *conditional probabilities:* E is associated with C if and only if the conditional probability of E given C is different from the absolute probability of E. This condition represents the intended idea that the incidence of E varies according to the presence or absence of C. Here we are concerned with claims of the following sort: "Marital status is causally relevant to suicide rates." Let E be the circumstance of a person's committing suicide and C be the property of the person's being divorced. The absolute probability of E is the incidence of suicide in the population as a whole; it may be represented as $P(E)$. The conditional probability of a divorced person committing suicide is the incidence of suicide among divorced persons within the general population; it may be represented as $P(E|C)$ (the probability of E occurring given C). The statistical relevance test constructed by Wesley Salmon (1984:32–36) may now be introduced: If $P(E) \neq P(E|C)$, then we have grounds for asserting that C is causally relevant to the occurrence of E; if they were *not* causally related, then we should expect that the conditional probability of E given C should equal the incidence of E in the general population. (This is tantamount to the *null hypothesis*, which states that there is no relationship between a pair of values. This idea is considered in greater detail in Chapter 8.)

Suppose we are interested in the causes of the pattern of distribution of superior mathematical ability among high school seniors, as measured by a score of 90 or above on a standard test. Of the total population taking the test only 1 percent falls within the "superior" range, so the absolute probability of a random student qualifying as superior is 1 percent. Now suppose that we break down the population into a series of categories: gender, ethnic background, parental income, parental years of schooling, and student's grade point average. Each classification is designed to be mutually exclusive and exhaustive: Each individual falls within one and only one category. We now produce a series of tables similar to Figure 2.1 for each classification and inspect the conditional probabilities defined by the various cells of the tables, such as the probability of receiving a superior score given a parental income in the $20,000–30,000 range. For some classifications there will not be a significant variation from one cell to another; each will be approximately 1 percent. In those cases we may judge that the properties defining the classification are not causally related to mathematical performance. In Figure 2.1, however, we find that there is significant variation from one cell to another. The incidence of superior performance among families with incomes of less than $30,000 is significantly below the population average (1 percent), whereas the incidence of superior performance among families with income above $30,000 is significantly above the population average. In other words, mathematical performance is associated with parental income. We may conclude from this finding that parental income is causally relevant to mathematical performance.

This conclusion does not establish the nature of the causal relation. Instead, it is necessary to construct a hypothesis about the causal mechanisms that connect these variables. Several such hypotheses are particularly salient. First, it might be held that superior mathematical capacity is closely related to the quality of mathematical instruction provided to the child and that families with more than $30,000 in income are able to purchase higher-quality instruction for their children. In this case high family income is a cause of high mathematical performance. Second, it might be held that a child's educational experience and the set of cognitive skills that the child develops most fully are highly sensitive to family attitudes toward education, which are in turn correlated with income; families with higher income tend to value education more highly than those with low income. As a result, children of high-income families put more effort into mathematical classwork and on average perform better than children of low-income families. In this case the causal factor is family attitudes toward education, which are (in this hypothesis) tied to income. So income itself is not a causal factor in determining mathematical performance. Finally, it might be held (as Jensen and Herrnstein argued unpersuasively in the 1970s) that performance generally is sensitive to the individual's genetic endowment and that the same genetic features that permitted the parents to attain high income lead to higher-than-average mathematical competence as well. Here we have an instance of collateral causation: Both family income and mathematical performance are effects of a common cause (genetic endowment).

How, then, does the statistical relevance test contribute to an explanation of probabilistic phenomena? Information about conditional probabilities allows us to begin to identify potential causal factors in the occurrence of a characteristic. If one cell of a partition of a population shows a substantially different conditional probability than the base population, the best explanation is that there is a causal factor common to individuals in this cell and not common to the general population that is relevant to the trait in question; otherwise the difference in probabilities can only be the result of random fluctuations that should even out over time. Thus the statistical relevance test supports the inference that there is a causal relationship between E and C. Properly understood, then, the statistical relevance test demands that we back such explanations with some account of the causal factors that give rise to the differing probabilities.

This establishes an important point: Evidence of association gives us reason to believe that there is a causal relationship of some kind affecting the variables under scrutiny, but it does not establish the nature of that relation. Instead, it is necessary to advance a hypothesis about the causal mechanism that produces the observed conditional probabilities. And this hypothesis in turn must be empirically evaluated (perhaps through additional statistical relevance testing [Simon 1971:6]). In the first instance above— wherein the correlation between income and performance is explained as the result of a hypothesized difference in the quality of education provided by higher-income families—it would be possible to design a new study that holds this variable constant and thereby determine whether the conditional probabilities still differ. Our study might compare a significant number of scholarship students from low-income families (with the background assumption that the quality of educational resources will now be equal) and a significant number of high-income students in the same school. If the resulting conditional probabilities are now equal, we have provided empirical support for the educational quality hypothesis. If they are not, then we must consider other hypotheses.

An example of a social explanation that depends explicitly on an inductive method is James Tong's study of collective violence in the Ming dynasty (Example 2.2). Tong's argument may be construed as a "conditional-probability" analysis. The absolute incidence of banditry is .21 events/hundred county-years (the total number of events divided by the total number of county-years embraced by the study). If the variables under scrutiny are causally irrelevant to the occurrence of banditry, then the incidence of banditry in each cell should be approximately .21. The incidence of banditry is broken down into nine cells in Figure 2.2, corresponding to the nine possible combinations of survival risks as peasant and outlaw. In the three cells in the upper right, we find that the incidence of banditry is lower than the absolute incidence for all county-years. In the other six cells, by contrast, the incidence of banditry is greater than the absolute incidence. (This is possible because each cell covers a different number of county-years.) Further there is an orderly progression from the bottom left to the upper right. The highest incidence occurs in the lower left, next come the adjacent cells, and so on toward the upper right cell. There is thus a correlation between the two independent variables and the incidence of banditry. This finding permits us to infer that there is a causal relation between the probability of survival as outlaw and peasant and the occurrence of banditry.

Now we need to identify the causal mechanism that underlies this pattern. Upon inspection it emerges that the cell with the greatest incidence of banditry is the cell in which survival prospects as a peasant are minimum and survival prospects as an outlaw are maximum. But the two cells in which the incidence of banditry is least are those in which survival as peasant is maximum and survival as outlaw is moderate or minimum. Therefore, this finding supports the hypothesis that the occurrence of banditry

Example 2.2   Inductive study of banditry in the Ming dynasty

Banditry and rebellion were common events in imperial China, and they tended to occur in clusters of events across time and space. What caused this temporal and spatial distribution of banditry? James Tong assembles a set of 630 cases of collective violence over the period 1368–1644, distributed over eleven of fifteen Ming provinces. He then evaluates three alternative causal hypotheses:

• Collective violence results from rapid social change;
• Collective violence results from worsening class conflict;
• Collective violence results from situations of survival stress on rational decisionmakers.

He argues that the third hypothesis is correct. He codes each incident in terms of the current "likelihood of surviving hardship" and "likelihood of survival as an outlaw" (Tong 1988:122–24). And he argues that when coded for these variables, the data vindicates the rational choice hypothesis (Figure 2.2).

| | Survival as outlaw | | | |
Survival as peasant	Maximum	Moderate	Minimum	Total
Maximum	0.39	0.11	0.12	0.19
Moderate	1.32	0.53	0.20	0.59
Minimum	1.79	0.90	0.82	1.15
Total	0.41	0.13	0.12	0.21

Fig. 2.2   Incidence of banditry per 100 county-years by likelihood of surviving as peasant and surviving as outlaw

Source: Data derived from Tong 1988:126

The most rebellions occur when the probability of surviving hardship is lowest and survival as an outlaw is greatest (1.79 rebellions/county-year), and the fewest occur in the two cells in the upper right (.12 rebellions/county-year). There is a positive association, then, between the variables that Tong isolates and the occurrence of rebellion. Moreover, Tong's causal mechanism to account for this correlation is straightforward; it depends on the rational decisionmaking processes of large numbers of anonymous persons.

Data: a large class of events of social disorder in Ming China culled from local histories
Explanatory model: inductive study used to support the hypothesis that the central causal variable in the occurrence of social disorder (banditry and rebellion) is the rational self-interest of the typical Chinese peasant in changing political and economic circumstances
Source: James Tong, "Rational Outlaws: Rebels and Bandits in the Ming Dynasty, 1368–1644" (1988)

is responsive to the circumstances defining the costs and benefits of banditry for rational agents. When the risks of banditry and the prospects of survival as a peasant are lowest, we should expect that rational agents will be most inclined to adopt the bandit strategy. This expectation is born out in the data produced by Tong.

Let us now evaluate the inductive regularity thesis. It is clear, to start with, that the discovery of an inductive regularity connecting two or more variables strongly suggests a causal relation between the variables. The discovery that electrical workers have substantially higher rates of cancer than the general population is strong evidence that there is some causal influence in their work environment that produces cancers—whether or not we can yet identify the cause. Thus the discovery of regularities, abnormal probability distributions, and correlations is substantial evidence of causal relations. However, the IR thesis claims more than this; it claims that the notion of a causal relation can be reduced to facts about correlation and conditional probabilities. Is this a defensible claim? It is not because, if applied rigorously, the IR criterion would generate two different sorts of errors (false positives and false negatives). And the best remedy for these failings is to identify the causal mechanisms that produce the observed regularities.

First there is the problem of a spurious correlation between variables (to be discussed at greater length in Chapter 8). Suppose that smokers tend to have nicotine stains on their fingers; that is, there is a correlation between being a smoker and having nicotine stains. If there is a statistical correlation between smoking and cancer, then there will also be a correlation between nicotine stains and cancer. But it is plainly not true that nicotine stains cause cancer. This possibility shows that IR claims too much. The presence of a regularity between two variables does not establish a causal link between them. In this case the IR criterion generates a "false-positive" error: It classifies a relation between two variables as causal when in fact it is not.

The IR criterion may also generate false-negative errors—conclusions that there is *no* causal relation between two variables when in fact there is. The most prominent source of this kind of error is the possibility of infrequent causal sequences. There may be causal relations among individual events whose covariance is masked when we move to classes of events. In considering a particular rebellion, for example, we may conclude that a famine was the proximate cause of the popular violence, based on an analysis of the particular circumstances and the mechanisms leading from famine to the outbreak of violence. But it may *not* be true that famines and rebellions are correlated; instead rebellions may be greatly dispersed over a variety of background social or economic causes. In this case the IR thesis imposes too coarse a test for causal relations.

To exclude both of these types of errors, we must fall back on an analysis of the possible causal mechanisms that mediate cause and effect. We can best exclude the possibility of a spurious correlation between variables by forming a hypothesis about the mechanisms at work in the circumstances.

If we conclude that there is no possible mechanism linking nicotine stains to lung cancer, then we can also conclude that the observed correlation is spurious. (If we identify the actual causal sequence leading from smoking to *both* nicotine stains and lung cancer, we can explain the occurrence of the spurious correlation between the latter variables.) Likewise, we can avoid a false-negative error concerning a particular causal sequence (e.g., the occurrence of famine stimulating a particular rebellion) by identifying the causal mechanism that led from one occurrence to the other.

I therefore conclude that the inductive regularity criterion is secondary to the causal mechanism criterion: There is a causal relation between two variables if and only if there is a causal mechanism connecting them. Facts about inductive regularities are useful for identifying possible causal relations, but investigation of underlying causal processes is necessary before we can conclude that a causal relation exists. The IR criterion should therefore be understood as a source of causal hypotheses and a method to evaluate them empirically—not as a definition of causation.

NECESSARY AND SUFFICIENT CONDITIONS

Causal claims involve identifying necessary and sufficient conditions for the occurrence of an event (principle NSC above). **C** is causally related to **E** if and only if **C** is either necessary for the occurrence of **E** or sufficient for the occurrence of **E** (or both). Let us define a *causal field* as the set of conditions that may be causally relevant for the occurrence of the explanandum. A *sufficient* condition **C** is one in which the presence of **C** guarantees the occurrence of **E**. The presence of solar radiation on the dark surface of an object is sufficient to heat the object. The idea that **C** is a sufficient condition for the occurrence of **E** corresponds to the intuitive notion that causes *produce* their effects or make the occurrence of their effects unavoidable in the circumstances. However, it is rarely true that any single condition is sufficient for the occurrence of any other. Instead, a group of conditions may be jointly sufficient. So, for example, the material properties of a pane of glass conjoined with the mass and momentum of a baseball are sufficient to cause the window to break. Moreover, causal explanations usually depend on the assumption that "normal conditions" obtain. Suppose that we explain a stock market crash as the effect of investor fears triggered by oil price increases. This explanation requires that we presuppose a set of ceteris paribus conditions: that investors want to maximize gain and minimize losses, that information about commodity prices is available, that investors are free to buy and sell stock, and so forth. But these conditions are part of the normal conditions of a stock market, so they may be taken as fixed. In actual causal arguments in the social sciences, it will often emerge that the claim that **C** is sufficient for **E** rests upon an unstated ceteris paribus clause: **C** is sufficient for **E** under normal circumstances.

A condition **C** is said to be *necessary* for the occurrence of an event **E** if **E** would not have occurred in the absence of **C**. The idea that **C** is a necessary condition for **E** reflects the notion that if **C** is a cause of **E**, then **E** would not have occurred if **C** had not occurred. The presence of oxygen is a necessary condition for the occurrence of combustion; if oxygen is absent, combustion will not occur. Suppose that it is maintained that the assassination of Archduke Franz Ferdinand was a cause of World War I. One way of refuting this claim is to argue that war would have broken out within months even if he had not been assassinated, i.e., the assassination was not necessary for the outbreak of war. This illustrates the phenomenon of *causal overdetermination:* causal fields in which multiple conditions are present, each of which is separately capable of bringing about the event. In such a case none of the circumstances is singly necessary (though it is necessary that one out of a set of circumstances should occur).

We may also distinguish between standing conditions and instigating conditions within a causal field. A standing condition is one that is present over a long period of time and was present for an extended time prior to the occurrence of the explanandum. It is sometimes argued that the naval arms race between Germany and Britain was one of the structural causes of World War I, but this is a condition that extended back to the 1890s. An instigating condition is an event localized in time whose occurrence at time **t** brought about the occurrence of the effect at time **t**. An instigating condition introduces the element of change into a state of affairs that produces the effect.

What establishes the relations of necessity and sufficiency among events or conditions? Philosophers have tried to capture these ideas in terms of the concept of natural necessity—the idea that, given the laws of nature and the background circumstances, the former leads unavoidably to the latter.[1] As we saw above this relation ultimately depends on the causal laws and mechanisms that link cause and effect. Causal laws are the lawlike generalizations—characterizing regularities of human agency, for example—that govern the behavior of the components of the conditions. In the natural sciences, therefore, causal reasoning relies on the assumption that there are laws of nature that establish necessary relations among events and conditions. The claim that the presence of oxygen is a necessary condition for the occurrence of combustion depends finally on our knowledge of the laws of chemistry that govern combustion. Put another way, laws of nature are the basis for our judgment that certain events influence others.

This treatment permits us to construct the following analysis of causal explanation:

A causes **B** if and only if:
1. **A** is a necessary condition for the occurrence of **B**;
2. **A** belongs to a set of conditions **C** that are jointly sufficient to give rise to **B**.

However, this account is unsatisfactory for several reasons. First, as we noted earlier, a single condition is almost never a sufficient condition for the occurrence of another event. Instead the conjunction of a set of conditions is normally needed to supply a sufficient condition; a condition, therefore, may be part of a set of conditions that are *jointly* sufficient for the outcome. The presence of oxygen *and* the presence of dry paper *and* the presence of a spark are together sufficient for the occurrence of combustion. Thus the presence of dry paper is not sufficient for the occurrence of the fire, nor is it necessary because other combustibles might equally well be present. For reasons of this sort, John Mackie refines the concept of necessary and sufficient conditions by introducing the idea of an INUS condition: an "insufficient but necessary part of a condition which is itself unnecessary but sufficient for the result" (Mackie 1976:62). His point is that there may well be alternative sets of conditions, each of which is sufficient to bring about the event. None of these is necessary because the other sets would do as well. And none of the individual conjuncts of each set is sufficient for the event. Thus Mackie holds that **A** is a cause of **P** if and only if it is a part of an INUS condition of **P**: "**A** is an INUS condition of a result **P** if and only if, for some **X** and for some **Y**, (**AX** or **Y**) is a necessary and sufficient condition of **P**, but **A** is not a sufficient condition of **P** and **X** is not a sufficient condition of **P**" (Mackie 1965:237).

The most important defect of the analysis of causal relations in terms of necessary and sufficient conditions is tied to the fact that some causal relations are probabilistic rather than deterministic. Consider the claim that poor communication among superpowers during crisis increases the likelihood of war. This is a probabilistic claim; it identifies a causal variable (poor communication) and asserts that this variable increases the probability of a given outcome (war). It cannot be translated into a claim about the necessary and sufficient conditions for war, however; it is irreducibly probabilistic.

This consideration suggests that the INUS condition is too strong; at best it holds in cases where we have deterministic laws governing the relations among events. But in the case of social phenomena particularly, it is implausible to suppose that the underlying regularities are deterministic. Fortunately, there is an alternative available, in the form of the concept of causal relevance (discussed in the previous section). The concepts of necessary and sufficient conditions can be generalized in terms of comparisons of conditional probabilities. If **C** is a necessary condition for **E**, then the probability of **E** in the absence of **C** is zero ($P(E|-C) = 0$). If **C** is a sufficient condition for **E**, then the probability of **E** in the presence of **C** is one ($P(E|C) = 1$). And we can introduce parallel concepts that are the statistical analogues of necessary and sufficient conditions. **C** is an *enhancing* causal factor just in case $P(E|C) > P(E)$, and **C** is an *inhibiting* causal factor just in case $P(E|C) < P(E)$. The extreme case of an inhibiting factor is the absence of a necessary condition, and the extreme case of an enhancing causal factor is a sufficient condition.

Consider an example that illustrates a necessary and sufficient condition analysis of social causation (Example 2.3). We may analyze the causal

---

Example 2.3   Poverty and instability in Latin America

Lars Schoultz analyzes the causal relationship between poverty and instability in Latin America (Schoultz 1987), and his account is summarized in Figure 2.3.

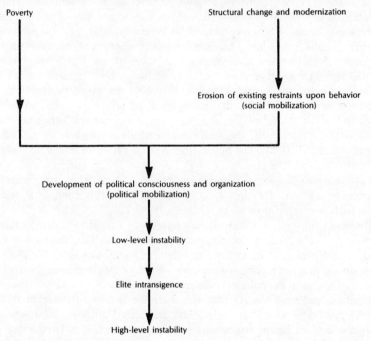

Fig. 2.3   Poverty as a cause of instability

Source: Adapted from Schoultz 1987:72

The arrows in the diagram represent causal mechanisms through which the condition at the top gives rise to the condition at the bottom; thus modernization leads to the erosion of traditional restraints. Schoultz describes this causal hypothesis in these terms: "To be destabilizing, poverty must first await the structural changes that erode traditional restraints upon behavior. Then, when two additional factors—political mobilization and elite intransigence—are also present, the result is instability" (Schoultz 1987:72).

Data: data describing income distribution and political instability in post-1945 Latin America

Explanatory model: causal explanation identifying standing and instigating conditions

Source: Lars Schoultz, *National Security and United States Policy Toward Latin America* (1987)

hypothesis in Example 2.3 using the framework we have now developed. Poverty is a standing condition in this analysis, and modernization is an instigating condition. Poverty and modernization are both necessary conditions for the eventual outcome (high-level instability). Poverty, modernization, political mobilization, and elite intransigence are a set of jointly sufficient conditions for high-level instability. Modernization is a historical development that brings its own causal properties—in this case it leads to a weakening of customary or traditional restraints on behavior. For each of these causal processes, we need to provide an account of the mechanisms and laws that give rise to the process. Here modernization erodes customary restraints by disrupting traditional social organization, diminishing the role of the family and traditional religion, stimulating rural-urban migration, and forcing people into market relations. Political mobilization is partly caused by poverty and structural change but not exclusively, which implies that there is an independent unknown causal factor at this point. Once political mobilization has occurred, low-level instability is the unavoidable result. Elite intransigence does not necessarily follow, however; instead we need another independent factor representing the conditions that determine whether elites will be intransigent or accommodating. Finally, if elite intransigence occurs, then high-level instability results through escalating conflict between elites and the poor.

FORMS OF CAUSAL REASONING

In this section I will consider the character of causal reasoning and explore the ways in which social scientists discover or establish causal relations. There are several broad approaches, corresponding to the main elements of the meaning of causal judgments. We will cover comparative analysis and analysis of causal mechanisms here and turn to a more extensive treatment of statistical reasoning in Chapter 8.

The case-study method

Suppose we are interested in explaining the occurrence and character of a particular event—e.g., the Chinese Revolution. Here the research topic may be stated in these terms: Why did the Chinese Revolution occur in the time and circumstances that it did and take the form of a radical peasant revolution rather than an urban liberal democratic movement? This is a causal question. A common approach to such a problem is the *case-study* method, in which the investigator examines the history of the event in detail to arrive at a set of causal hypotheses about its course. The investigator's goal is to discover circumstances in the history of the event that are causally relevant—that is, circumstances that had credible effects on the occurrence, timing, or character of the event. The central difficulty in this type of problem is that we are dealing with a unique series of events, all of which are antecedent to later events in the historical process. Consider three historical circumstances that occurred in China in the 1930s. First, the Great

Depression disrupted the world economy in the 1930s and significantly affected the Chinese rural economy as well. Second, large numbers of Japanese-educated Chinese students returned to China in the 1930s. And third, the Chinese Nationalist movement under Chiang Kai-shek violently expelled the Communist Left from the party in this decade. Each of these circumstances is antecedent to the emergence of a peasant-based political movement aimed at Communist revolution in the late 1930s, and it is possible to interpret each as a causal variable in the occurrence and character of the Communist movement. It might be held that the first and third factors were causally relevant to the Communist revolution but that the second was not. The global depression worsened the economic situation of the peasantry, making that group more easily mobilized by a revolutionary movement. And the Nationalist Party's attack on the Communists impelled the Communist movement to redirect its attention from urban workers to rural peasants. But the return of foreign-educated students had no significant effect on the course of subsequent events. However, this causal analysis must be defended on credible grounds. So it is critically important for the investigator to arrive at a warranted basis for assigning causal importance to diverse factors.

The most common way to support such a causal analysis is by providing an account of the particular causal mechanisms linking various parts of the story. This is one purpose of historical narrative: to establish the series of events that lead from cause to effect. Some links may be non-law-governed— for example, a spontaneous decision by a crucial actor—and others may be governed by social regularities—for example, a price rise in rice relative to wheat leads consumers to shift toward wheat consumption.

To credibly identify causal mechanisms we must employ one of two forms of inference. First, we may use a deductive approach, establishing causal connections between social factors based on a theory of the underlying processes. In this case we note that singular event **a** is followed by event **b**, and we argue that this is to be expected on theoretical grounds. Suppose, for example, that it is held that falling prices for cotton in the international market in the 1930s caused Chinese peasant activism. This causal judgment may be supported by a theoretical analysis of peasant political motivation, focusing on the connection between peasant economic security and political behavior.

Second, we may use a broadly inductive approach, justifying the claim that **a** caused **b** on the ground that events of type **A** are commonly associated with events of type **B**. This reasoning may depend on statistical correlations or on comparative analysis (discussed below). But in either case the strength of the causal assertion depends on the discovery of a regular association between event types.

The construction of a causal story based on a particular case, then, requires two things: fairly detailed knowledge about the sequence of events within the large historical process and credible theoretical or inductive hypotheses about various kinds of social causation. Consider the hypothesis that the depression increased the likelihood that a revolutionary peasant movement would succeed. This hypothesis depends on several kinds of knowledge. It presupposes a theory of political behavior: Peasants are concerned about their economic welfare, and the worse their economic circumstances, the more likely they are to support radical political movements. It also requires fairly detailed historical knowledge about the rural economy and peasant political behavior in the 1930s: We need to know whether the rural economy did in fact worsen during the 1930s and whether peasants did in fact become more responsive to radical movements as conditions worsened. If these assumptions are not born out, then the causal hypothesis fails. Finally, this causal argument is much strengthened if it can be supported with comparative and inductive evidence. If the researcher can show that radical political movements in other settings (Vietnam, Cuba, Ming China) have been sensitive to worsening economic circumstances, this provides empirical support for the singular causal judgment in this case as well.

These considerations lead us to some conclusions about the case-study method. It involves the detailed study of a particular sequence of social events and processes. And it depends on identifying particular causal links among historical events and circumstances. But the claim of causal connectedness unavoidably requires more than the knowledge of temporal succession among the events; we also need a theoretical or inductive basis for asserting that a given historical circumstance affected the occurrence and character of a subsequent circumstance. This leads us, then, to several other forms of causal reasoning, especially the comparative method and analysis of particular causal mechanisms.

Consider an example of a case-study analysis of social causation—Elizabeth Perry's explanation of the Nian rebellion in North China (Example 2.4). Perry's analysis is based on a detailed study of one extended historical event—a major peasant rebellion. And she arrives at a hypothesis about the conditions that caused this event: a set of environmental and social circumstances that provided individuals with an incentive to support bandit and rebel organizations in order to survive. Finally, her account depends on the theoretical analysis of individual decisionmaking within a particular environment of choice.

The comparative method

Another important approach to causal analysis is the comparative study of cases that embody a range of similar characteristics with certain salient differences. What explains different outcomes in apparently similar circumstances? For example, why do some poor villages become more cohesive in the face of famine, war, or flood and others become less so? Are there general factors that account for these differences? Or are the differences the result of historical accident?

In the comparative approach the investigator identifies a small number of cases in which the phenomenon of interest occurs in varying degrees and then attempts to isolate the causal processes that lead to different

---

Example 2.4   Peasant rebellion and strategies of survival

Peasant rebellions were a recurring feature of nineteenth-century China. What caused these rebellions? Elizabeth Perry analyzes the Nian rebellion that occurred in North China in the 1850s. After detailing the precarious ecology of North China, Perry holds that the central concern of peasants in this area was to find and pursue a strategy of survival. She identifies two broad families of such strategies: predatory and protective. Predatory strategies include salt-smuggling, petty theft, and banditry; protective strategies involve largely village-level defense organizations (militias, fortification, etc.). She argues that the Nian rebellion was the unintended outcome of the interaction between these strategies: As bandit gangs became more attractive to desperate peasants, bandit predations became more dangerous to villages and conflict escalated between militias and bandit gangs. Eventually bandit gangs grew large enough to attract the attention of the state, and in self-defense they organized themselves to repel military attack by state forces. Thus Perry holds that the Nian rebellion should be understood on the basis of factors at the level of the peasant household and village, not national or regional political factors. And she pays close attention to the circumstances at the local level that made it rational for individual peasants either to support local militias or to join bandit gangs.

Data: nineteenth- and twentieth-century peasant political behavior in the North China plain

Explanatory model: rebellion was the aggregate result of individually rational strategies of survival that escalated to large-scale collective action

Source: Elizabeth Perry, *Rebels and Revolutionaries in North China 1845–1945* (1980)

---

outcomes. This method requires a close scrutiny of the details of the cases, along with an effort to develop a hypothesis about the cases' causal dynamics. Thus comparative studies look at the details of a few cases in order to probe the mechanisms of change, the details of the processes, and the presence or absence of specific factors. The comparative study often uses a form of Mill's methods (discussed below), reasoning that if a given outcome is present in one case and absent in the other, there must be a causal factor present in the first case that is lacking in the latter. And the comparative method looks directly for causal mechanisms through which differing outcomes result from given social circumstances.

Theda Skocpol is a prominent exponent of the comparative method for social science. She describes her method in these terms: "The overriding intent is to develop, test, and refine causal, explanatory hypotheses about events or structures integral to macro-units such as nation-states" (Skocpol 1979:36). The comparative method is applied to a fairly small number of cases involving large social units in which the explanandum phenomena are found. The method then proceeds by identifying a set of relevantly similar cases involving the phenomenon to be explained—in Skocpol's case, the occurrence of successful revolution in France, Russia, and China. As

Charles Ragin describes it, "Comparativists are interested in the similarities and differences across macrosocial units" (Ragin 1987:6). The investigator then tries to determine whether there are factors that covary across the cases in such a way that they can be potential causes of the phenomenon to be explained.

Consider a hypothetical example. Suppose we are concerned with the occurrence of popular social conflict—riots, eat-ins, rebellions, etc. Using the comparative method we would identify several cases in which there is a substantial history of such conflict—say colonial Vietnam, seventeenth-century France, and Qing China. We would first pursue a detailed understanding of the processes of social conflict in each of the cases. Then we would try to determine whether there are similar patterns in the several cases. Now suppose that it is suggested that sharp class conflicts are a necessary and sufficient condition for the occurrence of social conflict. A comparative study can do two things. It can determine that revolutions have occurred in the absence of class conflict—thus refuting the claim that class conflict is a necessary condition for revolution. And it can determine that there are circumstances in which there was intense class conflict but no revolution—thus refuting the claim that class conflict is a sufficient condition.

Suppose that we find that class conflict was present in all the positive cases and absent in the negative ones, i.e., that class conflict covaries with revolution exactly (which it does not, in fact). Does this establish that class conflict is a necessary and sufficient condition for the occurrence of revolution? It does not, for two reasons. First it is possible that the covariance is accidental or artifactual; whenever we are restricted to an examination of a small number of cases, it is always possible that covariance is the result of random events. And second we have the familiar problem of spurious correlation: It may be that both class conflict and successful revolution are the collateral effects of some third factor. To exclude these possibilities we must construct a theory of the mechanism connecting cause and effect— the pathway by which the explanans gives rise to the explanandum.

Theda Skocpol's analysis of the causal conditions of successful revolution represents an important instance of comparative analysis (Example 2.5). Skocpol's analysis treats social unrest as a standing condition that is present in virtually all agrarian societies. Therefore, she suggests, social unrest cannot be the immediate cause of revolution—otherwise all agrarian societies would undergo revolution. It is therefore necessary to find a factor that is present in the instances in which revolution occurs and absent otherwise. And Skocpol argues that the factors that vary in the appropriate way are the competence and coherence of the state and its capacity to preserve itself in the face of popular opposition. Note, however, that this argument does not demonstrate that social tension is not a causal factor in the occurrence of revolution, only that it is not a sufficient condition. On this account, social tension is a necessary condition for the occurrence of revolution, and, when it is experienced in a society characterized by a weak state, revolution ensues.

Example 2.5   State structure and revolution

What explains the success of revolutions in a small number of cases and the failure of revolutionary movements in many others? Theda Skocpol offers a comparativist analysis of the causes of revolution in China, France, and Russia to answer this question. She argues for a complex causal hypothesis: that peasant unrest is a necessary but not sufficient condition for social revolution in pre-industrial societies, that such unrest is virtually ubiquitous and that the critical variable determining whether revolution occurs is the status of the state structure. Her causal account therefore focuses on the administrative capacity and competence of the state. She holds that the three revolutions studied all showed the same pattern: Old regime states were confronted with international crises they could not handle, and in those circumstances endemic class conflicts broke out that the repressive and political powers of the state were incapable of eliminating. She writes, "I have argued that (1) state organizations are susceptible to administrative and military collapse when subjected to intensified pressures from more developed countries abroad and (2) agrarian sociopolitical structures that facilitated widespread peasant revolts against landlords were, taken together, the sufficient distinctive causes of social-revolutionary situations commencing in France, 1789, Russia, 1917, and China, 1911" (Skocpol 1979:154). In this account the critical factors that determined whether rebellion would occur were the structure of the state and the social and political arrangements that governed local life.

Data: comparative study of the social, economic, and political circumstances that preceded the French, Russian, and Chinese revolutions

Explanatory model: a structural-causation model, according to which variations in the political structures of several societies account for the success or failure of revolution in those societies

Source: Theda Skocpol, *States and Social Revolutions: A Comparative Analysis of France, Russia, and China* (1979)

Consider a second example of comparative analysis: Atul Kohli's analysis of the politics of poverty reform in India (Example 2.6). Kohli's analysis begins by identifying the factor to be explained across cases—the existence and effectiveness of poverty-alleviation programs. He then attempts to determine the features of social and political institutions that covary with this factor and plausibly represent the primary causal mechanisms that account for differences in the factor. His account presupposes a specification of the causal field—that is, the factors that are potential causal variables prior to investigation. (So, for instance, Kohli does not consider ethnic composition as a potential causal variable.) Finally, he argues that there is a complex political factor whose presence or absence covaries in the predicted way with the existence and effectiveness of poverty programs—the political ideology and competence of the regime in power. He concludes that this factor is the primary causal variable in producing the different outcomes. This argument, it should be noted, proceeds both inductively and deductively.

Example 2.6   Poverty reform in India

Atul Kohli notes that the situation of the poor in India has scarcely changed since independence in 1947, in spite of the economy's respectable rate of growth in that period. However some states in India have done better than others in poverty alleviation. What are the social and political factors that influence the welfare of the poor in the process of third-world economic development? Kohli undertakes a comparative study of the economic policies of three Indian states (West Bengal, Karnataka, and Uttar Pradesh). He finds that the welfare of the poor is not correlated with the overall prosperity of a state. Instead, the critical variable is the type of regime in power during the process of economic development. Regimes formed by strong, competent political parties of the Left succeed in tilting the process of development toward poverty alleviation, whereas weak regimes and those dominated by the propertied classes have a poor record of performance in poverty reform. The Communist Party, Marxist (CPM) in West Bengal succeeded in bringing tangible benefits to the poor through poverty reforms including tenancy reform and rural credit and employment programs. CPM is a leftist party with a coherent redistributivist ideology, competent party organization extending down to the village level, and effective leadership. The Urs regime in Karnataka also possessed a redistributivist ideology but lacked effective political organization and had a fragmented leadership; its efforts at poverty reform were not successful. And the Janata Party in Uttar Pradesh was dominated by the rural landowning class and lacked the will to implement poverty reforms. Kohli explains the presence or absence of poverty alleviation in a state, then, as the result of the presence or absence of a regime that has both the will and the means to implement poverty reform.

Data: economic and political data drawn from three Indian states in the 1970s
Explanatory model: a causal explanation of poverty reform in India based on
   comparative analysis of the political aims and capacities of different regimes
   and parties
Source: Atul Kohli, *The State and Poverty in India: The Politics of Reform* (1987)

The inductive side corresponds to the point about covariance between regime type and poverty performance, but the deductive side takes the form of a theoretical argument designed to show why this result is a plausible one. In other words, Kohli's position relies on an argument about the causal mechanisms through which poverty policies are adopted and implemented in state governments in India.

Mill's methods

The comparative method depends heavily on an analysis of causal reasoning provided by John Stuart Mill in his *System of Logic*: the methods of agreement and difference. These are methods aimed at identifying the cause of an event by observing variations in antecedent conditions for repeated occurrences of the event.[2] Suppose that we are interested in discovering the cause of an event **P** in a causal field of a range of possibly

	P		A	B	C	D	E
I_1	p		p	p	a	a	p
N_1	p		p	a	p	a	a

Fig. 2.4   Mill's method of agreement

	P		A	B	C	D	E
I_1	p		p	p	a	a	p
N_1	a		a	p	a	a	p

Fig. 2.5   Mill's method of difference

relevant factors $\{A,B,C,D,E\}$. For vividness, suppose that the event **P** is the success of a union-organizing drive and the causal factors are: **(A)** falling real wages, **(B)** urban setting, **(C)** skilled labor force, **(D)** authoritarian management style, and **(E)** industrial company. That is, we are interested in discovering a factor that is necessary and sufficient for the occurrence of **P**. The method of agreement instructs us to find two or more cases in which **P** occurs and in which only one of the possible causal factors is present in all cases (factor **A** in Figure 2.4). (The letters **p** and **a** signify the presence or absence of the factor in question.) In this example, then, we need to find two or more instances of union-organization drives that lead to success and then determine the state of factors **A** through **E**. If the set of factors surveyed is exhaustive and if there is a single necessary and sufficient condition for the occurrence of **P**, then the factor that is present in every case must be the necessary and sufficient condition. Here it is the "real wage" variable that is constant across the cases, so the method of agreement would lead us to conclude that the direction of change of real wages is the cause of success or failure in union-organizing drives.

Turn now to the method of difference. In this instance we are instructed to find a pair of cases in the first of which **P** occurs and in the second of which it is absent. Once again we are to survey the set of relevant factors $\{A,B,C,D,E\}$. If there is a single factor that covaries with **P**, we can conclude that A is the cause of **P**. In Figure 2.5 there are two cases, one in which **P** occurs (I_1) and one in which **P** does not occur (N_1). We now survey the two circumstances and find that **B**, **C**, **D**, and **E** remain fixed through both cases, and **P** and **A** vary from the first case to the second. We can conclude from this analysis that **C** and **D** are not necessary conditions for **P** because they are absent in I_1. The only factor that is present when and only when **P** occurs is **A**. If **B** were a sufficient condition for the occurrence of **P**, then **P** ought to have occurred in N_1 as well. Therefore, the method of difference permits us to conclude that **B** is not a sufficient condition for the occurrence of **P**.

But do these findings permit us to conclude that **A** *is* a sufficient condition for **P**? They do so only if we can assume that $\{A,B,C,D,E\}$ is an exhaustive set of causal factors for the occurrence of **P**; otherwise it is entirely possible that the covariance of **A** and **P** is accidental. However this is a highly unrealistic assumption; in the typical case it will be an open question whether there are other as yet unidentified causal factors. If we do not know that $\{A,B,C,D,E\}$ is exhaustive, then the best we can conclude is that only **A** out of the set $\{A,B,C,D,E\}$ is potentially a necessary and sufficient cause of **P** and only **A**, **B**, and **E** are potentially necessary conditions for **P**. To have further reason to suppose that **A** is sufficient and necessary, we need to survey a number of other possible cases. Ideally it will emerge that **A** always covaries with **P**, and neither **B**, **C**, **D**, nor **E** is necessary for the occurrence of **P**.

What Mill's methods cannot handle are complex causation and probabilistic causation. Suppose that **A** causes **P** when in the presence of **F** and **B** causes **P** when in the presence of **G**. Then there will be cases where **A** is absent, **B** is present, and **P** is present; there will be cases where **A** is present, **B** is absent, and **P** is present; and there will be cases where **A**, **B**, and **P** are all present. The first such case would indicate that **A** is not a cause of **P**, and the second indicates that **B** is not a cause of **P**. Likewise suppose that **A** is the only cause of **P**, but it is a probabilistic cause: If **A** occurs, then there is a 90 percent chance that **P** will occur as well. If our set of cases includes one of the rare instances where **A** occurs and **P** does not, the method of difference will exclude **A** as a cause of **P**. Thus Mill's methods are well designed only for cases where we have single conditions that are necessary and sufficient for the occurrence of the outcome. Moreover, these methods require relatively demanding conditions for their application: a complete list of potentially relevant causal conditions, a pair of observations in which **P** occurs and does not occur, and information about the occurrence or nonoccurrence of each of the relevant conditions. In spite of these limitations, however, Mill's methods underlie much reasoning about causation in the social sciences.

CONCLUSION

The fundamental idea underlying causal reasoning in social science is that of a causal mechanism: To claim that **C** caused **E** is to claim that there is a causal mechanism leading from the occurrence of **C** to the occurrence of **E**. We have seen that this concept is the basis for two other prominent ideas about causation: the ideas that causal judgments correspond to inductive regularities and express claims about necessary and sufficient conditions. We have also seen that the discovery of an inductive regularity between two variables is a strong reason to expect a causal connection between them, although the connection itself takes the form of a causal mechanism. Likewise if it is true that there is a causal mechanism connecting **C** and **E**, then it follows that the occurrence of **C** enhances the probability of the occurrence of **E** (the most general version of the necessary and sufficient condition thesis).

Subsequent chapters will show that causal explanation plays a very prominent role in social science. We will find that materialist, functionalist, and structuralist explanations may be seen as specialized forms of causal explanations. And it will emerge that statistical explanations in social science, when they are genuinely explanatory, depend on the availability of credible hypotheses on underlying causal mechanisms. It is commonly held that there are distinctive *non*causal explanations available to the social sciences— for example, structuralist, rational-intentional, or interpretive explanations. But arguments in later chapters will cast doubt on this view. We will show that the central causal process underlying social change derives from rational-intentional behavior on the part of individuals. Thus there is an intimate connection between causal and rational explanation, which will be explored in the next chapter. The sole exception to the idea that social explanations are primarily causal explanations is the interpretive social science paradigm— a framework that we will consider in Chapter 4. And Chapter 5 will show that functional and structural explanations, when valid, are specialized forms of causal explanations.

NOTES

1. Rom Harré (1970) develops this view in detail. Related views may be found in Salmon (1984).

2. Mill's methods are described in Mill (1950). Discussion of the methods can be found in Mackie (1974:68 ff.).

SUGGESTIONS FOR FURTHER READING

Elster, Jon. 1983. *Explaining Technical Change.*
Mackie, J. L. 1974. *Cement of the Universe.*
Miller, Richard W. 1987. *Fact and Method.*
Ragin, Charles C. 1987. *The Comparative Method: Moving Beyond Qualitative and Quantitative Strategies.*
Salmon, Wesley C. 1984. *Scientific Explanation and the Causal Structure of the World.*
Skyrms, Brian. 1980. *Causal Necessity: A Pragmatic Investigation of the Necessity of Laws.*

3
RATIONAL CHOICE
THEORY

Social phenomena result from the activities of human beings, and human beings are *agents* whose actions are directed by their beliefs, goals, meanings, values, prohibitions, and scruples. Human beings, that is, are *intentional* creatures who act on the basis of reasons. This has a number of implications for the social sciences. First, it implies that social regularities derive from a rather different type of causal relation than do natural regularities. The latter stem from the fixed, objective features of the entities involved and the laws of nature that govern them, while the former stem from the intentional states of the agents. Second, the intentional character of social phenomena makes possible a type of explanation for social science that is not available in natural science. Many social phenomena can be explained as the aggregate consequence of the purposive actions of a large number of individuals. By coming to understand what those persons wanted, what they believed, and how they expected their actions to further their goals, we can explain the occurrence of the aggregate consequence as well.

In this chapter we will examine a model of explanation based on this feature of social life—*aggregative* explanations that attempt to account for social patterns as the aggregate result of the rational actions performed by large numbers of participants. Rational choice theory provides a formal analysis of rational decisionmaking on the basis of a set of beliefs and goals, and it incorporates several areas of economic theory—probability theory, game theory, and the theory of public goods. In the previous chapter we found that causal explanations of social science require some account of the mechanisms that mediate between cause and effect. The rational choice paradigm offers a general account of such mechanisms among social phenomena. If we can assume that individuals in a variety of social settings make calculating choices based on their beliefs and goals, we may be able to explain numerous social arrangements as the aggregate effect of such choices. This paradigm is controversial, however, for some social scientists believe that the rational choice approach abstracts too much that is culturally specific in human action, with the result that rational choice "theorems" have little to do with actual social behavior. This chapter presents some of the fundamental ideas of the rational choice paradigm. And in later chapters

---

Example 3.1   Feudal labor services and economic rationality

European feudalism was characterized by a legal obligation of the peasant to provide labor services for the lord. This is one system of surplus extraction, but there are many others—fixed wages, fixed rents, or some combination. Why were compulsory labor services selected by the manorial economy as the form of surplus transfer from peasant to lord? Douglass North and Robert Paul Thomas interpret feudalism as an exchange of goods between lord and peasant; the lord provides various public goods—chiefly security—and the peasant provides part of his surplus as income to the lord. North and Thomas argue that the labor service contract is the most acceptable arrangement to both lord and peasant in the context of a nonmarket economy. Fixed wages require the lord to assume the risks of cultivation (because wages must be paid whether the crop is successful or not), and fixed rents require the peasant to assume the risks; in either case the costs of negotiation between lord and peasant are high because the necessities of life are difficult to evaluate in the absence of a monetized economy. A labor service arrangement, on the other hand, provides a standard arrangement that is easy to negotiate and enforce and automatically adjusts to both good and bad years. "The contractual arrangement of the classic manor can now be seen as an efficient arrangement for its day. The obligation of the serf to provide labor services to his lord and protector, an input-sharing arrangement, was chosen because given the constraint of high transaction costs involved in trading goods it was the most efficient. . . . The 'quaint' organization of the classic manor is therefore understandable as an appropriate response in the general absence of a market economy" (North and Thomas 1973:31–32).

Data: historical data about the manorial economy and the legal relations
   between lord and tenant
Explanatory model: explain patterns of human behavior as the outcome of
   deliberation within the framework of economic rationality
Source: Douglass C. North and Robert Paul Thomas, *The Rise of the Western
   World: A New Economic History* (1973)

---

we will see how these ideas are applied to concrete problems of social explanation in economic anthropology, public choice theory, and Marxist theory.

Example 3.1 illustrates the aggregative mode of explanation. Here North and Thomas explain the system of bonded labor as the most advantageous to both serfs and lords; they hold that the labor service contract was selected by participants within feudal society because it was the most economically efficient arrangement available and was in the interest of both lord and peasant. On this account, then, a key feature of feudalism is explained as the aggregate consequence of the rational choices made by large numbers of peasants and lords over time.

AGGREGATIVE EXPLANATION

The rational choice paradigm of explanation rests on one central premise and a large set of analytical techniques. The premise is that individual behavior is goal-directed and calculating. Individuals are assumed to have a set of interests against which they evaluate alternative courses of action; they assign costs and benefits to various possible choices and choose an action after surveying the pros and cons of each. Rational choice explanations thus depend upon the "means-end" theory of rational action. An action is rational just in case it is an appropriate means of accomplishing a certain end, given one's beliefs about the circumstances of choice. Therefore, to explain an individual's action is to identify his or her background beliefs and goals and to show how the action chosen is a reasonable way to achieve those goals given those beliefs.[1]

This account of rationality may be described as a "thin" theory of human action.[2] It depends on an abstract description of goals in terms of interests, utilities, or preferences and postulates a simple mode of reasoning—utility maximization, for example. On the basis of these simplifying assumptions, rational choice theorists hope to explain a variety of human behaviors. The advantage of this approach is explanatory parsimony and power; to the extent that these assumptions bear some relation to human behavior, they provide the basis for explaining a wide range of social phenomena in a variety of cultural settings. However, a primary criticism of rational choice analysis arises at this point because interpretive social scientists postulate the need for "thick" descriptions of human action—detailed accounts of norms and values, cultural assumptions, metaphors, religious beliefs and practices—in order to account for human behavior. Furthermore, they deny that more abstract descriptions of human action are of much explanatory value. We will return to these criticisms in the next chapter.

So far we have not considered the content of the goals that guide individuals' actions. Economists, however, tend to include at least one substantive assumption in their account of rationality—the assumption of egoism. They assume that each economic agent is solely concerned with maximizing his own *private* interests—minimizing labor, maximizing income, maximizing leisure, and so forth. However this assumption is not essential to rational choice theory; it is possible to leave open the question of the nature of the agent's goals. In this light, the problem of rational choice theory is how to specify the best way of deciding among a range of choices *given* one's ends. The content of the agent's ends is left open; some individuals may attach utility to self-interest, the interests of various other persons, and the public good, while others may be solely concerned with self-interest.

A final issue raised by the thin conception concerns the rationality of beliefs about the environment of choice. This factor reflects the fact that rational action depends on the agent's possessing beliefs about (1) the options that are available to him or her and (2) the probable consequences of each action. This presents us with a choice in formulating a thin theory of rationality: Shall we require that the agent's beliefs about the probable consequences of the outcomes are themselves rationally grounded—that is, shall we require that the agent has rational beliefs—or shall we take the agent's beliefs as given and focus only on the problem of choice relative to those beliefs? I will assume that the thin theory involves both rational beliefs and rational choices, so that I will also assume that rational agents come to their beliefs about the consequences of their actions on the basis of appropriate inductive methods.

How does the concept of individual rationality give rise to explanations of *social* phenomena—the occurrence of collective action, enduring social institutions, or processes of social and economic change? The rational choice approach seeks to explain social outcomes as the aggregate result of large numbers of individuals acting on the basis of rational calculations. Malthus's predictions about the relation between economic trends and population curves depends on this assumption, as do Marx's analysis of the capitalist economic system and contemporary "political economy" approaches to politics in peasant societies. What these theories have in common is an explanatory strategy: explaining a social pattern as the aggregate consequence of the rational actions of a large number of participants, given the circumstances of the social and natural environment within which they deliberate. Why do strikes often collapse before they gain their objectives? Because defection has advantages for individual strikers. Why do prices tend to oscillate around the cost of production plus an average rate of profit? Because rational entrepreneurs enter and exit industries according to the rate of profit. Why do arms agreements tend to break down? Because participants fear unilateral defection by their opponents. Thus Elizabeth Perry explains the emergence of Nian armies as the aggregate result of local predatorial strategies of survival (Example 2.4); Samuel Popkin explains the failure of collective action in village societies as the effect of free-rider choices (Example 7.1); and Robert Brenner explains the stagnation of French agriculture as the absence of incentives and opportunities for technological innovation on the part of landlords and peasants (Example 6.6). In each case the author identifies a pattern of rational individual behavior that responds to a particular set of incentives and constraints and then attempts to show how this pattern of individual behavior aggregates into the observed macropattern.

These efforts may be described as *aggregative explanations*, which seek to explain large-scale social, economic, and political phenomena as the aggregate and often unintended outcome of rational decisionmaking at the individual level. Here the formal tools of rational choice theory are of value for they offer a variety of analytical techniques for deriving the aggregate effects of the actions of a large number of rational decisionmakers. Game theory, collective action theory, and marginalist economic theory each provide aggregation techniques for a range of situations within which rational decisionmakers act: strategic conflict and cooperation, public goods problems, and markets. The motivational and systemic conditions defined by social institutions impose discernible patterns on society in this sense: They define both the interests that guide various actors within society and the prohibitions and incentives that influence deliberation. They thus represent a highly structured system within which individuals act, and they impose a pattern of development and organization on society as a whole. Explanation therefore consists of showing the process through which these conditions shape the

Example 3.2   Residential segregation

Noting the common pattern of segregation between ethnic groups in U.S. cities, Thomas Schelling attempts to construct an explanation of this in terms of a hypothesis about the preferences of individuals. "This chapter is about the kind of segregation . . . that can result from discriminatory individual behavior. . . . It examines some of the *individual* incentives and individual perceptions of difference that can lead *collectively* to segregation" (Schelling 1978:138). He shows that rather weak assumptions about individual preferences are sufficient to produce sharply segregated residential patterns in the aggregate. In particular, if we assume that members of each ethnic group will tolerate an ethnically mixed neighborhood up to a certain ratio and will move if the proportion rises above that ratio, in a variety of neighborhood models it emerges that the stable equilibria are those in which the two groups are sharply segregated. This aggregate result stems *not* from the fact that each person prefers to live in a segregated neighborhood but rather from the ripple effects that follow as residents in unsatisfactory neighborhoods move into new neighborhoods, thereby altering the proportions in the new neighborhood and stimulating new movement.

Data: descriptive data concerning residential patterns in a variety of cities in the world
Explanatory model: aggregative explanation based on a hypothesis about agents' neighborhood preferences
Source: Thomas Schelling, *Micromotives and Macrobehavior* (1978)

observable features of the social system. Examples 3.2 and 3.3 illustrate this mode of explanation.

Schelling's explanation (Example 3.2) is a simple one. On the basis of an uncomplicated hypothesis about individual preferences, he derives the aggregate consequence of those preferences within a simple model. Marx's model in Example 3.3 is slightly more complex but essentially similar. It can be summarized in the following way: A given feature of capitalism occurs because capitalists are rational and are subject to a particular set of incentives, prohibitions, and opportunities. When they pursue the optimal individual strategies corresponding to these incentives, prohibitions, and opportunities, the explanans emerges as the aggregate consequence of the resulting choices. Each of these is thus an aggregative explanation because it attempts to show that a social feature is the unintended consequence of the rational strategies chosen by large numbers of participants within a particular environment of choice.

The rational choice approach, then, rests upon a simple explanatory strategy. To explain a given social phenomenon it is necessary and sufficient to provide an account of:

• the circumstances of choice that constitute the environment of action;

Example 3.3 Marx's economics

Nineteenth-century capitalism displayed a number of systemic characteristics—for example, crisis, concentration of capital, a falling rate of profit, and a pool of chronically unemployed workers. Marx sought to explain these characteristics (which he called "the laws of motion of the capitalist mode of production") through analysis of the defining economic institutions of capitalism: production for profit organized around independent, privately owned, labor-hiring firms. The capitalist economy is defined by a set of social relations of production (property relations). These relations determine relatively clear circumstances of choice for the various representative actors (the capitalist, the worker, the financier). And these circumstances are both motivational and conditioning: They establish each party's interests, the opportunities available to each, and the constraints on action that limit choice. The problem confronting Marx is that he must demonstrate, for a given characteristic of the capitalist mode of production (e.g., the falling rate of profit), that this characteristic follows from his account of the primary institutions of capitalism through reasoning about rational behavior within the circumstances of choice. Capitalists strive to maximize the rate of profit in their firms, which leads them to adopt cost-cutting new technologies that are typically capital intensive; when these innovations are adopted by all producers, the rate of profit falls.

Data: economic indicators of nineteenth-century capitalism (rate of profit, size of firm, wage data, etc.)

Explanatory model: aggregative explanation based on (1) rational individual capitalist behavior, (2) the constraints and incentives created by the capitalist economic structure, and (3) use of classical economic models to derive consequences from these findings

Source: Karl Marx, *Capital*, vol. 1 (1867/1977)

- the strategies that rational, prudent persons would pursue in those circumstances;
- the aggregate effects of those strategies.

Social phenomena, in this view, are the result—often unintended—of the purposive actions of large numbers of rational agents, and explanation consists in showing how the circumstances of individual action stimulate the patterns of behavior that in turn give rise to the observed social phenomena.

This model requires further analysis at two points. First, we need a formal account of the structure of rational decisionmaking so that we can arrive at determinate predictions about rational choice in particular social circumstances. Second, we need an analysis of some of the situations of interactive social behavior to which the rational choice approach may be applied, specifically strategic rationality and collective action. The following sections will consider each of these aspects of the aggregative model of explanation.

DECISION THEORY

This section will offer a closer examination of the details of the rational choice framework. I will also discuss the foundations of rational choice theory—the notions of utility, probability, and a decision rule.

Utility and preference

The thin theory of rationality may be stated as follows: "Agents act rationally insofar as they choose their actions from the range of available *options* that best serve their *ends*, given their *beliefs* about available options and their probable consequences." The thin theory assumes that agents have a consistent set of aims or purposes, rationalized by either a utility scheme or a complete preference ranking; that they deliberately consider a range of possible actions and their consequences; and that they choose an action based on its contribution to achieving these aims. This description requires that we focus attention on the agents' *goals* and *beliefs* and the *rules of choice* through which rational agents select one action from a range of alternatives.

We may begin with the problem of characterizing the goals of action, the goods that actions are designed to achieve. Individuals perform actions in order to acquire various things—income, leisure, education, and so on. And their actions impose costs on these agents: labor expended, wages forgone, risks run. To make rational decisions about various possible actions, then, it is necessary to have some way of weighing trade-offs between heterogeneous goods and bads because various goods and bads will commonly be produced by each possible choice. Is it worth it to me to give up an afternoon with my friends in order to hear an instructive philosophy lecture? If I have no way of comparing the goods associated with these two activities, then I have no basis for choosing between them.

Rational choice theorists use the concept of *utility* as a basis for comparing heterogeneous goods and bads or benefits and costs. A theory of utility is designed to provide a common measure for a variety of goods—income and leisure, nutrition and cost, intellectual challenge and social environment. The intuitive idea is that we can assign comparable values to heterogeneous goods because we do in fact manage to choose among them. The theory of utility is intended to formalize that capacity. The basic logical requirements for this theory are (1) that utility is a function that takes goods as a variable and specifies the value of the good to the agent as a result, (2) that a rational agent always prefers outcomes with greater utility, and (3) that the utility scale is continuous (so it is possible to add utilities).

We assume, then, that decisionmakers are able to assign utilities to all the goods that they value and that these utilities provide a basis for making choices among goods. For example, a prospective vacationer may judge that a trip to St. Tropez will produce better meals, worse beaches, and higher costs than a trip to Martinique. The decisionmaker needs a way of comparing the trade-offs of meals, beaches, and costs so that he or she can choose the best vacation, all things considered. Utility theory offers a basis for doing just that (at a conceptual level, at least); it requires that the agent decide how much he or she would sacrifice in the quality of meals in order to improve the beach payoff, and so on for each of the goods in question. Notionally the agent might reason as follows: The meals at St. Tropez will produce a utility of 5 units compared to 3 units for Martinique; the beaches at St. Tropez produce 2 units, compared to 4 units for Martinique; and the cost of St. Tropez is −6 units, compared to a cost of −4 units for Martinique. This produces an overall utility of 1 unit for St. Tropez compared to 3 for Martinique—dictating the choice of Martinique over St. Tropez.

In some cases income is a suitable surrogate for utility, but it is not always so for it is reasonable to hold that income is subject to a law of *diminishing marginal utility*. That is, the benefit a worker derives from an increase in income from $10,000 to $15,000 is greater than the increase from $25,000 to $30,000. This implies that it may be rational for the worker to accept a more dangerous or unpleasant job to gain the first increase but not the second; the utility of the first $5,000 increment is greater than the disutility of the unpleasant job, whereas the disutility of the job is greater than the utility of the second $5,000 increment.

Several problems confront utility theory. How should we interpret the claim that "person p assigns utility u to outcome y"? Is this a psychological fact about the agent? Does it represent the amount of pleasure that the agent attaches to the outcome? Neither of these options has provided a plausible basis for the theory of utility. Instead, it is preferable to regard utilities as an abstract construct representing the value that the agent attributes to outcomes, permitting us to explain the choices and comparisons that the agent makes among them.

A second issue concerns the problem of "interpersonal comparisons" of utility. How are we to understand sentences like "p_1 assigns the same utility to outcome y as p_2 does"? This is a particularly vexing problem if we assume that utilities are psychological magnitudes; it is less of a problem, however, if we regard utility as a theoretical construct in terms of which we can analyze agents' choices. Moreover, most applications of rational choice theory do not require interpersonal comparisons of utility because we are typically concerned with an actor's choices given his or her utility scale. (The problem of interpersonal comparisons arises in a serious way, however, in welfare economics, where the central task is to select policies that produce the greatest overall utility across a number of persons.)

An alternative approach to analyzing the agent's goals is to describe the agent's preference ranking of the outcomes rather than attempt to assign utilities to the outcomes. This approach is an *ordinal* framework (as compared to a *cardinal* utility framework). A preference ranking provides information concerning the agent's ranking of all pairs of outcomes, but it provides no information about *intensity* of preference. Let us understand the expression "xPy" to mean "the agent prefers x to y or the agent is indifferent between x and y." (Preference is thus conceived along the lines of the greater-than-

or-equal relation between numbers.) Suppose the range of options include (a,b,c) and the agent's preference rankings are: **aPc, cPb, aPb**. This is a *complete* preference ranking of the options in this sense: For each pair of alternatives $\{x,y\}$, it specifies whether **xPy** or **yPx**. And it is a *transitive* ranking in this sense: If **xPy** and **yPz**, then **xPz**. What a preference ranking does not offer, however, is information about how close together various choices are—information about *intensity of preference*. It might be, intuitively, that the agent's preference for **a** over **c** is very great, whereas the preference for **c** over **b** is slight, but a preference ranking cannot embody this information. Such information is, intuitively at least, relevant to decisionmaking. Fortunately it is possible to infer intensity of preference if we assume that agents have preferences between sets of outcomes specified probabilistically. Suppose that Jones prefers **a** to **b** and **b** to **c**. Now suppose that we offer him a series of choices between **b** and a lottery ticket with a fixed chance of winning **a** and the balance of winning **c**. There will be a probability **p** such that Jones is indifferent between **b** and the lottery ticket $\{$ **a** at probability **p**; **c** at probability $1-p\}$. Intuitively, this thought experiment can be understood as posing this question: How probable would a lottery ticket have to be in order to make it worthwhile to give up the certainty of **b** for the chance of gaining **a**? If Jones strongly prefers **a** to **b** and only slightly prefers **b** to **c**, then we would expect that the probability would be low. Let **k** be the probability at which the agent is indifferent between **b** and the lottery ticket. We can now assign notional utilities to **a**, **b**, and **c**: $U(a)=1$, $U(b)=k$, $U(c)=0$. The greater that **k** is, the closer together **a** and **b** are in Jones's preference space. This, then, is a technique for converting information about preference rankings into information about utilities. Therefore I will assume in what follows that it is possible to assign utilities to outcomes.

Probability

The theory of utility gives us a way of representing the goals of action. Now we need to consider the problems of *risk* and *uncertainty*. It is rarely possible to determine the outcome of an action with certainty; instead, in choosing a line of action, the agent must take into account the fact that there are multiple possible outcomes. The concept of risk refers to the common circumstance that a given action may have several possible outcomes with known probabilities, some of which are desirable and others undesirable. If I know that one out of ten plates of sushi are contaminated, then my choice of sushi for lunch is subject to risk: I have a 90 percent chance of enjoying my lunch and a 10 percent chance of food poisoning. Uncertainty refers to the fact that it may not be possible to determine the relative frequencies of outcomes. For example, if I know that some sushi is contaminated but do not know how common this problem is, then my decisionmaking is subject to uncertainty.

The central concept used in describing risk and uncertainty is that of the *probability* of an event or outcome. In general the probability of an event is an estimate of the likelihood of its occurrence, ranging between 0 and 1. An event with probability 0 is one that cannot occur; an event with probability 1 is one that is bound to occur. But what is the meaning of fractional probability values for a given event? There are two primary interpretations available: a frequency interpretation and a degree-of-belief interpretation. (The two interpretations are sometimes referred to as *objective* and *subjective* probabilities.) The frequency interpretation requires that we identify the universe of possible outcomes; the probability of a given outcome **e** is then the frequency of **e** within this universe of outcomes. For example, the probability of getting the ace of clubs in a bridge hand is .25—that is, one out of four randomly drawn bridge hands contains the ace of clubs. The other central interpretation construes a probability estimate as an indication of the strength of the agent's grounds for expecting the occurrence of the outcome, based on available evidence. When the weatherman judges that there is a 33 percent likelihood of rain, his statement rests upon the evidence available (the incoming low-pressure front), along with some rudimentary theory about the causal properties of the weather phenomena in question. (We may construe this as corresponding to the odds that the agent would accept in a wager concerning the event.) The subjective interpretation is most useful in discussion of uncertainty. In cases of uncertainty, we have no way of estimating relative frequencies of outcomes. We are therefore forced to assign equal a priori likelihood to each outcome—which is equivalent to saying that we have no greater reason to expect that **e** will occur than that any of the other possible outcomes will. (Discussion of these interpretations may be found in Glymour 1980.)

There is also a hybrid interpretation that relies on both these accounts. Here the judgment that "the probability of **e** is **r**" should be understood as representing *two* probabilities. (We may call this the *predicted frequency* interpretation of probability.) The probability claim itself can be understood as an estimate of the frequency of **e** within the universe of outcomes, and the degree of confidence that we have in the judgment is **w** (for warrant). Both **r** and **w** are values between 0 and 1, but there is no necessary relation between them. It may be that I have high warrant in believing that the incidence of failures in a nuclear power plant is low; in this case, **w** is high and **r** is low. For an example that runs in the opposite direction, suppose that the current theory of star formation implies that it is highly probable that the sun will burn out within one million years and that the evidence available for this theory is weak. The probability judgment that derives from this theory assigns a high probability **r** to the sun's burning out in one million years, but the warrant **w** that this judgment bears is low.

In general the frequency interpretation is preferable for scientific explanation; this is because we do not want to explain an event in the world on the basis of facts about our own states of mind (as is the case in the subjective interpretation). The difficulty is that for many events there is no straightforward way of computing the absolute incidence of the event in question. For example, suppose that it is held that there was a .33 probability of war between the United States and the Soviet Union at the time of the

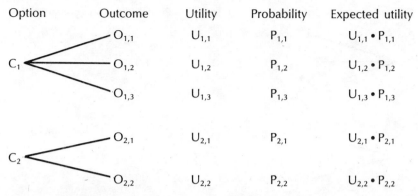

Option	Outcome	Utility	Probability	Expected utility
C_1	$O_{1,1}$	$U_{1,1}$	$P_{1,1}$	$U_{1,1} \cdot P_{1,1}$
	$O_{1,2}$	$U_{1,2}$	$P_{1,2}$	$U_{1,2} \cdot P_{1,2}$
	$O_{1,3}$	$U_{1,3}$	$P_{1,3}$	$U_{1,3} \cdot P_{1,3}$
C_2	$O_{2,1}$	$U_{2,1}$	$P_{2,1}$	$U_{2,1} \cdot P_{2,1}$
	$O_{2,2}$	$U_{2,2}$	$P_{2,2}$	$U_{2,2} \cdot P_{2,2}$

Fig. 3.1 Choices, outcomes, and probabilities

Cuban missile crisis. This is a nonrepeatable event; there is no existing universe of outcomes that can be used as a basis for frequency computations. Instead the frequency interpretation depends on counterfactual judgments: If the circumstances existing at the time of the crisis were rerun a large number of times, the incidence of war outcomes would be .33. Plainly this is an experiment that cannot be run, so our judgment that the probability of war was .33 must rest on other grounds—our theory of the causes of war. The predicted frequency alternative serves us best in this case: The meaning of the claim involves a hypothetical incidence of outcomes among possible alternatives, whereas the *warrant* for the claim depends on our theories of the causes of war applied to the particular circumstances of the missile crisis. Throughout, then, I will interpret probability judgments as estimates of relative frequencies, and I will set aside the problem of measuring the degree of warrant that these judgments possess.

Let us now consider a simple rational choice problem. The agent is faced with a range of alternative actions that may be performed, and each action has one or more possible outcomes with varying probabilities (the circumstances of risk and uncertainty). Figure 3.1 represents a simple example. The agent has two possible actions (C_1 and C_2); C_1 has three outcomes ($O_{1,1}$, $O_{1,2}$, and $O_{1,3}$), and C_2 has two outcomes ($O_{2,1}$ and $O_{2,2}$); and each outcome is associated with a payoff ($U_{i,j}$) and a probability ($P_{i,j}$). We assume, first, that the agent is able to assign values to the payoffs of each possible outcome. We may refer to these values as utilities. Second we assume that the agent can assign probabilities to each outcome; these probabilities may be construed as representing predicted frequencies of outcomes in repeated trials.

Decision rules

This analysis provides an abstract framework for analyzing the problem of rational decisionmaking. Now we must tackle the problem of articulating an appropriate decision rule. Return to the problem of choice described in

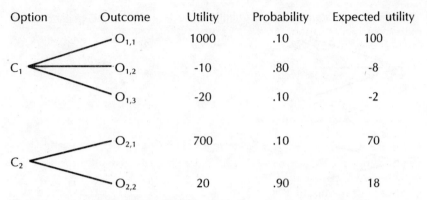

Option	Outcome	Utility	Probability	Expected utility
C_1	$O_{1,1}$	1000	.10	100
	$O_{1,2}$	-10	.80	-8
	$O_{1,3}$	-20	.10	-2
C_2	$O_{2,1}$	700	.10	70
	$O_{2,2}$	20	.90	18

Fig. 3.2   A specific expected utility example

Figure 3.1. How should the agent decide what to do? One prominent basis for choice is the *expected utility* rule (sometimes referred to as Bayes' rule [Levi 1967:43–45]). In this approach the agent assigns a weighted value to each option that consists of the sum of the expected utilities for each of its outcomes (the utility of the outcome discounted by the probability of the outcome—$U_{i,j} * P_{i,j}$). The agent then chooses that outcome with the greatest expected utility. The advantage of this rule is that it leads to the greatest utility *when applied over a large number of choice situations*. If the problem of choice is one of deciding which lottery ticket to purchase and if the agent faces this choice frequently, the expected utility rule will lead to the highest possible winnings over time.

However suppose that the values of $U_{i,j}$ and $P_{i,j}$ are as described in Figure 3.2. In this example the expected utility of C_1 is 90, and that of C_2 is 88, so the expected utility rule would dictate the choice of C_1. However there is a 90 percent probability that the payoff for C_1 will be negative, whereas the payoff for C_2 is guaranteed to be positive (either 20 or 700). Finally suppose that this choice is a one-time opportunity, so that a loss today will not be evened out by future gains. Under these circumstances the expected utility rule does not seem to be a sensible rule of choice; it leads the agent to run a high risk of a loss when a gain can be guaranteed at only a small cost in the best case (by adopting C_2 over C_1).

Another rule that might be applied is called the *maximin* rule of choice. In this case the agent considers each alternative and identifies its worst outcome, then chooses that action that has the best worst outcome. (This rule leads the agent to maximize the minimum payoff received.) In the example of Figure 3.2, the worst outcome for C_1 is −20, and for C_2 it is 20; the maximin rule therefore dictates that the agent should choose C_2. The maximin rule is a "risk-aversive" rule; it protects the agent against catastrophic losses—even though it may also guarantee that the best achievable outcome will be lower than what might otherwise be gained.

These two rules differ in their treatment of risk and uncertainty, but each is a maximizing rule and requires that the decisionmaker choose the option that optimizes with respect to a particular variable (expected utility or worst outcomes). Not all rational behavior depends on maximizing, however. Instead Herbert Simon has shown that much rational action derives from a decisionmaking process that he refers to as *satisficing* (Simon 1979). In this procedure the agent determines the minimal parameters that must be fulfilled in solving a problem. He or she then looks for a solution that satisfies these parameters and selects the first such solution. This process will not lead to the optimal solution to the problem, but it will produce a satisfactory one.

Satisficing behavior reflects an important constraint on rationality: the fact that there are information costs associated with the search for an optimal solution to a problem. If I want to eat the cereal that gives me the greatest nutritional payoff for the lowest possible cost, I must expend a good deal of effort evaluating all available cereals. There will be trade-offs between different nutritional parameters, so I will have to construct an appropriate metric assigning an overall nutritional value to each cereal. And finally I will have to balance cost and nutritional value. If, on the other hand, I want to eat a cereal that is "good enough," all I need to do is set a minimal standard of nutritional adequacy and a price standard and then choose the first cereal that I encounter that satisfies both requirements. (It might appear that satisficing choices maximize utility once we take information costs into account. However this is not quite accurate because to pursue a maximizing rule including information costs we would have to collect data on information costs and select an optimal solution in light of the new problem of choice. The satisficing approach dispenses with the need to collect additional information altogether once we have arrived at an acceptable solution.)

This approach to decisionmaking is particularly important in circumstances of complex choice-situations, in which there are many options and many possible outcomes. The cost of surveying all possible options and outcomes rapidly grows with an increase in the number of options; significantly, however, many real problems of choice do in fact involve large numbers of options. The satisficing rule thus appears to be an important basis for decisionmaking in complex real-life situations.

GAME THEORY AND THE PRISONERS' DILEMMA

Strategic rationality

The discussion to this point has analyzed rational choice on the assumption that the decisionmaker is confronted with a range of options with determinate outcomes (what Elster describes as "parametric" rationality [Elster 1983:74 ff.]). These cases involve the assumption that the outcomes are fixed by the properties of nature and that the decisionmaker's problem is simply to select one out of a menu of choices based on the probable consequences of each option. This framework covers a wide range of decision problems but not all. The most important class of cases that parametric rationality excludes are those in which outcomes depend on the deliberate choices of other rational decisionmakers. This is the situation of *strategic* rationality, and problems of strategic rationality have a different structure than problems of parametric rationality. In particular the expected utility rule is no longer relevant as a rule of choice because outcomes are not probabilistic. In cases of strategic rationality, the payoff to the individual depends on the choices made by the other players. So each decisionmaker must consider the rational calculations of the others and choose that option that maximizes his or her payoff *given* the assumption that all the others make a rational decision as well.

Strategic rationality is particularly germane to social science because it bears on interactive social behavior: Individuals make choices based on their predictions about the actions other agents will perform, and the outcomes that individuals receive depend on the choices of other agents. This topic is the subject for investigation for several areas of rational choice theory, such as game theory and collective goods theory. In this section I will discuss the main ideas of game theory; in the next section I will turn to collective action theory.

Game theory is generally concerned with problems of strategic rationality— problems in which the rational decisionmaker must take into account the fact that the outcomes of various possible actions available to him or her are influenced by the choices made by other rational decisionmakers. Whereas the rational gambler chooses among alternative actions on the basis of the probabilities of win and loss that he or she assigns to each bet, the rational general must take into account both probabilities (e.g., concerning the weather) and the strategic rationality of his counterparts in the contending army. The opposing general is attempting to work out an optimal strategy given his understanding that the opponent is a rational agent; consequently each participant will act on the basis of assumptions about the other's intentions. This problem may look deeply intractable because **A** reasons that **B** reasons that **A** reasons that . . . , but the central finding of game theory is that there are optimal and stable solutions for several general classes of problems of choice of this sort.

Let us begin with the main ideas of two-person game theory. Game theory is premised on the assumption of rational self-interest and the theory of utility. Each "player" is assumed to have a set of private interests and a way of comparing the various possible outcomes in terms of their contribution to those interests. A *zero-sum* game is one in which each player's gain is exactly equal to the other player's loss; the sum of the two players' payoffs is zero. A non-zero-sum game is one in which the sum of payoffs for a given outcome may be positive (or negative, for that matter). An example of a zero-sum game is a bet on the toss of a coin; an example of a non-zero-sum game is an agreement between a worker and a capitalist to produce a good. It is evident that zero-sum games do not permit cooperation between the players because each player's gain is exactly offset by the other's loss. A zero-sum game is a game of pure competition. A positive-sum game, by contrast, *does* permit cooperation. For example, the winner may secure

Column

		$S_{2,1}$	$S_{2,2}$	.	.	.	$S_{2,m}$
	$S_{1,1}$	4,2	-1,3	.	.	.	5,-3
	$S_{1,2}$	6,3	2,0	.	.	.	-3,0
Row	.		.	.	.	.	.
	.		.	.	.	.	.
	.		.	.	.	.	.
	$S_{1,n}$	-2.1	3,0	.	.	.	0,3

Fig. 3.3   Game matrix

the loser's cooperation by compensating him for his loss and still come out ahead. Thus a positive-sum game is a mixed game of competition and cooperation.

A *strategy* is a detailed rule of play for the whole of a game. It specifies the player's play for every possible move by the opponent at each stage of the game. (It is worth noting that this conception of a game strategy is extremely demanding; even in the game of checkers, the list of logically possible strategies for one player is impossibly long.) Each player is assumed to have a list of available strategies ($S_{i,j}$), each is assumed to know both his or her own list of strategies and that of the opponent (in a game of perfect information), and each is assumed to know the outcome for each player of a given pair of strategies.

There are two ways of representing a game. A game may be described in terms of its *game tree*. (This is termed as the *extensive form* of the game.) A game tree begins with the first player's options at the first move. For each of these options it specifies the options available to the second player and so on until the end of the game. Each complete branch of the game tree represents a pair of strategies for the two players. The advantage of the game tree is that it displays the game as a sequential series of plays by the two players. A finished game tree permits us to analyze the strategic situation of both players from the endstates backward. Each assumes that the other player is perfectly rational. At any stage of the game, the player can determine which set of options is available to the opponent on the next play. More generally earlier moves determine what sets of outcomes will be accessible later in the game. Because the opponent is assumed to be rational, the problem for each is to choose a strategy that forces the opponent to permit him to arrive at the best-worst payoff (an application of the maximin principle). There is a combinatorial explosion, however, that quickly threatens to overwhelm the analysis of any but the simplest of games; if each player has three choices at each play and if the game continues through five moves for each player, the total number of branches in the tree is 19,683 (3^9).

A game may also be summarized in the form of a "game matrix": a two-dimensional matrix listing player **A**'s strategies in the rows and player **B**'s strategies in the columns (Figure 3.3). (This is described as *normal form* or *strategic form*.) Each entry in the matrix is an ordered pair that represents A's payoff and B's payoff for the selected pair of strategies. (The combinatorial explosion is equally significant in the case of normal-form descriptions of a game. For example, tic-tac-toe presents at least $9*7^8*5^{48}$ strategies to the first player.) A *game of perfect information* is one in which each player has full information about the strategies available to the other and about the state of the game at each stage of play. (That is, there are no hidden moves.) The central problem for two-person game theory, then, is to determine whether there are rational procedures for choosing strategies for games analyzed along these lines.

Let us begin with the analysis of two-person zero-sum games. The simplest strategic situation is the game in which each player has a *dominant strategy*—a strategy that is best for that player no matter what choice the opponent makes. In this case the player can effectively ignore the possible choices that the opponent may make; whatever my opponent does, my best strategy is fixed. In games in which each player has a dominant strategy, the outcome is easily determined: It is the intersection of the pair of dominant strategies. And if only one player has a dominant strategy, the problem of choice is also simple. If my opponent has a dominant strategy, then I know that he or she will play that strategy, and I should choose the strategy that gives me the greatest payoff on that assumption. In the more interesting cases, however, neither player has a dominant strategy; instead each must take into account the strategies available to the opponent and select a strategy accordingly.

Game theorists have shown that there are two classes of two-person zero-sum games. Some have a pure equilibrium point: a pair of strategies for players **A** and **B** with the property that—if these strategies are chosen—neither **A** nor **B** can improve the payoff by defecting to another strategy. (Such a position is also called a saddle point—an entry in a game matrix that is a maximum for one player and a minimum for the other.) That is, given that **A** chooses $S_{1,i}$, **B** can do no better than to choose $S_{2,j}$; given that **B** has chosen $S_{2,j}$, **A** can do no better than to choose $S_{1,i}$. (This is sometimes referred to as a *Nash equilibrium*.) Under these circumstances both players have a best available strategy, and the game is solved. How can we determine whether a given game has an equilibrium point? Here the maximin rule described above is the appropriate tool of analysis for each player. (I will refer to the players as "Row" and "Column.") Row should rank his strategies according to their worst outcomes and provisionally choose that strategy $S_{1,j}$ with the best worst outcome. Now he should consider what options are available to his opponent: If Column knew that Row is playing $S_{1,j}$, what strategy would he choose? On the assumption that Column would choose $S_{2,i}$, could Row improve his payoff? If he could, then $S_{1,j}$ does not provide an equilibrium point; if he could not, then $\left\{ S_{1,j},\ S_{2,i} \right\}$ is an equilibrium point. Games in which such an equilibrium exists likewise have an optimal solution: Each player should choose a strategy that falls on an equilibrium point. If there is a saddle point, then each player can do no better than choose a strategy that leads to this saddle point.

The second class of games is more difficult. These are games without a saddle point; consequently no single pair of strategies represents an equilibrium. (If Row chooses $S_{1,i}$ on the assumption that Column will play $S_{2,j}$, then Column can improve his payoff by choosing another strategy. Row, foreseeing this possibility, determines not to play $S_{1,i}$.) Game theorists have shown that these games too have a solution for both players. In this case, however, the solution is a *mixed* strategy: a distribution among several different strategies determined by a fixed set of probabilities assigned to them (to be applied using a randomizing process). The advantage of a mixed strategy is that it makes it impossible for my opponent to exploit knowledge about what I will do. If he knows that I must play $S_{1,j}$, he can choose the best response available on that assumption. But if he knows that I will choose randomly among $S_{1,j}$, $S_{1,k}$, and $S_{1,l}$, then he must be prepared for each of these strategies.

The analysis up to this point is restricted to zero-sum games. However many cases of strategic interaction are not zero-sum; instead many games produce outcomes in which both parties may be better off if they cooperate. A game of *pure cooperation* is the polar case. In this situation the optimal outcome for both players is possible if they properly coordinate their strategies. There is no conflict of interest between the parties; each is concerned only to coordinate with the other. (An example of this is the problem of locating a friend in a crowded stadium. It does not matter whether the friends meet at the ticket booth or the 50-yard line, as long as they both arrive at the same place.) The more interesting case is that in which there is both harmony of interest and conflict of interest between the players. In such a case both do better by coordinating with each other, but each prefers some of the cooperative outcomes to others. Thus there is a conflict of interest between the players over which of the cooperative outcomes will be selected.

This case is of particular interest in the social sciences. Given that the game is non–zero-sum, a negotiated solution is possible. (In a zero-sum game there is no overlap of interest between the two players that would permit a negotiated solution.) Here certain outcomes are preferred by all players over other outcomes, and if players are permitted to communicate with each other, they may be able to reach an agreement that enables them to coordinate their choices and arrive at one such outcome. Game theorists have tried to analyze the conditions that affect what the bargaining solution will be, based on the payoffs to the parties. Intuitively the general conclusion is that, if I am the party with the most to lose, I will be forced to accept a bargained solution that favors my opponent for he can use his "threat advantage" to reason that failure to reach agreement will hurt me more than him. (See Shubik 1982 for an extensive discussion of the large literature on bargaining theory.)

The prisoners' dilemma

These are the basic notions of game theory. And—as game theorists themselves point out explicitly—the theory has few direct practical appli-

	Cooperate	Defect
Cooperate	1,1	-2,2
Defect	2,-2	-1,-1

Fig. 3.4   Prisoners' dilemma

cations because of the impossibly strenuous assumptions it makes about each player's knowledge and computational abilities. Along the way, however, the game theorists have analyzed several simple games that have surprising properties. Central among these is the *prisoners' dilemma*. This is a non-zero-sum game that models a number of common strategic situations. Consider the game matrix in Figure 3.4. Each player is faced with two possible strategies: cooperate and defect. The payoffs to each are as indicated; A's strategies are listed on the left side, and B's are listed across the top; A's payoff is the first quantity, and B's payoff is the second quantity. If both choose to cooperate, then both receive 1 unit; if both defect, both lose 1 unit. Finally, if one cooperates and the other defects, the defector gains 2 units and the cooperator loses 2 units.

If we now analyze this game according to the assumptions of rational self-interest outlined above, we will see immediately that it has an equilibrium point because each player has a dominant strategy. The dominant strategy is defection: Each sees that he is better off defecting regardless of whether the opponent defects or cooperates. And the equilibrium point is the pair of defecting strategies—with a loss of 1 unit for both A and B. Both players prefer the cooperate-cooperate outcome to the defect-defect outcome, but they are unable to arrive at this outcome through rational decisionmaking. Here we have arrived at something like a paradox of collective rationality. Each player chooses rationally, each selects a strategy that maximizes his own outcome, and the net result is an outcome that is worse for both than another possible outcome (joint cooperation). It would seem, then, that individual rationality in this case leads to collective harm.

There are many instances of social behavior that appear to embody the structure of the prisoners' dilemma—for example, arms races, the breakdown of price-fixing agreements, and the failure of cooperative practices. In each case participants have a collective interest in a cooperative solution that is undermined by the cost-free incentive to defect. Prisoners' dilemmas thus involve the role of *trust:* If parties to a cooperative agreement trust that other participants will keep the agreement *and* if each participant has a normative motivation to keep fair agreements, then prisoners' dilemma situations can be overcome.

The situation of a prisoners' dilemma changes if the situation of choice is a repetitive one.[3] Here the chief finding may be summarized rather simply: Defection is no longer the optimal strategy for each player when each knows that he confronts an open-ended series of prisoners' dilemma decisions with a given opponent.[4] Each player can foresee that defection on the first play— even if it gains a one-time advantage over the opponent—will lead the opponent to defect on the second play and will result in a stable run of "defect" plays by each player for the whole series of games. Each can see that both players lose on this scenario; consequently it is rational to make a tacit "offer" to cooperate through playing "cooperate" on one play and seeing if the opponent reciprocates on the next. Robert Axelrod (1984) and Michael Taylor (1987) have analyzed the structure of cooperation from the point of view of prisoners' dilemmas; see Example 3.4 below for Axelrod's analysis. These arguments show that conditional cooperation is a rational strategy in repeated prisoners' dilemma situations.

Applicability of game theory to empirical social science

It is reasonable to ask, in at least a preliminary way, to what extent game theory is relevant to empirical social science. The technical apparatus of game theory is probably less useful than the basic ideas that game theory provides: strategic rationality, the prisoners' dilemma, reasoning about the choices of others in a circumstance of interactive outcomes, and bargaining and coalitions. The technical achievements of game theory—that various classes of games are in principle solvable—are of questionable relevance. Suppose that a peasant community and its lord in a particular historical context are in a conflict with a game structure that locates it within a class of games T. Suppose further that some axiomatization of game theory shows that T is solvable using a particular mixed strategy. Nothing follows from these facts for the behavior of the participants, even if we assume that they are rational, for the participants do not know that T is solvable, and, in any case, they lack the mathematical machinery for solving T. The fact that they are rational does not imply that they will act in accordance with the requirements of a fully developed scheme of strategic rationality. In fact, if their actions do conform to the solution to T, we have an even harder problem—explaining how this fortuitous outcome emerged. This situation parallels arguments for the applicability of game theory to evolutionary biology in the form of the concept of evolutionarily stable strategies. It is held that species may evolve genetically determined "mixed strategies" in which individuals are programmed to alternate strategies in a fixed ratio and that the ratio is that required by the solution to the game in which the species finds itself in a given environment. (See Elster 1982 and Dawkins 1976 on these applications.) The biological explanation would go along these lines: Those subpopulations that accidentally hit the right strategic mix have an advantage over those that do not.

How would this affect the peasants/lord game discussed above? Not at all. The behavior of peasants and lords is not genetically programmed but rather intentional and rational. If they do not possess the machinery of game theory, they could only hit the optimal mix of strategies through trial and error, not through rational calculation.[5]

The general framework of analysis provided by game theory, however, is useful for social science explanation. Consider Example 3.4. Here Robert Axelrod uses some nontechnical elements of two-person game theory to

---

Example 3.4   Cooperation and repeated prisoners' dilemmas

In World War I the violence of trench warfare was often reduced by apparent unofficial truces by units on both sides. Each side would continue to fire its weapons but without inflicting much damage on the other. Robert Axelrod explains this "live and let live" strategy in terms of the phenomenon of *reciprocity* (strict conditional cooperation). He argues that rationally self-interested agents will find it in their self-interest to cooperate conditionally with other agents in circumstances where each side has something to gain from cooperation and something to gain from defection: The short-term gains of defection are more than offset by the long-term gains of cooperation. Axelrod's model of cooperation derives from study of repeated prisoners' dilemmas. He shows that the structure of the prisoners' dilemma changes in an open-ended series of plays of the game. Conditional cooperation ("tit for tat") is the best strategy for each player and the most robust over a wide variety of contexts. "Tit for tat" opens with cooperation and then plays whatever its opponent played on the previous move—that is, it responds cooperatively to cooperation and immediately punishes defection with defection. Axelrod identifies a set of conditions under which cooperation (strict reciprocity) is the optimal strategy for each player. Players must first be able to recognize and reidentify their opponents from one play to the next, and they must be able to remember the opponents' previous history of play. These conditions are necessary to make the cooperator selectively responsive to different strategies. Then players must judge that the probability of future interaction with the opponent is sufficiently great to justify weighing future gains from cooperation against present gains from defection. Under these circumstances Axelrod shows that the optimal strategy for each individual when confronted with opportunities for cooperation with others is conditional cooperation. Axelrod holds that the "live and let live" process found in trench warfare is explained as rational behavior making use of the strategy of conditional cooperation on both sides.

Data: examples of cooperative behavior, game theoretic analysis of repeated prisoners' dilemmas, historical data from World War I
Explanatory model: explanation of patterns of cooperative behavior as the result of the rational self-interest of each of the players
Source: Robert Axelrod, *The Evolution of Cooperation* (1984)

---

account for cooperation among rational agents. This analysis is useful in explaining a range of social phenomena, from tipping behavior to the practice of aiming high in trench warfare. In this instance we have a situation that embodies a repeated prisoners' dilemma between the two sides. On any given occasion each side prefers the outcomes in this order: unilateral shooting, joint nonshooting, joint shooting, and unilateral nonshooting. (That is, each side would prefer to impose harm on the enemy without cost to itself.) If each unit encountered an enemy only once, we would expect that each side would shoot. Given the situation of trench warfare, however, in which opposing units face each other over an open-ended series of opportunities for conflict, the strategy of conditional cooperation is superior to noncooperation for each party; each is better off if it continues to cooperate in response to previous cooperation by the enemy. (We should also expect this pattern of cooperation to break down as one side or the other comes closer to withdrawal from the front.)

COLLECTIVE ACTION THEORY

Let us turn now to another important area of applied rational choice theory: the theory of collective action. A generation of economists writing on public goods problems have shown that there is conflict between private rationality and collective action: A group of rationally self-interested individuals will not act effectively in pursuit of public goods (goods that are indivisible and nonexcludable—for example, clean air and water). In a classic work Mancur Olson (1965) advanced a theory of group behavior that drew certain counterintuitive conclusions. There is a long-standing tradition of thought that took it as self-evident that groups and organizations would act collectively in pursuit of the common interest of the group. Olson showed, however, that this assumption commits something akin to a logical fallacy because groups consist of individuals who make independent decisions. Consequently it is not sufficient to show that an action would serve the group's interest if all or most members of the group were to perform it; it is necessary to show in addition that all (or most) individuals in the group have a rational interest in acting in that way. (Russell Hardin uses the term "fallacy of composition" to describe the error [Hardin 1982:2].) In fact Olson argues that in the most common circumstances a group will *not* act effectively in pursuit of common interests. Rather, if we assume that a group is composed of rational agents concerned with maximizing private interests, Olson shows that each member will have a rational incentive to take a "free ride." Each potential contributor to the public good will choose to become a free-rider and hope that other members of the group will make the contrary decision.

Assume that a group is composed of rational individuals who have a common interest—an outcome that would benefit each of them if it were to occur. Individuals are motivated by self-interest, described by a consistent set of utilities. Every individual has a range of private interests and chooses among available actions according to the costs and benefits that each presents in terms of those private interests. Assume that a common interest is a good whose attainment would improve every individual's welfare, according to his or her own private scheme of interests. (That is, there is no conflict of interest over the attainment of the good; every member of the group would prefer the presence of the good to the absence of the good.) Assume that this common good is a *public good*—a good that, if it is available to any member of the group, "cannot feasibly be withheld from the others in the group" (Olson 1965:14). (That is, a public good is characterized by nonexcludability.) Finally the collective action of the group is the action that is expected of each member in order to achieve the common good. The problem of collective action is this: Under what circumstances will a group succeed in acting in concert to bring about its common interest?

Consider an example that embodies these assumptions. Let the group be an association of mail-order merchants, let the common good be a decrease in the postage rate on the mailing of catalogs, and let the collective action in question be a contribution to a lobbying fund designed to get Congress to write appropriate legislation. Assume, further, that the lobbying effort is almost certain to be successful if funded at a sufficiently high level—say, 90 percent compliance with each member donating $1,000. Finally, assume that the savings in postage that each member would realize would average $800 per year, over a predicted time frame of five years. The good in question in this example is a common good; each member would benefit from the decrease in postage rates. Further, it is a public good; it is not possible to exclude noncontributors from the benefits of lower postage rates. Finally, the individual rationality assumption is satisfied if we simply assume that merchants decide whether to contribute strictly according to their individual costs and benefits of contribution or noncontribution.

We are now ready to consider what I will refer to as Olson's "theorem of collective action." "In a large group in which no single individual's contribution makes a perceptible difference to the group as a whole, or the burden or benefit of any single member of the group, it is certain that a collective good will not be provided unless there is coercion or some outside inducements that will lead the members of the group to act in their common interest" (Olson 1965:44). His argument reduces in large part to the following point: "Though all of the members of the group . . . have a common interest in obtaining this collective benefit, they have no common interest in paying the cost of providing that collective good. Each would prefer that the others pay the entire cost, and ordinarily would get any benefit provided whether he had borne part of the cost or not" (Olson 1965:21). The theorem follows from two points: the fact that rational individuals make their decisions based on private interests and the fact that the common good is nonexcludable. Given nonexcludability, individuals can reason that the good will either be achieved or not achieved independent from their own choices of action. With either outcome, personal interests are best served by not contributing. If the good is achieved, they will enjoy the benefits without the cost of contribution. If it is not achieved, then the individuals are spared the cost of contribution. Each member will thus decide not to contribute, and the good will not be achieved—thus the "theorem of collective action."

This problem of collective action is referred to as the "free-rider" problem: Rationally self-interested individuals are under an unavoidable incentive to take a "free ride" in circumstances of collective action—that is, to refrain from contribution and hope that others make a contrary choice.

We might informally test this result against the assumptions of our example above. Assume a representative merchant has just received the request for a contribution to the lobbying fund, reminding him that the association determined that this course will best serve the common interest. He has two choices: to contribute or not to contribute. And there are two possible outcomes: successful collective action and unsuccessful collective

	Success	Failure
Contribute:	3000	-1000
Don't contribute:	4000	0

Fig. 3.5   Collective action payoffs

action. These choices are represented in Figure 3.5. This table of outcomes shows that the merchant has a best strategy available regardless of the success or failure of the joint enterprise: noncontribution. This strategy leads to $4,000 versus $3,000 in the event of collective success; it leads to $0 versus −$1,000 in the event of collective failure. Therefore our representative merchant elects to refrain from contribution. But each participant is faced with the same scheme of costs and benefits. Therefore none contributes, the lobbying effort fails, and the good is not achieved.

Olson qualifies his analysis in two ways. First he distinguishes between large and small groups and shows that small groups are sometimes "privileged"; individuals in such small groups may derive enough benefits from the supply of the public good that it is individually rational to purchase the good. Large groups, however, are "latent": They normally do not succeed in undertaking collective action. Second he points out that groups may be able to arrange a schedule of in-process benefits or penalties that are sufficient to change the individual's rational calculus.

Russell Hardin shows that Olson's analysis of group size is too simple, however, and that a more complete analysis proves that size is relevant in other respects as well. In particular Hardin shows that more relevant than absolute size is the ratio of benefits to costs and the extent of stratification of benefits within the group (Hardin 1982:40 ff.). If the benefit-to-cost ratio is sufficiently high, there may be a subgroup within the larger group that would benefit from the collective good even if it provided the whole funding of the collective project. "Let us use **k** to designate the size of any subgroup that just barely stands to benefit from providing the good, even without cooperation from other members of the whole group" (Hardin 1982:41). Hardin shows that it is the size of **k** rather than the absolute size of the group that influences the feasibility of collective action. Suppose that a thousand people would benefit from extending road service to a remote village and that benefits are unequally distributed. Most people would save $100 a year on the cost of hiring a donkey to convey them to the city, but a small group of ten merchants would gain $5,000 a year in increased trade. Finally suppose the cost of the road is $10,000. The benefits to the 990 ordinary villagers are $99,000—much greater than the cost of the road. But, for reasons deriving from Olson's analysis, it will be difficult to secure cooperation from this group. The benefits to the ten merchants are $50,000, so it is in their interest to fund the whole cost of the road rather than have the project fail. Moreover this is a small enough group that we may expect that it will succeed in implementing this collective effort.

This case no doubt strikes the reader as closely related to the prisoners' dilemma sketched above. And in fact Russell Hardin argues that the problem of collective action is formally equivalent to the n-person prisoners' dilemma (Hardin 1982:25–28). Both the prisoners' dilemma and the collective action theorem have apparently paradoxical consequences for group rationality. (They represent "the back of the invisible hand," in Hardin's felicitous phrase.) Both results appear to show that groups composed of rational individuals will be incapable of acting to secure collective benefits—even when all participants can rehearse the full story of Olson's argument and the prisoners' dilemma. And the only solutions that seem to be available for these problems in their most abstract form are either irrational conduct (choosing a less-than-optimal strategy) or coordination under coercive conditions (in which individuals can commit themselves not to defect from the collective action).

The theory of collective action provides the basis for the explanation of a wide variety of social behavior: strikes, the success or failure of rebellion, and the instability of price-fixing agreements. In Example 3.5, Allen Buchanan uses the collective action problem to explain worker passivity in the face of opportunities for revolutionary action.

CRITICISMS OF NARROW ECONOMIC RATIONALITY

This completes my treatment of the main tools of rational choice theory. In this final section I return to the issue with which we began: the specification of the notion of individual rationality. A number of writers have offered criticisms of the conception of individual rationality at work here, on the ground that it is insensitive to features of human action and deliberation that are in fact quite central.

Some authors have criticized various aspects of the theory of narrow economic rationality. Particularly important among these is A. K. Sen's critique. Sen—himself an economist of the first rank—criticizes the assumption of pure self-interest that is contained in the standard conception. "The purely economic man is indeed close to being a social moron" (Sen 1982:99). Against the assumption of self-interested maximizing decision-making, Sen argues for a proposal for a more structured concept of practical reason, one that permits the decisionmaker to take account of *commitments*. This concept covers a variety of nonwelfare features of reasoning, but moral principle (fairness and reciprocity) and altruistic concern for the welfare of others are central among these. Sen believes that the role of commitment is centrally important in the analysis of individuals' behavior with regard to public goods. For example, he suggests that the voters' paradox may be explained by assuming that "voters are not trying to maximize expected utility, but . . . to record one's true preference" (Sen 1982:97). And he draws connections between the role of commitment and work motivation. "To run an organization entirely on incentives to personal gain is pretty much a hopeless task" (Sen 1982:98). He argues, therefore, that to understand different areas of rational behavior it is necessary to consider both utility-maximizing decisionmaking and rational conduct influenced by commitment; furthermore,

---

Example 3.5 Revolutionary motivation

Marxist theory predicts that workers have objective class interests that make it rational for them to support revolutionary movements to overthrow capitalism. Marx writes, "The proletarians have nothing to lose but their chains. They have a world to win" (Marx and Engels 1848/1974:98). But proletarian activism and revolution are the exception, not the rule, among working-class groups throughout the world. Why is this so? Allen Buchanan explains this phenomenon by accepting the point that workers have a collective interest in revolution but pointing out that revolution is a "public good" for members of the working class. Buchanan argues, "Even if revolution is in the best interest of the proletariat, and even if every member of the proletariat realizes that this is so, so far as its members act rationally, this class will not achieve concerted revolutionary action" (Buchanan 1979:63). Any worker will be able to enjoy the benefits of socialism whether he has contributed to the revolution or not. Therefore rational workers elect to become free-riders. As a result working-class collective action is infrequent. Thus Buchanan derives working-class passivity from three assumptions: (1) workers have a group interest in revolution, (2) workers are individually rational decisionmakers, and (3) rational decisionmakers are usually ineffective at securing collective action. Therefore the working class is generally incapable of mounting collective action in support of its interests.

Data: historical patterns of working-class political behavior
Explanatory model: application of the theory of collective action to a
  hypothetical group of rational proletarians
Source: Allen Buchanan, "Revolutionary Motivation and Rationality" (1979)

---

it is an empirical question whether one factor or the other is predominant in a particular range of behavior (Sen 1982:104).

Sen's arguments show that there are good analytic and empirical reasons for judging that much actual human behavior is not explicable on the basis of a simple utility-maximizing scheme. This finding might lead us to suppose that human beings are typically not rational or it might lead us to question the concept of rationality associated with the standard conception. Sen suggests the latter course and proposes that we attempt to build a more structured concept of practical reason that permits us to take account of moral, political, and personal commitments as well as concern for welfare. Moreover he shows that the former cannot be subsumed under the simple concepts of utility-maximizing or preference rank-ordering. (Sen's main contributions are contained in "Rational Fools" and "The Impossibility of a Paretian Liberal" in Sen 1982.) Thus he holds that an adequate theory of rationality requires more structure than a simple utility-maximizing model would allow; in particular it must take account of moral principles and commitment.

This argument suggests that the concept of rationality must incorporate normative principles in some way. How might this be done? Recent work in moral philosophy offers some insight into this problem. Various moral philosophers have argued that practical rationality is more comprehensive than narrow economic rationality. Thus Thomas Nagel provides a series of arguments to the effect that rationality requires altruism—recognition of the reality of the interests of others and a direct willingness to act out of regard for those interests (T. Nagel 1970). The egoism assumption is neither mandatory nor plausible as a basis for rational choice analysis. Instead it is perfectly consistent to postulate that individuals define a range of goals, from narrow self-interest to the interests of the family to the interests of more encompassing groups, and choose their actions according to the degree to which various alternatives serve this ensemble of interests. All that the rational choice requires is that these be *individual* goals—that is, goals established and pursued by individual agents. But the content of the goals may be other-regarding. It is the structure of means-end rationality rather than the particular character of the ends that individuals pursue that is essential for the rational choice approach.

This line of thought directly addresses the egoism assumption of the standard conception. It does not, however, do quite enough for it does not give us a way of incorporating the idea of moral principles (or other normative requirements) into the decisionmaking process. But other recent moral philosophers have outlined the sort of structured decisionmaking process necessary to take account of the role of principle in decisionmaking: The decisionmaker can combine a set of side constraints on action (normative commitments, in Sen's terms) as well as a set of goals (personal interest, social goals, the welfare of others, etc.).

In particular a number of philosophers have attempted to incorporate the idea of *fairness* into the concept of rational decisionmaking.[6] A reason for my performing an act is that I benefit from widespread performance of this sort of act, and I recognize that fairness requires that I pay my share of the cost of these public benefits. John Rawls's *A Theory of Justice* represents an extended argument to the effect that there are principles of justice that should regulate the just society, derived from the principle of fairness. His construction is at some distance from our primary concern because he is concerned with global features of justice and we are concerned with individual rationality. But the kernel of Rawls's construction is relevant here: If individual rationality involves evaluating alternative lines of action in terms not only of the costs and benefits of each alternative but of the fairness of each alternative, then we have arrived at a structured concept of rationality. And it is a concept that involves the imposition of side constraints on the decisionmaking process. A more structured decisionmaking process is necessary to take account of the role of principle in decisionmaking: The decisionmaker can combine a set of side constraints on action as well as a set of goals. And the decisions he or she arrives at will be a complex function of constraints and goal-maximizing actions.

How do these findings relate to our central concerns? First they suggest that the narrow conception of economic rationality is not a comprehensive theory of practical reason because it fails to consider certain features of the decisionmaking process that are intuitively crucial in some contexts. Further these considerations suggest an alternative model of the decisionmaking process that promises to be a more adequate analysis of the concept of human rationality. Moreover this richer conception of practical reason promises to offer a new set of solutions to different classes of collective action problems: If individuals are altruistic to some degree (that is, responsive to the interests of others) and if they are principled (that is, moved by considerations of fairness, reciprocity, or justice), then they will be practically motivated to act differently, when confronted with occasions for collective action, than the theory of collective action predicts.

These findings have direct import for the applicability of rational choice models in social explanations. For example, consider the problem of free-riding and public goods problems. Once we consider a more complex theory of practical deliberation, formal arguments predicting the emergence of public goods problems in real social groups will be found to be misleading. On a more complex and more empirically adequate account of practical reason, altruism, cooperation, and reciprocity are rational choices; therefore we would expect a social group consisting of rational individuals to show marks of cooperation and altruism.

We must be careful not to draw an overly strong conclusion, however, for no one would maintain that human beings are indifferent to private welfare. Indeed generally speaking it would seem reasonable to assume that each decisionmaker places a high priority on personal and familial welfare; human beings generally do not behave like impartial utilitarians. This finding suggests that human behavior is the result of several different forms of motive, such as self-interest and altruism, and several different types of decisionmaking processes, including maximizing and side-constraint testing. (See Margolis 1982 for an attempt to formalize some of these contrasts.) And to the degree that self-interest and maximizing behavior are prominent in a particular type of circumstance, the collective action theorem will be empirically significant. These criticisms, then, do not discredit the rational choice approach; rather they suggest the need for further development of the theory of individual rationality.

CONCLUSION

This chapter has surveyed the foundations of the rational choice approach to social explanation. The general idea is to explain specific social phenomena as the aggregate result of large numbers of rational persons making choices within a specific social and natural environment. What gives social content to this approach is the level of detail provided about specifics of the social environment. So, for example, rational persons within a traditional peasant society may show substantially different patterns of behavior from those of persons in modern industrialized societies. And these differences may derive not from differences in the psychology or agency of the persons involved but from substantive differences in each group's environment of choice.

The rational choice approach underlies several important research programs in social science that will be considered in greater detail below. The *public choice* paradigm attempts to explain social and economic behavior of persons in non-Western societies on the basis of fairly narrow assumptions about individual rationality. This paradigm forms the basis of work in *economic anthropology*. And the rational choice paradigm has close affinities with *materialist explanation* and Marxist theory, for materialists and Marxist social scientists attempt to explain aggregate social structures as the result of rational individuals pursuing their material interests.

Before we turn to these applications of the rational choice approach, however, we must consider a powerful line of criticism against this approach— the view that social science requires *interpretation* of culturally specific norms, values, and meanings. This view suggests that the rational choice framework is fundamentally flawed because it attempts to abstract from the culturally specific content of agency and replace it with an abstract, universal model of rationality. In the next chapter, then, we will consider the interpretive paradigm of social explanation.

NOTES

1. For a brief but clear discussion of this type of theory of rationality, see Philip Pettit, "Rational Man Theory," in Hookway and Pettit, eds. (1978). Von Wright (1971) provides a more extensive analysis of rational-intentional explanations. My *Understanding Peasant China* (1989) explores the application of this model to China studies.

2. For a useful discussion of "thin" and "thick" theories of rationality in area studies, see Michael Taylor's useful essay, "Rationality and Revolutionary Collective Action," in Michael Taylor, ed. (1988). This collection provides a number of strong examples of the rational choice approach in application to area studies.

3. Particularly important are Axelrod (1984), Rapoport and Chammah (1965), Hardin (1982), and M. Taylor (1976).

4. The qualification of open-endedness is important. If the series ends at the hundredth game, then each party foresees that the other will defect on the last game. But if the opponent is determined to defect on the hundredth game, then the player should defect on the ninety-ninth game and so forth back to the first game. See Hardin (1982:146 ff.) on this paradox.

5. Kenneth Oye provides a thoughtful consideration of the relevance of game theory to applied social science in his introduction to *Cooperation Under Anarchy* (1986). He writes, "The equilibrium solutions identified by formal game theorists may stabilize convergent expectations among mathematicians, but unless equilibria can also be reached through 'alternative less sophisticated routes,' such solutions may have little influence on international outcomes" (Oye, ed. 1986:2).

6. See, for example, the extensive literature on utilitarianism and fairness (Regan 1980, Griffin 1985, and Harsanyi 1985).

SUGGESTIONS FOR FURTHER READING

Axelrod, Robert. 1984. *The Evolution of Cooperation.*
Becker, Gary. 1976. *The Economic Approach to Human Behavior.*
Bonner, John. 1986. *Introduction to the Theory of Social Choice.*

Elster, Jon. 1979. *Ulysses and the Sirens.*
Elster, Jon, ed. 1986. *Rational Choice.*
Rapoport, Anatol. 1966. *Two-Person Game Theory.*
Schelling, Thomas C. 1978. *Micromotives and Macrobehavior.*
Sen, Amartya. 1987. *On Ethics and Economics.*
Shubik, Martin. 1982. *Game Theory in the Social Sciences: Concepts and Solutions.*
Simon, Herbert A. 1983. *Reason in Human Affairs.*
Taylor, Michael. 1987. *The Possibility of Cooperation.*

4
INTERPRETATION THEORY

In the previous two chapters we have examined approaches to social science that emphasize the importance of generalizations in social explanation. In this chapter we turn to an approach that emphasizes instead the importance of the particulars of different cultures and holds that the central goal of social inquiry is the *interpretation* of meaningful human practices. This approach distinguishes between explanation and understanding: Explanation involves identifying general causes of an event, whereas understanding involves discovering the meaning of an event or practice in a particular social context (Von Wright 1971:5–6). The goal of social inquiry is to reconstruct the meaning or significance of social arrangements and practices. This approach is thus *hermeneutic*: It treats social phenomena as a text to be decoded through imaginative reconstruction of the significance of various elements of the social action or event. The interpretive framework thus holds that social science is radically unlike natural science because it unavoidably depends upon the interpretation of meaningful human behavior and social practices. Natural science is concerned with objective causal processes, but social science is concerned with meaningful actions and practices. The former may be objectively described and explained; the latter require interpretation and understanding. Explanation, then, is the goal of the natural sciences, and understanding is the goal of the social sciences.

The philosopher Charles Taylor describes the interpretive framework in his essay "Interpretation and the Sciences of Man" (C. Taylor 1985b). He argues that social science *must* be interpretive and hermeneutic and that social inquiry that depends exclusively on objective factors (causal relations, social structures, abstract rationality) will inevitably fail. Thus he writes, "My thesis amounts to an alternative statement of the main proposition of interpretive social science, that an adequate account of human action must make the agents more understandable. On this view, it cannot be a sufficient objective of social theory that it just predict . . . the actual pattern of social or historical events. . . . A satisfactory explanation must also make sense of the agents" (C. Taylor 1985b:116).

The interpretive program for social science can be represented as maintaining a number of interrelated points:

- Individual actions and beliefs can only be understood through an act of interpretation, by which the inquirer attempts to discover the meaning or significance of those actions or beliefs for the agent.
- There is radical diversity across cultures concerning the way in which social life is conceptualized, and these differences give rise to diverse social worlds.
- Social practices (bargaining, promising, going to work, parenting) are constituted by the meanings that participants attribute to them.
- There are no "brute facts" in social science—facts that do not allude to specific cultural meanings.

The import of these positions is fairly clear. To provide a satisfactory analysis of a given social phenomenon, it is necessary to arrive at an interpretation of the meanings that agents within that culture assign to their actions and social relations. Social science is therefore unavoidably hermeneutical, and those social sciences that fail to provide such understanding are fundamentally misdirected.

Consider an example of interpretation by a leading interpretive anthropologist, Clifford Geertz (Example 4.1). In Geertz's interpretation of the cultural significance of cockfighting in Bali, he attempts to connect this apparently superficial social practice to deep elements of Balinese selfhood. He interprets the pattern of large-scale betting on cockfights as emblemizing social relationships in local society—kinship, village, and status relationships. And he construes the cockfight itself as an emblem—positive or negative— for elements of Balinese life. Note what this account does not provide. It does not tell us what processes or mechanisms brought about cockfighting (a causal explanation). And it does not attempt to show how individual Balinese men pursue their own interests or purposes through cockfighting (a rational choice explanation). This account, then, does not provide an explanation of the practice; instead it offers a reading of the practice in its context, intended to elucidate the meaning of the practice for us.

INTERPRETATION AND AGENCY

The central notion in the approach studied in this chapter is that of an *interpretation* of an action or practice. Interpretation involves viewing individual actions and social practices as expressive of human meanings. We may use the conception of *agency* to refer to the fact that human beings are deliberate, symbolic actors who act on the basis of their understanding and wants. Agents' understanding consists of a number of features: a representation of the world in which they find themselves, a set of values and purposes characterizing their wants, a set of norms determining the limits on action beyond which transgression is shameful, a conception of their own powers and capacities, and so forth. The rational choice model of explanation adopts a particularly thin and abstract perspective on agency, emphasizing causal beliefs, material interests, and instrumental reasoning.

Example 4.1   A Balinese cockfight

Balinese men spend a great deal of time involved in cockfights—grooming and training the birds, feeding them, watching the fights and betting on them, discussing the strengths and weaknesses of the competing birds, and so on. Why is this activity (sport?) such a prominent part of Balinese village life? Clifford Geertz offers a detailed interpretation of the significance of cockfighting in Bali that aims to locate the activity within the larger compass of Balinese culture. He discusses the jokes and language associated with cockfighting and the social meanings to which cockfighting is related. Particularly important, in Geertz's account, is the Balinese distaste for animal-like behavior in human beings; animals represent the "Powers of Darkness" (Geertz 1971e:420). Geertz construes the fascination with cockfighting as a surrogate for the struggle between good and evil: "In the cockfight, man and beast, good and evil, ego and id, the creative power of aroused masculinity and the destructive power of loosened animality fuse in a bloody drama of hatred, cruelty, violence, and death" (Geertz 1971e:420–21). He concludes, "To treat the cockfight as a text is to bring out a feature of it . . . that treating it as a rite or a pastime, the two most obvious alternatives, would tend to obscure: its use of emotion for cognitive ends. . . . In the cockfight, then, the Balinese forms and discovers his temperament and his society's temper at the same time. . . . The culture of a people is an ensemble of texts, themselves ensembles, which the anthropologist strains to read over the shoulders of those to whom they properly belong" (Geertz 1971e:449, 451, 452).

Data: ethnographic findings in a Balinese village
Explanatory model: interpretation of the significance of a complex cultural practice
Source: Clifford Geertz, "Deep Play: Notes on the Balinese Cockfight" (1971e)

But it is also possible to specify more nuanced descriptions of the state of agency of the individual, including extensive description of the individual's values, worldview, assumptions, and modes of thought. And the central claim of interpretive social science is that more detailed accounts of agency are needed if we are to make sense of individual and social action.

To give an interpretation of an action, then, involves giving a description of the cultural context and state of mind of the agent in a way that makes his or her action intelligible to us. The goal of interpretation is to make sense of an action or practice—to discern the meaning of the practice in the context of a system of meaningful cultural symbols and representations. Consider a simple example. Suppose we observe a man walking down the street. He passes under a ladder, looks up, and then hurries to a wooden bench nearby. He taps on the bench with his knuckles, mops his brow, drops his bag, and then continues along the street. An alien observer would find this sequence of events and actions puzzling; it is plainly a series of deliberate actions undertaken in response to the shifting environment, but it appears to be unmotivated. The man's action does not wear its meaning on its sleeve. Now suppose that we offer an interpretation of the scene. The man is a poorly educated peasant, with strong but simple religious beliefs. He believes that certain events in ordinary life are portents of things to come: Black cats, ladders, and broken mirrors portend bad luck. He believes that there are things one can do to ward off bad luck, such as knocking on wood. Seeing that he has inadvertently walked under a ladder (bad luck!), he hurries to the nearest wooden object and knocks on wood (a remedy). Relieved that he has done what he can to protect himself, he mops his brow (a customary, reflexive way of expressing relief in his culture) and resumes his walk. Dropping the bag is just an accident; it has no meaning and supports no further interpretation.

The story I have just told amounts to an interpretation of the man's behavior; it is an account of his beliefs and understanding of the meaning of events in the world that makes sense of his subsequent actions. This story represents interpretation at two levels: first an interpretation of common social meanings in the man's culture (the significance of black cats and ladders), and second an interpretation of particular actions by the man (knocking on wood and mopping his brow).

There is a strong and deliberate parallel between interpreting human action and interpreting a literary text. The investigator is presented with an ensemble of meaningful elements and attempts to discover the significant connections among them. (This is what makes interpretation a *hermeneutic* process.) Once such a description has been provided, the investigator has shown that the agent's behavior is not "irrational"; rather it fits into a larger cultural and normative system, and the whole system is coherent. The conception of means-end rationality is one possible model of human action that may give us an interpretive framework within which to understand the agent's action. But we may also interpret an action as a symbolic display, as a dramatic device, as a ritualistic performance, etc.

How should the social scientist investigate meaningful social action? Is there an "interpretive method" that can guide him in making an interpretation? An important formulation of this idea of a method appropriate to social science can be found in Max Weber's concept of *verstehen*.[1] This method distinguishes between social science and natural science, according to Weber. In *The Methodology of the Social Sciences*, he describes the method in these terms: "In the social sciences we are concerned with psychological and intellectual phenomena the empathic understanding of which is naturally a problem of a specifically different type from those which the schemes of the exact natural sciences in general can or seek to solve" (Weber 1949:74). A few pages later he writes, "We have designated as 'cultural sciences' those disciplines which analyze the phenomena of life in terms of their cultural significance. The *significance* of a configuration of cultural phenomena and the basis of this significance cannot however be derived and rendered intelligible by a system of analytical laws. . . . The concept of culture is a *value-concept*" (Weber 1949:76).

According to the method of interpretation, the goal of the social scientist is to arrive at a hypothesis about the agent's state of mind in performing a given action—the beliefs, values, and purposes that bring the agent to perform the action. Weber refers to this process as "explanatory under-standing": "This is rational understanding of the motivation, which consists in placing the act in an intelligible and more inclusive context of meaning" (Weber 1978:8). He sometimes uses the term "empathy" to characterize this process, but he does not suppose that there is a distinctive faculty that permits us to interpret the agent's state of mind. Instead it is a matter of considering possible beliefs, purposes, and values that *might* generate the action and then attempting to determine through direct and indirect evidence whether the interpretation is correct (Weber 1978:8–9). The method of *verstehen*, then, is based on a process of hypothesis-formation through which the investigator forms a conjecture concerning the state of mind of the agent and then tries to test this conjecture against the agent's actions and speech.

Clifford Geertz describes an interpretive method in many of his works. He writes in *Local Knowledge*:

> What the anthropologist has to do . . . is tack between the two sorts of descriptions—between increasingly fine-comb observations . . . and increasingly synoptic characterizations . . . in such a way that, held in the mind together, they present a credible, fleshed-out picture of a human form of life. "Translation," here, is not a simple recasting of others' ways of putting things in terms of our own ways of putting them . . . but displaying the logic of their ways of putting them in the locutions of ours; a conception which again brings it rather closer to what a critic does to illumine a poem than what an astronomer does to account for a star. (Geertz 1983:10)

It is reasonable to conclude from the vagueness of both Weber's and Geertz's descriptions that there is *no* distinctive method of interpretation—no set of rules that permits us to derive an interpretation from a description of social behavior. Instead the problem confronting the interpretive social scientist is the familiar one of hypothesis-formation. The interpretive social scientist must arrive at a hypothesis about the meaning of an action that makes sense of the action in light of the known facts. And—as in other areas of science—there is no recipe for a good hypothesis.

When presented with an interpretation of an action or practice—for example, the story about the man and the ladder—we are forced to consider the problem of verification: How are we to determine whether the inter-pretation is true or false? What criteria of adequacy are available for deciding between conflicting interpretations? What empirical tools can be used to probe the meaning of the actions and practices we observe? The criterion that plays the most prominent role in discussions of method by interpretive social scientists is *coherence*—the requirement that the elements of the interpretation should hang together as a consistent, meaningful whole. This approach raises two problems, however.

First, what sort of coherence is at issue? The notion of logical coherence is available but too weak to do the job for it requires only that there be no logical contradictions in the account provided. Suppose, for example, that the story of the man and the ladder is modified so that the man is a highly educated engineer. Our interpretation now appears somewhat inconsistent for we are attributing superstitious beliefs to a man who is by profession trained to be rational about causal processes. There is nothing logically contradictory about such an assumption; rather the traits of superstitiousness and causal rationality seem unlikely to go together. It is difficult to provide a convincing account of the notion of incompatibility that is at work here. It is akin to an expression of aesthetic coherence— the idea that some symbolic elements do hang together, whereas others do not. But this idea is too subjective to serve as a useful criterion of truth.

Second, the requirement of coherence is too weak because it does not give us a basis for making empirical judgments about interpretations. When we are offered an interpretation of an event or practice, we want to know more than that it is a consistent interpretation (that is, true in some possible world). We want a reason to believe that it is *true* (that is, true in this world). And this appears unavoidably to require that we offer empirical evidence in support of the interpretation; we need some way of using our observations of the participants and their background culture to support certain interpretations and exclude others.

Fortunately it is possible to offer empirical support for an interpretation. We can turn to the evidence of the agent's own avowals or avowals from other members of the same culture. We can ask the man, in the case above, why he knocked on wood, and he may reply along lines that strongly support the interpretation we have advanced. But it is also possible that his testimony will discredit our interpretation. For example, he may say that his hand had fallen asleep and he tapped his knuckles to shake off an unpleasant sensation. This explanation discredits our interpretation because it implies that there is no connection between his walking under the ladder and his tapping the wooden bench. The agent's testimony is not decisive, of course; we may judge that he suffers from self-deception, that he does not understand his own motives, that he is embarrassed to admit his superstitiousness, and so on. But such a claim on our part requires that we have other sources of empirical support for our contrary interpretation. We may also consider the evidence of behavior. If we have observed other such incidents, with similarly adaptive behavior, we may regard the resulting behavioral regularities as evidence for the truth of the interpretation that members of this culture are superstitious.

Let us now pose a question of central concern in this book. Is an interpretation of an action or practice *explanatory*? Or is it rather a distinctive kind of description? It is clear, to start with, that a plausible interpretation of an action or practice is explanatory in the weakest sense; it provides us with information we did not previously have, in the context of which the action or practice is intelligible or comprehensible. When we ask why the man knocked on wood, the reply—that he is superstitious—satisfies us because it permits us to understand his action. However it seems reasonable to state that explanation requires more than this. Recall our discussion of "why-necessary" questions in Chapter 1. There it was held that explanations paradigmatically involve identifying necessary or probable sequences of events. In this light we have explained an event when we have identified the antecedent circumstances that made the event necessary or probable. An interpretation does not conform to this model. Instead we may better construe an interpretation as a description of a semiotic state of affairs (the way things stand in terms of meanings for a culture or individual). Here, then, to provide an interpretation is to provide a description of a distinctive sort; what it describes is a configuration of meanings in a culture or individual.

It can also be argued that interpretations provide the basis for genuine explanations of social phenomena. Here we may follow the line of argument that Donald Davidson pursues in his analysis of reasons as causes (Davidson 1963/80). According to Davidson, the fact that a person has a reason to do x is properly understood as a *cause* of his actually doing x. We may extend this argument to interpretations by holding that the fact that a person understands an action in a certain way—for example, he regards it as the proper ritual performance in the circumstances—is a *cause* of his subsequent performance of the action. Thus interpretations capture states of the world that can function as causal conditions (states of agency), and therefore interpretations can serve as the basis for explanations.

Consider an example of a social analysis that depends on analysis of social meanings—Michael Adas's account of millenarian rebellions in the colonial world (Example 4.2). Adas attempts to understand millenarian rebellions "from within"—in terms of the religious ideas and practices that characterized these movements. He then tries to provide a causal analysis of the emergence of these symbol systems in various parts of the non-Western world. This latter effort takes him a step away from Geertz's analysis of Balinese cockfighting in Example 4.1, however, for Geertz implies that interpretation is the beginning and end of social explanation and that causal analysis is out of place in social inquiry.

SOCIAL ACTION

Let us now look more closely at some of the elements of interpretation theory. A central topic in this approach is the view that social action is inherently meaningful: It is not possible to provide meaning-neutral descriptions of social actions or practices. Weber writes of the concept of social action in these terms: "Sociology . . . is a science concerning itself with the interpretive understanding of social action and thereby with a causal explanation of its course and consequences. We shall speak of 'action' insofar as the acting individual attaches a subjective meaning to his behavior—be it overt or covert, omission or acquiescence. Action is 'social' insofar as its subjective meaning takes account of the behavior of others and is thereby oriented in its course" (Weber 1978:4). This passage makes two central points: first that actions are by definition partially constituted by a subjective meaning or intention on the part of the agent; second that a social action

Example 4.2 Millenarian rebellion

Religiously inspired rebellions occurred against colonial rule in various parts of the non-Western world in the nineteenth and twentieth centuries: Java, New Zealand, India, East Africa, and Burma. In each case colonial bureaucracies had infiltrated local society to impose taxes and regulations, and each rebellion was organized around a syncretic religion and a charismatic leader prophesizing a changing age—a *millenarian* ideology. Michael Adas attempts to explain the relations between these circumstances. This problem breaks down into two topics: Why did rebellion occur against colonialism? And why did it so commonly take the millenarian form? Adas believes the answer to the first question is straightforward: Colonized peoples had many pressing and legitimate grievances that could not be resolved except through violent protest. His answer to the second question, however, is more complex. There were millennial traditions in several (though not all) of these societies. It was critical, however, that there should be a prophetic leader who could mold a coherent ideology capable of mobilizing followers (Adas 1979:116). And given the apparently overwhelming strength of European colonial powers—military resources, scientific knowledge, and administrative capacity—millenarian, magical ideologies were the most effective way of inducing large numbers of followers in local society. "Through these prophetic figures and their divinely inspired revelations, a belief in the efficacy of resistance and the possibility of escape from their troubles was born and nurtured among deprived, colonized peoples" (Adas 1979:121). Millenarianism, then, was an intelligible ideological response to the material power of colonial states, and it provided the basis for large-scale mobilization against the colonial powers.

Data: data describing millenarian protest movements in Asia, Africa, and the Pacific

Explanatory model: millenarian movements can be understood as a common cultural response to the economic and ideological incursions of Western cultures into non-Western societies

Source: Michael Adas, *Prophets of Rebellion: Millenarian Protest Movements Against the European Colonial Order* (1979)

---

is one whose subjective meaning is oriented toward the actions of others. When I return a library book on the due date, the meaning of the action is my intention to avoid the fine. When I get up at dawn to drive to the beach early and avoid the traffic, my action is a social action because my intention is oriented toward the actions of others (in this case to avoid the consequences of the actions of other persons).

It is clear enough what is meant in stating that action is meaningful; this simply reflects the intentional character of action, the idea that agents have purposes and their own understanding of the meaning of their bodily motions. But what does it mean to say that all social phenomena are intrinsically meaningful? Here the idea is that social phenomena are not objective in the way that natural entities are. Instead social phenomena are (partially) constituted by the assumptions, concepts, and intentions of the persons who participate in them. Electromagnetic fields have objective properties that are independent of the ways in which human beings conceive of them. It is plausible to hold, by contrast, that human institutions and practices are inherently dependent on the ways in which participating persons conceive of them—or at least that is the position taken by interpretation theory. Clifford Geertz makes the point in these terms: "Interpretive explanation . . . trains its attention on what institutions, actions, images, utterances, events, customs . . . mean to those whose institutions, actions, customs, and so on they are. As a result, it issues not in laws like Boyle's, or forces like Volta's, or mechanisms like Darwin's, but in constructions like Burckhardt's, Weber's, or Freud's: systematic unpackings of the conceptual world in which *condottiere,* Calvinists, or paranoids live" (Geertz 1983:22).

The interpretation theorist concedes that there are meaning-neutral things that we can say about types of social relations—e.g., exchange systems, kinship systems, or patron-client relations—but holds that these characterizations do not give us insight into how such social relations work in a particular cultural context. Consider the idea of a kinship system. We might make a preliminary effort to define this concept in meaning-independent terms as *the structure of social relations among blood relations and marriage relations in a particular culture.* This definition then allows us to identify kinship systems in a variety of cultures—e.g., Nuer, Berber, and Boston Brahmin cultures. However interpretation theorists hold that this is a pointless abstraction because it takes us no closer to an understanding of how kinship works in these different cultures—what the social significance of kinship is for Nuer, Berber, and Boston Brahmin men and women. And in order to address this question we must descend from the abstract plane to the level of the concrete subjective understandings of kinship relations found among the participants in these various cultures: what values constrain the choice of marriage partners; what obligations are experienced toward one's elders; what forms of loyalty, affection, or aversion are experienced toward brothers, sisters, cousins, and children. Only when we have provided a specific account of the significance of kinship relations for Berber men and women have we made a genuine contribution to the understanding of kinship at all for the kinship system only has social effects through the particular meanings that participants attribute to it.

These arguments suggest that the human sciences require interpretation, then, on two levels. To understand individual meanings and actions it is necessary to interpret them, and to understand social practices it is necessary to understand the meanings and values that their participants attribute to them. Interpretation of individual action may take a variety of forms, either as goal-directed activity action or as symbolic participatory action. Social phenomena are in part *constituted* by the interpretive schemes that members of a society employ to organize their social worlds, to explain their own behavior, to justify or condemn the actions of others and the workings of institutions, and the like. It is impossible, then, to properly understand social practices and institutions unless we properly interpret the significance of the actions and meanings of the persons who embody them.

MODELS OF SOCIAL ACTION

To interpret meaningful social action we need some paradigm examples of types of meaningful human behavior; that is, we need some background ideas about the various forms that meaningful social action takes. We have already seen one such paradigm—Geertz's frontal assault on the meaning of a given social practice (Balinese cockfighting). In this case Geertz attempts to piece together an account of the cultural symbols that frame the cockfight, much as a literary critic might identify the literary conventions in the context of which we should read *The Brothers Karamazov*. There are several other models that have influenced the general perspective of interpretive social science, however, and, without hoping to offer a complete treatment, I will discuss several of these models in the next few pages—ritual, drama, rule-following, and practice. The utility of the interpretive approach as a contribution to social science depends chiefly on the degree to which interpretive social scientists succeed in identifying symbolic structures within human behavior.

An important concept in interpretive social science is that of *ritual*: a rule-guided sequence of behavior consecrated by religious meanings (Geertz 1971b:112). Here we have a conception of social meaning that emphasizes repetitive symbolic behavior. The central model is not goal-directed action but dramatic participation. Weber's conception of social action remains rationalistic; it recommends that we understand an action in terms of the purposes and intentions of the agent. But anthropologists like Geertz and Victor Turner have broadened the notion of meaningful action by focusing on other paradigm examples—behavior that is participatory, rule-guided, and dramatic rather than prudential and goal-pursuing.

Consider, for example, Geertz's description of a Javanese funeral. "The mood of a Javanese funeral is not one of hysterical bereavement, unrestrained sobbing, or even of formalized cries of grief for the deceased's departure. Rather, it is a calm, undemonstrative, almost languid letting go, a brief ritualized relinquishment of a relationship no longer possible. Tears are not approved of and certainly not encouraged; the effort is to get the job done, not to linger over the pleasures of grief. . . . The whole momentum of the Javanese ritual system is supposed to carry one through grief without severe emotional disturbance" (Geertz 1971d:153). Here we have a model of social action that involves individuals' carrying out a sequence of actions that are prescribed by social convention and that correspond to meaningful human needs—grief, in this case—but that are not prudential or goal-directed. Instead we can say that the participants are taking part in a socially regulated performance that collectively embodies a meaningful response to a biological event—death.

Another important contributor to interpretive social science is Victor Turner. He approaches the problem of interpreting social action by using the organizing concept of a *drama*. The notion of a drama—an extended interaction between a number of characters over time—permits him to emphasize the temporal structure of social action and the creative agency through which social actions unfold. "Social dramas and social enterprises . . . represent sequences of social events, which, seen retrospectively by an observer, can be shown to have structure. Such 'temporal' structure, unlike atemporal structure . . . is organized primarily through relations in time rather than in space" (Turner 1974:35–36). The notion of a drama is thus a device in terms of which to represent meaningful human activity extended over time. "Social dramas . . . can be isolated for study in societies at all levels of scale and complexity" (Turner 1974:33). A social drama is a structured and temporally extended situation in which a number of actors play out their interests, concerns, and intentions within the context of a culturally defined world. Turner writes, "Social dramas, then, are units of aharmonic or disharmonic processes, arising in conflict situations. Typically, they have four main phases of public action. . . . 1. Breach of regular, norm-governed social relations occurs between persons or groups with the same system of social relations. . . . 2. Following breach of regular, norm-governed social actions, a phase of mounting *crisis* supervenes. . . . 3. This brings us to the third phase, *redressive action*. In order to limit the spread of crisis, certain adjustive and redressive 'mechanisms' . . . informal or formal, institutionalized or ad hoc, are swiftly brought into operation by leading or structurally representative members of the disturbed social system. . . . 4. The final phase I distinguished consists either in the *reintegration* of the disturbed social group or of the social recognition and legitimization of irreparable schism between the contesting parties" (Turner 1974:37–41).

Turner offers, then, a paradigm of interpretation of social processes: To understand a social arrangement or outcome we must focus on the process through which that outcome emerged, and that process may be understood in the framework of social drama. Therefore we can understand a wide variety of social phenomena in a range of cultures using the framework of a social drama. This leads the investigator to focus on both the meanings that participants attribute to a sequence of events *and* their interactive behavior over time—the ways in which their behavior is affected by previous actions of other participants.

Another important theoretical attempt to provide a framework for interpreting repetitive behavior (e.g., ritual, etiquette, or marriage practices) is Pierre Bourdieu's *Outline of a Theory of Practice* (1977). Many aspects of human behavior appear to be rule guided, such as grammatical speech, polite behavior in formal social occasions, marriage patterns, and religious ritual. Anthropologists have often attempted to conceive of such behavior in terms of a model of rule-following, with the result that a given behavior is merely the instance of the rule applying in particular circumstances. The rules generate the behavior. Bourdieu argues that this model is deeply misleading, however, because it does not give sufficient priority to human *practice* (practical, deliberate human action within the context of social, cultural, and material constraints). As the model of human social behavior, he offers the analogy of an extended interaction between two intelligent actors (for example, two boxers jockeying for advantage within the context of the rules of a prize fight) in place of the idea of an authoritative system of rules. "In dog-fights, as in the fighting of children or boxers, each move triggers off a counter-move, every stance of the body becomes a sign pregnant with a meaning that the opponent has to grasp while it is still incipient, reading in the beginnings of a stroke or a sidestep the imminent future, i.e., the blow or the dummy" (Bourdieu 1977:1).

Bourdieu considers the idea that repetitive behavior might be best characterized by the notion of rule-governed action and argues that this framework underplays the role of deliberation and strategic thinking. He introduces the idea of a "habitus"—"the durably installed generative principle of regulated improvisations [that] produces practices which tend to reproduce the regularities imminent in the objective conditions of the production of their generative principle" (Bourdieu 1977:78). One of the virtues of this concept is the fact that it permits us to consider habitual behavior as *both* rule guided and agent centered; it offers yet another model in terms of which to understand the meanings that underlie human action.

Bourdieu considers the two paradigms in application to kinship systems and the practice of exogamy (marriage restricted to women from outside the man's lineage). The "legalistic" (rule-following) model holds that a set of kinship rules determine kinship behavior, whereas Bourdieu contends that kinship and marriage behavior is the outcome of many independent strategic choices by individuals and families. "Thus, far from obeying a norm which would designate an obligatory spouse from among the whole set of official kin, the arrangement of marriages depends directly on the state of the practical kinship relations, relationships through the men usable by the men and relationships through the women usable by the women, and on the state of the power relations within the 'house,' that is, between the lineages united by marriage in the previous generation, which allow and favour the cultivation of one or the other field of relationships" (Bourdieu 1977:52).

The symbolic, dramaturgical, and practice-oriented approaches give rise to a rich program of research for the anthropologist can identify the rituals, conventions, and symbolic performances that underlie much collective life in a given culture and can then piece together the meaningful connections among various elements of these performances. This provides a basis for understanding social action at two levels. The agent's action is understood once we have located it within a particular conventionally defined symbolic performance, and the performance type itself is understood when it is located within the larger system of symbolic activities.

Consider two examples that illustrate concrete investigations of the meaningful conceptions and self-identities of various human groups (Examples 4.3 and 4.4). Each of these examples involves the use of interpretive tools to make sense of historical phenomena. In Example 4.3 Arthur Wolf provides an interpretation of Chinese folk religion. This account focuses on establishing the relationships between the meaning of a complex of religious beliefs and practices and the "social metaphysics" characteristic of rural

---

Example 4.3   Popular culture in China

Poor rural people in China practiced a religion that included rituals directed to gods, ghosts, and ancestors. These practices were significantly different from official and high-culture religion in China. Arthur Wolf attempts to provide a coherent interpretation of the significance of these beliefs and rituals and show that this system of meanings corresponds closely to the way in which poor Chinese rural people perceived the social world around them. "This significance is largely determined by the worshippers' conception of their social world. . . . The most important point to be made about Chinese religion is that it mirrors the social landscape of its adherents" (Wolf, ed. 1978:131). For example, Wolf finds that the local gods were organized in "districts" that paralleled the administrative organization of officials; as there was an official responsible for a certain locale, so there was an "earth god" (T'u Ti Kung) with parallel responsibilities. Each earth god is represented by a clay figure in a small temple. And when earth gods fail in their responsibilities—for example, when they cannot control the weather—they may be punished in the same way that officials are punished: They can be banished to other areas or destroyed. Wolf quotes an observer: "A year or so ago, at Nanling Hsien during a drought, a god was publicly tried by the magistrate for neglect of duty, condemned, left in the hot sun to see how he liked it himself, and finally, after enduring every kind of insult, was broken in pieces" (Wolf 1978:144). He construes popular Chinese religion, then, as a projection of the social worldview of the Chinese rural lower class.

Data: ethnographic data drawn from interviews with poor rural Taiwanese in the 1960s
Explanatory model: interpretation of religious beliefs and explanation of those beliefs in terms of a correspondence between the spiritual world and the bureaucratic structure of the Chinese imperial state
Source: Arthur P. Wolf, "Gods, Ghosts, and Ancestors" (1978)

Chinese society. In Example 4.4 E. P. Thompson considers the historical processes through which members of a group come to share important symbolic understandings of their group and its place in the social world. He provides a detailed reconstruction of the historical development of the English working class—the meanings, values, and commitments that a historically specific group came to share over the better part of a century.

SOCIAL VARIABILITY AND THE PRIMACY OF CULTURE

One distinctive aspect of the interpretive framework, in contrast to the causal and rational choice approaches considered in previous chapters, is its inclination to insist that social inquiry must be culturally specific. There is no antecedent framework—whether instrumental rationality, materialism, or anything else—that will provide an explanatory key to a given society.

Example 4.4 The English working class

Classical Marxism maintains that classes tend to become class-conscious: They identify themselves as a class, identify the material interests they have in common, and crystallize as a collective agent. E. P. Thompson argues that the process of class formation is not mechanical or inevitable in the ways suggested by this account. Instead classes come to a state of conscious class-identity only through extended historical experiences in particular social circumstances. "By class I understand an historical phenomenon, unifying a number of disparate and seemingly unconnected events, both in the raw material of experience and in consciousness" (Thompson 1963:9). In *The Making of the English Working Class*, he explores in detail the historical route through which workers and artisans in England came to regard themselves as a class in the eighteenth and nineteenth centuries. "The class experience is largely determined by the productive relations into which men are born—or enter involuntarily. Class-consciousness is the way in which these experiences are handled in cultural terms: embodied in traditions, value-systems, ideas, and institutional forms" (Thompson 1963:9–10). He considers in detail both the changing technological circumstances and the political and cultural experiences that shaped the English working class—the Industrial Revolution, popular political movements, workingmen's self-improvement associations, unitarianism, the extinction of some trades and the creation of new categories of work, and so on. "The making of the working class is a fact of political and cultural, as much as of economic, history. It was not the spontaneous generation of the factory-system. Nor should we think of an external force—the 'industrial revolution'—working upon some nondescript undifferentiated raw material of humanity. . . . The factory hand or stockinger was also the inheritor of Bunyan, of remembered village rights, of notions of equality before the law, of craft traditions" (Thompson 1963:194).

Data: historical data concerning the circumstances of labor in eighteenth- and nineteenth-century England
Explanatory model: to explain the emergence of political identity and class-consciousness, it is necessary to examine the particular cultural, social, and economic circumstances in which a given class was forged
Source: E. P. Thompson, *The Making of the English Working Class* (1963)

Rather the values, meanings, practices, and the like that make up the given culture must be explored without presupposition about the sorts of processes that will be found. This preference for cultural specificity is connected with the primary emphasis on social meanings for this reason: If social phenomena are constituted by the workings of human consciousness and if human creativity is diverse, then there is no reason to suppose that different cultures will produce similar social processes and structures.

Thus the interpretive paradigm insists on the fundamental cultural variability of human meanings, with the result that frameworks that abstract from the cultural particulars will unavoidably disregard the essential. Geertz maintains that a systematic unpacking of local meanings is mandatory for social inquiry because there are few, if any, transcultural universals in either society or individual. Even the conception of the person is culturally specific. So it is impossible to make generalizations about even the most basic features of human aspiration and self-conception. Geertz writes, "The Western conception of the person as a bounded, unique, more or less integrated motivational and cognitive universe, a dynamic center of awareness, emotion, judgment, and action organized into a distinctive whole and set contrastively both against other such wholes and against its social and natural background, is, however incorrigible it may seem to us, a rather peculiar idea within the context of the world's cultures" (Geertz 1983:59). In light of this radical diversity of human selfhood across cultures, the anthropologist is strictly obliged to attempt to work out the *local* system of values, conceptions, beliefs, and the like through which local people conceive themselves and constitute their social world. It would appear to follow from this, however, that social science inquiries that are premised on some set of core characteristics of human motivation—e.g., material environment or rational self-interest—are radically misguided.

From this perspective the question of socialization is a fundamental one. Through what processes do children acquire the "correct" attitudes and understandings of the institutions into which they are born? It is essential to the interpretation theory approach that meanings are subjective but not individualistic; they are socially shared meanings. And this, in turn, has much to do with the processes by which persons internalize a system of implicit rules governing a social activity—for example, rules of social etiquette, playground basketball, or courtship ritual. The young Berber who aberrantly regards deference to his elders as a humiliating loss of self does not by himself reconstitute the elder-junior relation; instead he is a social misfit who has not correctly absorbed Berber social values and understandings. Berger and Luckmann (1966:57–63) consider these processes in *The Social Construction of Reality*. Their account defines social relations as both objective and subjective in this sense: They are objective in that they constitute a more or less fixed world of relations and ideas into which a child is introduced, and they are subjective in that they are constituted by the meaningful actions and representations of the persons who participate in them.

Turn now to a position intimately associated with interpretation theory: the view that cultural systems are autonomous from other social structures—in particular from economy and politics—and, even more strikingly, that local cultural forms must be understood before it is possible to identify economic and political structures. The underlying idea here is that symbolic forms constitute the terms and character of social action. Therefore it is necessary to understand the symbolic and meaningful context of action before we can properly interpret economic or political behavior within a particular culture.

Thus Marshall Sahlins criticizes attempts to explain social phenomena as the result in the aggregate of "practical reason"—individual action aimed at satisfying material needs. He draws a rough distinction between two broad families of social sciences—materialist science and cultural science. He writes in *Culture and Practical Reason* (1976):

> The alternatives in this venerable conflict between utilitarianism and a cultural account may be broadly phrased as follows: whether a cultural order is to be conceived as the codification of man's actual purposeful and pragmatic action; or whether, conversely, human action in the world is to be understood as mediated by the cultural design, which gives order at once to practical experience, customary practice, and the relation between the two. (Sahlins 1976:55)

Sahlins holds, then, that a society can only be understood through careful analysis of the specifics of its cultural elements—values, beliefs, symbols, practices, and the like. Against a materialist or rational choice framework, he rejects the premise that it is possible to explain *any* social phenomena on the basis of a rational adjustment to material circumstances: "One evident matter—for bourgeois society as much as the so-called primitive—is that material aspects are not usefully separated from the social, as if the first were referable to the satisfaction of needs by the exploitation of nature, the second to problems of the relations between men" (Sahlins 1976:205). Rather, Sahlins holds that needs and interests are unavoidably culturally specific, with the result that interpretation and cultural analysis are required before we can even begin the materialist's program. Sahlins states, then, that social science must contain a central element of interpretation of the significance of culturally specific practices, beliefs, and values. (See Example 7.5 in Chapter 7, which is drawn from Sahlins's work.) We will discuss the validity of his position in that chapter, where it will be argued that there is a core of human interests and beliefs that are cross-cultural, and, as a result, it is possible to motivate materialist and rational choice arguments without specific information about local culture.

One theoretical ground for this insistence on cultural specificity derives from the definition of social phenomena themselves. Interpretation theorists maintain that it is not possible to refer to social practices and institutions except through the specific complex of meanings and understandings found within the culture itself. Here essentially we have a thesis of social ontology: There are no universal or cross-cultural social entities. Rather each such prospective entity (class, contract, state) upon closer analysis turns out to be so closely dependent on the specific values and meanings of the local culture that it is inappropriate to use the same concept to refer to these practices.

Consider now the idea that social phenomena are radically dependent on the self-understandings of the participants in those phenomena. Alasdair MacIntyre provides an extensive discussion of the notion that social phenomena are constituted by the meanings participants attribute to them. "It is an obvious truism that no institution or practice is what it is, or does what it does, independently of what anyone whatsoever thinks or feels about it. For institutions and practices are always partially, even if to differing degrees, constituted by what certain people think and feel about them"

(MacIntyre 1973:174). Thus we cannot properly characterize the institution of a political party, for example, except in terms of the understandings that participants have of the institution. And these understandings may be significantly variable across different national cultures—making it impossible to arrive at an abstract, meaning-neutral concept of "political party" that can be applied across cultures.[2]

Is this position a compelling one? Is it plausible to conclude that social relations can only be described in terms of the particular meanings and attitudes that participants attribute to them? It is not; rather, it is possible to concede that the structures depend on local interpretations but then provide abstract and cross-cultural characterizations of these. Arguments in Chapters 6 and 7 will attempt to show that it is possible and useful to formulate "thin" conceptions of social structures and processes that characterize institutions and practices in terms of their salient effects on the interests and needs of participants. Paradigm examples of concepts of institutions, structures, or practices that are applied cross-culturally in various areas of social science include:

- forms of labor organization: family farming, wage labor, cooperative labor;
- surplus extraction systems and property: taxation, interest, rent, corvée labor;
- institutions of village governance: elites, village council;
- commercialization: exchange, markets, prices, subsistence and cash crops, systems of transportation and communication;
- organized social violence: banditry, piracy, local militias;
- extralocal political organizations: court, military, taxation, law.

These represent a variety of institutions, practices, organizations, and social forms that may be found in various social contexts, such as China, Vietnam, Indonesia, and medieval France. They constitute part of the social and material environment in the context of which rural people live their lives and to which these folk adapt their behavior. And various authors have shown that it is possible to explain some features of all these rural societies without any more specific information about local meanings and interpretations.

Does this mean that these are "value-neutral" descriptions of institutions? It does not. Rather these institutions and practices can be understood in the context of a core conception of agency as goal-directedness. Peasants, in this perspective, are presumed to consider existing circumstances of commercialization and choose strategies accordingly. That is, they attribute the appropriate economic significance to markets, prices, cash incomes, etc. Likewise they are presumed to be aware of the implications of various land-tenancy arrangements, credit arrangements, and tax-distribution schemes and to prefer those that minimize their obligations and risks. Once again we assume that they take a rational interpretive stance toward these arrangements. In short the core idea of agency permits us to put forward a conception of material and social institutions and practices and to postulate that peasants orient their behavior toward these practices accordingly.

Does this position imply that there are *not* important cultural particulars in terms of the significance that peasants attribute to these practices and institutions? It does not; thus tenant-client relations may be embedded in moral or religious understanding as well as economic-political calculations of advantage. What this view is committed to, however, is that the economic-political aspects of land-tenancy systems are universally salient and play some important role in explaining the behavior of the peasant and that in some cases it is not necessary to have a fuller and culturally informed interpretation of the self-interpretation of these social relations.

CONCLUSION

The interpretive approach to social phenomena amounts to the following thesis: All human action is mediated by a subjective social worldview; no social science is possible that does not penetrate the individual's social world. Thus all social action is framed by a meaningful social world. To understand, explain, or predict patterns of human behavior, we must first penetrate the social world of the individual—the meanings he attributes to the environment (social and natural), the values and goals he possesses, the choices he perceives, and the way he interprets other individuals' social action. Only then will we be able to analyze, interpret, and explain his behavior. But now the action is thickly described in terms of the meanings, values, assumptions, and interpretive principles the agent employs in his own understanding of his world.

Let us take this claim in its strong sense, then, as a normative prescription for the social sciences. Is it reasonable to hold that all social sciences must make use of a hermeneutical approach? If so, then the explanatory frameworks discussed in the previous two chapters—causal and rational choice explanation—must be rejected. In later chapters we will consider this issue more closely; Chapter 6 will present the case for materialist explanation, and Chapter 7 will examine the grounds for the application of the concept of rationality to non-Western cultures. But it is possible to anticipate the conclusions of those chapters briefly now. Examples provided here establish that the interpretive framework is a legitimate approach to some problems in social science. However the suggestion that all social inquiry should be conducted in this manner is not persuasive. There are substantial areas of social science and explanation within which problems of significance and interpretation do not arise and in which objective factors—material interests, social structures, coercive institutions—play the central explanatory roles. And there are many research topics in the social sciences for which hermeneutic analysis is neither mandatory nor insightful.

In particular, arguments will be offered in Chapter 7 to show that it is legitimate to apply the concept of rational self-interest cross-culturally and that it is reasonable for social scientists to postulate that a great deal of social history may be understood as the aggregate consequence of individuals acting out of a prudent regard for self- or family-welfare. This rational choice framework is not suited for every topic of social inquiry, to be sure, but for many problems in social research—technological change, rebellion, social cooperation, and economic decisionmaking—the rational choice framework is a defensible one. If this is conceded, it follows that these constitute important areas of social science where the central problem is *not* to discover culturally specific meanings and values. Rather it is to discover the specific social arrangements and institutions that constrain individual activity into certain channels and have the result in the aggregate of producing a given pattern of social life.

It might also be noted that it is unclear what social science would look like on a purely interpretive approach. Would it offer explanations, generalizations, and models? Or would it be simply a collection of concrete hermeneutical readings of different societies? Would any notion of law or regularity emerge? Should causation have a place in such a science? Strict adherence to the interpretive dogma would seem to lead to a form of social analysis that is highly descriptive and not at all explanatory.

Thus the interpretation theory assault fails in its general goal of discrediting rational choice theory and materialist social science. There are substantial areas of social science that are premised on a sophisticated set of assumptions about rationality and material circumstances of life that are theoretically legitimate and empirically fruitful. And these frameworks are compatible with the basic truth of interpretation theory—the meaningful character of human action. They share the assumption, implicitly or explicitly, that social science must flow through an understanding of human agency—choice, belief, reasoning, action. What distinguishes these programs is not agency but rather at what level it is possible to characterize agency. The interpretive program implicitly assumes that there is no culturally neutral and nontrivial level at which to describe agency and personhood; the materialist program denies this. It maintains that there is a significant core of human agency that is species-specific but not culturally specific and that the content of this description is sufficient, in many social circumstances, to generate good social explanations of social patterns.

Does this mean that the interpretive approach is itself misconceived? Are hermeneutic social science, interpretive social inquiry, and cultural investigation of meanings legitimate programs for social science? They certainly are, and it is clear that they provide answers to questions that other approaches cannot. These points suggest essentially that rational choice theory, materialism, and culture science are competing research programs, each founded on a valid insight into one aspect of human behavior and society. Both deliberative reason and cultural meanings influence behavior, social practice, and history. The question is: To what extent and in what circumstances is the influence of goal-directed rationality sufficiently strong to let us explain and predict outcomes without extensive interpretation of cultural factors?

And the premise of rational choice theory and materialism is that there are such areas, particularly involving the social arrangements of production, the political behavior of persons when political outcomes substantially affect interests described in the core, and the economic structures that regulate material life.

NOTES

1. A useful survey of the *verstehen* method may be found in Outhwaite (1975).

2. Other instances of this sort of argument include Charles Taylor's analysis of bargaining (C. Taylor 1985a:32–36) and Geertz's discussion of the unsuitability of the ensemble of European political concepts (state, power, advantage) in application to Bali (Geertz 1980:121–22).

SUGGESTIONS FOR FURTHER READING

Berger, Peter L., and Thomas Luckmann. 1966. *The Social Construction of Reality.*
Bourdieu, Pierre. 1977. *Outline of a Theory of Practice.*
Davidson, Donald. 1963/80. "Actions, Reasons, and Causes."
Geertz, Clifford. 1971. *The Interpretation of Cultures.*
Outhwaite, William. 1975. *Understanding Social Life: The Method Called Verstehen.*
Sahlins, Marshall. 1976. *Culture and Practical Reason.*
Taylor, Charles. 1985. *Philosophy and the Human Sciences: Philosophical Papers 2.*
Turner, Victor. 1974. *Dramas, Fields, and Metaphors: Symbolic Action in Human Society.*
Von Wright, Georg Henrik. 1971. *Explanation and Understanding.*
Weber, Max. 1949. *The Methodology of the Social Sciences.* Trans. and ed. by E. Shils and H. A. Finch.

PART II
VARIATIONS AND
ELABORATIONS

We have now explored several fundamental ideas about the basis of social explanation. In this part I turn to elaborations of these models in a variety of directions. Functional and structural explanations (Chapter 5) will be seen to take the form of causal explanations. Materialist explanations (Chapter 6) combine elements of both rational choice explanation and causal explanation, along lines prepared in Part I. Economic anthropology (Chapter 7) attempts to explain patterns of social behavior in the premodern world using the tools of rational choice theory. And statistical explanations of social phenomena (Chapter 8) attempt to discover causal relations among social processes on the basis of analysis of patterns of covariance among social variables.

It emerges from this discussion that causal explanations based on an analysis of the circumstances of choice confronting rational individuals play a central role in each of these patterns of explanation. The forms of explanation considered here thus build upon the foundations described in Part I.

5
FUNCTIONAL AND STRUCTURAL EXPLANATION

We saw in Chapter 2 that the model of causal explanation plays a central role in social science. Some social scientists hold, however, that there are several modes of explanation that are distinct from causal explanation and particularly pertinent to social phenomena. *Functional explanations* seek to explain a feature of society in terms of the beneficial consequences it has for the larger social system. Why do hunter-gatherer peoples practice prolonged lactation? Because this reduces fertility, promoting sustainable levels of population growth. This is a functional explanation; the practice of prolonged lactation is explained in terms of its contribution to an important need of an ongoing hunter-gatherer society (retaining low population density).

A second common model of social explanation is *structural explanation*. This model seeks to explain a feature of society as the predictable consequence of certain structural characteristics of society. Why did rice prices correlate in nineteenth-century Beijing and Shanghai but not in Shanghai and Sian? Because the market system of traditional China embodied direct, low-cost transport links between Beijing and Shanghai but not between Shanghai and Sian. This is a structural explanation; the price correlation data are explained as the result of the structure of the traditional Chinese marketing and transport system.

In this chapter we will find that neither of these forms of explanation is fundamentally distinct from causal explanation, however. Functional explanations, it will emerge, depend essentially on the availability of a causal explanation establishing the postulated functional relationship. Lacking such an account, the functional explanation is defective. And structural explanations will turn out to be legitimate but simply a subcategory of causal explanation. They are causal explanations that attribute causal powers to structural characteristics of societies.

FUNCTIONALISM

A functional explanation of a phenomenon is one that places the explanandum within an interactive system in a process of controlled change or dynamic equilibrium. It explains the presence of the feature in terms of its beneficial effects on the system. Examples of functional explanations include:

1. Birds have hollow bones in order to facilitate flight.
2. Water mills have flywheels to smooth out the flow of energy.
3. The custom of bride-price among the Lele serves to enhance social interdependence across generations (Douglas 1958/67).
4. Religious practices among the Andaman Islanders existed in order to secure social cohesion (Radcliffe-Brown 1922/64).

The explanans specifies the function of the explanandum within the larger system and the benefits that the feature confers upon the smooth working of this system. The explanandum is to be explained, that is, in terms of the beneficial consequences it confers on the system as a whole. (Such an explanation can be described as a *consequence* explanation; it explains the occurrence of the explanandum in terms of its consequences.)

This description immediately raises the problem of teleology (explaining a circumstance in terms of its future effects). A cause cannot occur later in time than its effects, but that would be required if, for example, it were held that a fish's having a dorsal fin at time t is explained by the stability conferred by the fin on the fish at some later time t^*. Accordingly, to avoid presupposing teleological relationships between present and future states, it is necessary to find some *current* characteristic of the system that causes the trait to persist. One straightforward way of solving this problem is to consider the *current* dispositional property of the trait to produce certain endstates, rather than the future endstates themselves. Thus we might maintain that a species of fish has a dorsal fin because of the current dispositional property of the fin in the present environment to produce stability under water. In this case, however, we must be able to specify how this dispositional property causally interacts with the current environment to lead to the persistence of the trait. Natural selection is myopic: It can only select for traits on the basis of the immediate benefits that those traits confer on the organisms that bear them.

How can dispositional properties of social features lead to their selection? Consider a simple example. Let "production contiguity" refer to the feature of industrial organization representing the circumstance that sequential production processes are located in adjacent parts of the factory. Raw materials are delivered to one end of the factory, and the partially finished product flows through the building, finally exiting at the loading docks. It is tempting to argue that the presence of this feature in modern factories is explained by the fact that it results in a more efficient production process than alternative arrangements. But how can we account for the emergence and preservation of this trait? It might be that early factories lacked production contiguity, with different production stages located at random throughout the factory. If we suppose that industrial designers generate alternative arrangements more or less readily and then evaluate them in terms of industrial efficiency, the production contiguity arrangement will soon evolve—perhaps through a series of small changes in that direction—because the designer will recognize the propensity of this arrangement to yield greater efficiency. Thus the current dispositional property of this arrangement to produce future effects is itself the cause of the arrangement's selection.[1]

Functional explanations are most appropriate in systems that establish what we might call "quasi-teleology"—a tendency toward self-regulation or self-correction, with the result that the system preserves some equilibrium state against the random perturbations of the environment. The system is postulated to have some preferred equilibrium state, and various structures within the system are then interpreted as contributing to the maintenance of this state. In the social sciences such states might be social order, economic efficiency, or homogeneity of value systems.

A simple system that embodies quasi-teleology is a negative feedback loop (for example, the simple thermostat controlling a boiler). As the system moves away from its target condition, the negative feedback loop cuts in to induce the system back into equilibrium. Consider the price mechanism within a competitive economy. Competitive buying and selling in circumstances in which production can be readily expanded or contracted leads to a condition in which the price of a commodity is relatively independent of fluctuating supply and demand. As demand for the good rises, the price tends to rise. Rising prices induce other producers to enter the market and current producers to expand production, leading to an increased supply of the good, and the price begins to fall again. The process works the same way in reverse in a situation of falling prices and demand.[2]

Functional explanations have the clearest application in connection with artifacts and artificial systems. The reason for this is that artifacts are the result of deliberate design, and design is the process by which the creator selects characteristics to accomplish certain systemwide effects. The function of the power button is to turn the machine on and off; the truth of this claim consists in the fact that the machine's designer selected this particular arrangement in order to control the power. And even if we do not know the particulars of the design process, it is reasonable to work on the assumption that particular elements of the machine's design are chosen in order to accomplish some intended purpose. Moreover if we have reason to doubt that a particular feature was intended to have a given beneficial consequence, then we have equal reason to doubt that the function of the feature is to have this effect.

The chief examples of functional explanations in science occur in relation to biological systems. An organism's physiological or behavioral feature is explained in terms of the reproductive advantage that feature confers on it. George Williams discusses the function of conspicuous flight mechanisms in deer and rabbits, for example: "Certain rabbits and deer, when they take flight, raise their tails and display conspicuous markings. I interpret this as accessory to reproduction. The marking and the tail raising are designed partly to warn dependent young of the approach of danger, and mainly to attract the attention of a possible predator" (Williams 1966:206). The function of this ensemble of features, according to Williams, is to enhance the survivability of offspring. For each functional explanation of this sort, moreover, it is possible to provide a nonteleological causal explanation of the functional correlation between traits and reproductive fitness: The feature came to have functionally adaptive traits through the process of natural selection. In the example above, the task of the evolutionary biologist is to show how individuals who possess this ensemble of features out-reproduce competitors who lack it. That is, we can demonstrate that the feature's dispositional property is causally involved in its occurrence.[3]

Functional explanation in social science

Functional explanations in social science explain a social institution or practice in terms of its beneficial consequences for the social system as a whole or for some important subsystem. The goal is to specify "the part played in the social or cultural system" by the factor (Merton 1967:76). Social systems are seen as dynamic systems in which the parts play functional roles, and the goal of the functional analysis is to identify the role played by a particular institution or practice. Radcliffe-Brown represents this approach in his study of the Andaman Islanders. "Every custom and belief of a primitive society plays some determinate part in the social life of the community, just as every organ of a living body plays some part in the general life of the organism" (Radcliffe-Brown 1922/64:230). Consider his explanation of ceremonial customs among the Andaman Islanders (Example 5.1). According to Radcliffe-Brown, then, ceremonial customs fulfill a crucial role in sustaining and transmitting the cultural identity of Andaman society. Were these customs to disappear, Andaman social arrangements would falter. And these customs persist *because* they fulfill this role.

A functional explanation of a social institution or practice **P** with benefits **B** within a larger social system **S** has this structure: A given practice **P** persists within a society **S** because of the benefits **B** that it confers upon the society (social cohesion, stability, economic efficiency, outlet to antisocial behavior, etc.). Let us put this somewhat less schematically. Suppose we are concerned with a society **S** that embodies a practice **P** and we explain **P** by asserting that it serves the function of providing benefit **B** in **S**. (Javanese village society [**S**] embodies agricultural involution [**P**], and the function of agricultural involution is to provide an economic niche for all villagers [**B**]; [Geertz 1963].) This assertion may be divided into three subordinate claims—one about the persistence of the feature, one about **P**'s causal powers, and one about **B**'s causal history:

1. **P** persists in **S**;
2. **P** has the disposition to produce **A** in the circumstances of **S**;
3. **P** persists in **S** because it has the disposition to produce **B**.

The first requirement expresses the discovery that **P** is a persistent pattern or feature within **S** (with the background assumption that features that do

Example 5.1 The Andaman Islanders

Many cultures embody ritual practices that appear to be socially pointless—university commencement exercises, ritual scarification, toasting the queen's health. In his study of the Andaman Islands, A. R. Radcliffe-Brown uses the term "ceremonial custom" to refer to such practices as mourning rituals, marriage rites, and consecration rites. Such rituals are distinct from "moral customs" (those determining proper relationships between persons) and "technical customs" (those that serve an immediate utilitarian purpose). Unlike moral and technical customs that appear to have direct utility for the people who engage in them, ceremonial customs seem pointless. Is it possible to explain the currency and persistence of ceremonial customs in Andaman society? Radcliffe-Brown believes that such customs serve a social function within and that they persist because they preserve the conscious identification of important cultural values, sentiments, and beliefs. "The ceremonial customs of the Andaman Islands form a closely connected system, and we cannot understand their meaning if we only consider each one by itself, but must study the whole system to arrive at an interpretation. . . . I have tried to show that the ceremonial customs are the means by which the society acts upon its individual members and keeps alive in their minds a certain system of sentiments. Without the ceremonial those sentiments would not exist, and without them the social organisation in its actual form could not exist" (Radcliffe-Brown 1922/64:324).

Data: ethnographic data based on fieldwork in the Andaman Islands
Explanatory model: explanation of a cultural practice depends on identifying the function or purpose of the practice within the workings of the social system
Source: A. R. Radcliffe-Brown, *The Andaman Islanders* (1922/64)

---

not have a causal explanation will tend to disappear through the random processes of social development). The second requirement embodies the idea that **P** has certain causal powers—in particular the dispositional property to produce certain outcomes. And the third requirement offers a hypothesis about the true causal explanation of the persistence of **P**—that its disposition to produce **B** at a later time explains its persistence at the present time. In terms of our example, agricultural involution persists in Java, agricultural involution has the disposition to guarantee villagers a niche, and the persistence of involution is caused by this disposition.

The causal history requirement is the most important part of the content of a functional explanation, so let us examine it more closely. This requirement holds that if **B** is the function of **P** within society **S**, it must be that:

P's disposition to produce **B**
causes
the persistence of **P** in **S**.

This point can also be put counterfactually: If **P** ceased to have the disposition to produce **B**, then the random fluctuations of social life would gradually

---

Example 5.2   Extended lactation and population density

Hunter-gatherer cultures succeeded in producing ample food to sustain the group throughout the year. However this affluence depended on keeping population density low. For example, Eskimos dependent on caribou maintain a population density of .3 persons per square mile (Harris 1978:18). Population growth beyond this level would put unsustainable stress on the food-producing capacity of the territory covered by the group. How did hunter-gatherer cultures manage to control fertility? Marvin Harris asserts that there were probably several mechanisms but that the most effective check on fertility in these cultures was extended lactation (prolonging the time during which a mother nurses her infant). A new mother typically does not resume ovulation until her body reaches a threshold proportion of fat (20–25 percent of body weight), and the calorie drain imposed by nursing delays the achievement of this level—thus delaying future pregnancies. "Bushman mothers, by prolonging lactation, appear to be able to delay the possibility of pregnancy for more than four years" (Harris 1978:23). He holds that extended lactation was widely practiced among hunter-gatherer groups and that this practice served the function of depressing fertility and population growth within these groups.

Data: data on the economies and cultures of several hunter-gatherer groups, present and past
Explanatory model: functional explanation relating human cultural practices to the material needs of the social group
Source: Marvin Harris, *Cannibals and Kings: The Origins of Cultures* (1978)

---

undermine the practice of **P** and **P** would disappear in **S**. (See Miller 1987:121 for further development of this point.) If this causal condition is not satisfied, then we do not have a valid explanation; if we cannot demonstrate that it is satisfied, then we do not know whether we have a valid explanatory relationship. School buses are bright yellow, which makes them easy to spot from the air. But because the fact that yellow buses are easily detected from the air is not part of the reason that the color was chosen, it is incorrect to say that the function of the yellow color is to make the bus easily spotted.

Consider Marvin Harris's hypothesis that extended lactation among hunter-gatherer societies serves the function of depressing fertility and population growth (Example 5.2). This hypothesis prompts investigation on several important questions. First we need to establish that hunter-gatherer societies are in fact characterized by longer periods of lactation than other forms of human society for if they do *not* differ from other social forms in this regard, then the functional claim is pointless. (That is, we must show that condition 1 above—that **P** persists in **S**—is satisfied.)

Harris's explanation involves, next, the assertion that prolonged lactation has the disposition to depress fertility—we must demonstrate that condition 2 above (that **P** has the disposition to produce **A** in the circumstances of **S**) is satisfied. To support this part of the claim, we need to establish that extended lactation does in fact have this effect. This question involves the biology of the reproductive system and the relations between lactation, fat levels, hormonal balance, and so forth. It emerges that there is good evidence that lactation does have the effect of delaying ovulation, so that the following regularity is established: The average time between pregnancies among women with prolonged lactation is about twice that of women with short lactation. (For an individual woman this means that her probability of a new pregnancy is reduced by prolonged lactation.)

Finally we must establish that the social practice of prolonged lactation is sustained by its disposition to reduce fertility (the causal history requirement above). It may be that the fertility effects of prolonged lactation are merely collateral results, whereas the practice of prolonged lactation is sustained by unrelated factors—e.g., the relative cost of lactation versus other forms of infant food. It might be, for example, that hunter-gatherer mothers breast-feed rather than gather grubs for their offspring through the age of four because it takes less time to do so. And if this is so, then once again it is plainly wrong to attribute the function of fertility-reduction to prolonged lactation. In terms of our example, the claim is that prolonged lactation (**P**) has the function of reducing fertility (**B**) in hunter-gatherer societies (**S**). To sustain this claim it is necessary to demonstrate that prolonged lactation has the disposition to reduce fertility in **S** and that this fact explains the persistence of prolonged lactation.

Significantly Harris's account addresses the first and second conditions but not the third (that **P** persists in **S** because it has the disposition to produce **B**). He does not provide evidence to support the judgment that prolonged lactation persists because it reduces fertility, and he does not provide an account of the causal mechanisms that might mediate this relation. His functional account is therefore defective, and we have no reason to accept his contention that prolonged lactation is explained by the need for reduced fertility among hunter-gatherers.

Examples of functional explanations

Functional explanations can be found in many areas of social science. Let us consider several examples.

John Foster's account in Example 5.3 attempts to show that the political reforms of the 1840s were a functional adaptation to a threat to bourgeois interests. This explanation is flawed, however, because it does not show the mechanism through which threatened bourgeois interests led to political reform. Foster seems to presuppose a process of social adjustment that works behind the backs of the participants to reduce the level of political crisis.

Another example of functionalist explanation—with a more adequate account of supporting mechanisms—is G. William Skinner's application of central place theory (Example 5.4). This too is a functional argument; the feature of spatial arrangement is explained on the basis of its contribution to the workings of the economy. But the mechanism that supports this function is visibly individualistic. It works through the decisions of consumers,

---

Example 5.3 Political reform and economic crisis

The mid-nineteenth century witnessed significant political changes in English society, including the extension of suffrage to workers, the creation of legal labor unions, and the creation of mass political parties. Jointly these changes may be described as a process of "liberalization." Why did this process occur? John Foster argues that these changes were a functional adaptation within capitalist society to the demands of a more effective and organized working class; they represent a way of preserving ruling-class interests under pressure from working-class militancy. Foster writes, "Liberalization was in fact a collective *ruling-class* response to a social system in crisis and integrally related to a preceding period of working-class consciousness" (Foster 1974:3). He conceives of English capitalism as a complex economic and political system organized to advance capitalist interests, and he attempts to explain political changes within this system as a functional adjustment to new constraints and challenges. Working-class militancy in the textile sector began to rise following the French Revolution, and this process led to effective mass action (strikes and political activism by workers) by the 1840s. This activism imposed a political crisis on society and a sense of crisis in the bourgeoisie. In the late 1840s party politics began to undermine working-class unity, with workers moving to both Tory and Liberal parties (Foster 1974:209). The parties took on much of the rhetoric of working-class radicalism, further undermining working-class unity. The end result of this process of fragmentation in the working-class movement was a reduction in the political crisis and a lessening of the risks to capitalist interests. "In Oldham at least the changes associated with liberalization (the extension of the vote, the development of mass parties, the legal recognition of trade unions) were quite obviously part of a process by which specifically capitalist authority was reimposed and the working-class vanguard pushed back into isolation" (Foster 1974:251). He explains these changes, then, as a functional adjustment within the social and political system to reduce political crisis and stabilize bourgeois interests.

Data: historical study of three towns of nineteenth-century industrial England
Explanatory model: functional explanation of political facts based on benefits
    conferred upon the stability of the capitalist system
Source: John Foster, *Class Struggle and the Industrial Revolution* (1974)

---

officials, and sellers who constrain their behavior to arrive at individually optimal outcomes. In this case, then, we have a functional argument that is appropriately supported by an account of the local-level processes that establish and reproduce the functional adaptation.

Possible mechanisms

The causal history requirement above is often the most difficult to satisfy in defending a functional explanation for it is almost always possible to come up with *some* beneficial consequences of a given social feature. Therefore to justify the claim that the feature exists *because* of its beneficial consequences

---

Example 5.4 Marketing systems in late-imperial China

Are towns and villages located according to sheer historical accident? Or is there an underlying order to the placement of settlements in a typical landscape? G. William Skinner analyzes the central places of rural Sichuan and finds two forms of regularities. First there is an orderly hierarchy of places, ranging from hamlets to villages, standard market towns, intermediate market towns, and higher-level places. This hierarchy is determined by the marketing functions provided at places within the hierarchy; higher-level places provide services not available at lower-level ones. (This hierarchy also provides a basis for explaining the periodicity of local markets—the daily and weekly schedule of marketing in various places.) Second this hierarchy is spatially organized as well: Higher-level places are surrounded by hexagonal rings of lower-level places, leading to a hexagonal network covering the countryside. Thus rural Sichuan conforms to the topology predicted by central place theory, and Skinner explains this fact on the basis that this arrangement optimizes marketing activity; it minimizes transport cost within the marketing system (Skinner 1964/65). He goes on to argue that rural Chinese social life is structured by market systems rather than villages and that ideas are transmitted and social intercourse occurs along the pathways established by the marketing hierarchy.

Data: data about the marketing functions provided by hundreds of villages and towns in Sichuan; maps showing the location of central places and the roads connecting them

Explanatory model: the arrangement of towns and villages conforms to the optimal topology of hexagonal rings that minimizes transport cost; this arrangement results from the fact that economically rational agents make deliberate decisions about residence and place of marketing activity

Source: G. William Skinner, "Marketing and Social Structure in Rural China" (1964/65)

---

we must account for the mechanisms that created and reproduced the feature in a way that shows how the needs of the system as a whole influenced the development of the institution. If a functional relationship is to be regarded as explanatory, therefore, it is necessary to have some idea of the causal mechanisms that establish and preserve the functional relationship.[4]

Let us consider one important example of functional explanation more fully—the idea that certain normative systems have currency in particular social settings *because* they satisfy some important need of the group, such as keeping population density down, eliciting cooperation, or distributing income to ensure the basic needs of all members of the group are met. (Examples 7.4, 7.5, and 7.6 in Chapter 7 illustrate claims of this sort.) Suppose that it is true that a given normative system has the postulated beneficial effects for the group and that it achieves these effects by constraining individual behavior appropriately. (For example, the norm requiring reciprocity among neighbors might be enforced by the probability of scorn, anger, and derision expressed by other villagers if one flouts the norm.)

Two questions must be posed concerning this scenario. What social factors brought this beneficial set of norms into existence in the social group in the first place? And what social processes at the level of individual activity work to reproduce this set of norms over time? The central point is that the fact that the system of norms is best for the group as a whole is *not* sufficient to explain the existence and reproduction of the normative system because group benefits do not automatically bring the social arrangements that would produce those benefits. To assume otherwise is to implicitly assume what we might call the principle of Panglossian functionalism—the expectation that those social arrangements will emerge within a given social setting that best satisfy the needs of the group affected.

These considerations impose a demanding constraint on functional explanation. To explain a phenomenon it is not sufficient to demonstrate that it has consequences that are beneficial for the economy or for the interests of a particular class. Rather it is necessary to provide an account of the micropathways by which the needs of the economy or the interests of a powerful class are imposed on other social phenomena to elicit beneficial consequences. Thus the functional explanation is insufficient unless it is accompanied by an analysis at the level of individual activity—a microanalysis—that reveals the mechanisms that give rise to the pattern to be explained. (We will return to this topic in our discussion of the problem of "microfoundations" for social explanations in Chapter 9.)

In biology functional explanations are underwritten by a single well-understood causal mechanism—the process of natural selection. Features that enhance the viability of a typical organism will tend to replace less advantageous features through the working of natural selection. It is more problematic, however, to identify mechanisms through which social systems come to embody benefit-conferring features. There are two mechanisms that are uncontroversial in this regard, both turning on the intentional choices of individuals. First it may be that the benefits produced by a social feature are anticipated and pursued by the persons whose behavior gives rise to the feature. Thus mothers in hunter-gatherer societies may recognize the relationship between lactation and pregnancy and choose prolonged lactation *in order* to reduce the frequency of pregnancy. Or, second, the mothers may not intend the beneficial effects but the practice may be encouraged by other powerful individuals who *do* understand the causal relationship between the practice and the benefit and who intend to produce the benefit by encouraging the practice. It might be, for example, that magic specialists of the society know that lactation delays pregnancy and encourage women to prolong lactation on other grounds—e.g., that the gods prefer this system. This would be an example of a practice working behind the backs of the practitioners but that nonetheless emerges as the intentional result of an influential social engineer.

In both cases we have a satisfactory answer to the question raised by the causal history requirement above. The practice is introduced and sustained by the fact that it produces the benefit, and its disposition to produce the benefit leads to its selection by intentional actors. Thus the disposition of the practice to produce the benefit *causes* its persistence because it leads agents to adopt this practice. The more difficult and more interesting case is the one in which the benefits associated with the practice are unknown and unintended by all participants. This would be true in our hunter-gatherer example if neither mothers nor specialists understood the causal relationship between lactation and pregnancy. Suppose, then, that our investigator comes to the conclusion that none of the participants intends the beneficial results of the practice and each is in fact quite ignorant of the causal conditions of pregnancy. In this case we cannot explain the currency of the practice as the result of the deliberate choice of the participants. What sorts of mechanisms might serve to establish unintended functional relationships between practices and consequences? There are several possible avenues that various social scientists have pursued.

First, we might explore the idea that there is an analogue to natural selection that is pertinent to social organization. Suppose we imagine that societies consist of small groups and communities, each characterized by its own ensemble of practices and values. Some of these practices have better-than-average effects on the welfare of the group, whereas others have worse-than-average effects. Now suppose that members of groups are free to move from one group to another based on their preference for higher predicted welfare and that a group (along with its values and practices) is extinguished when it falls below a threshold size. Under suitable formal assumptions (for example, about the initial distribution of practices across groups), we can conclude that there will be a tendency toward a mix of practices suited to the welfare needs of groups at a given level of technology. However, these assumptions are highly unrealistic (the assumption of easy entrance and exit from groups, for example, flies in the face of most ethnography of premodern societies). So the "social selection" principle appears unpromising.

A second possibility also exploits the idea of selection, this time at the level of social features rather than social groups. Here the guiding intuition is that practices that have negative consequences for social functioning—dysfunctional economic institutions, for example, or social practices that tend to provoke needless social conflict—will tend to be extinguished over time, replaced by more felicitous practices. Consider, for example, a mountain peasant community in which communal lands are periodically redivided. There is a variety of soil qualities ranging from fertile valley land to rocky mountain slopes, and the current practice is for the village council to attempt to divide it into parcels that balance size with soil quality, so that each family receives a plot of equal value. Such a system is guaranteed to provoke dissension among families every time it is applied as each family jealously compares its plot with those of its neighbors. Therefore we might expect this system to be replaced by one that gives each family an equal share of land of each quality. One way of doing this is to allocate land in the form of vertical strips going up the mountainside. The new system reduces the

social conflict engendered by periodic redivision, but it also reduces agricultural efficiency because no family can effectively exploit a significant
quantity of valley land. Thus each system of division has some beneficial
features, and it is difficult to justify a judgment that one is more causally
relevant than the other. This "selection of features" approach, therefore,
looks unpersuasive as well.

We might tackle the problem from the other end and consider what
result would occur if a society *lacked* a particular type of functional characteristic. So it might be argued that if hunter-gatherer societies lacked all
fertility-depressing cultural practices, then they would have swiftly increased
in population to the point where a hunter-gatherer economy was no longer
possible. This counterfactual appears to be true; however, it takes us no
closer to an answer to the question confronting us now. There is no metasocial
principle of functionality establishing that societies will produce practices
that satisfy their long-term needs.

The problem with each of these approaches to unintended functional
relationships is that they presuppose an excessively optimistic metatheory,
holding that societies will tend to evolve toward more functional characteristics—what was referred to as "Panglossian functionalism" above. This
theory is groundless, however. Societies that fail to embody practices that
secure their basic long-term needs (feasible economy, adequate level of social
cohesion, sustainable population growth, etc.) will simply be replaced by
social forms that are more capable of satisfying these needs. The fact that
Roman slavery needed a regular replenishment of slaves through conquest
to compensate for low domestic slave fertility did not guarantee that this
need would be satisfied; instead, it led to the dissolution of slavery and
the emergence, eventually, of feudalism.

Considerations of these sorts lead to a skeptical conclusion: Functional
explanations are suspect in social science and are in the best cases inherently
incomplete in social science (though not in biology). In particular, they must
be supplemented by detailed accounts of the social processes through which
the needs of social and economic systems influence other social processes
to elicit responses that satisfy those needs.

STRUCTURALISM

Let us turn now to another supposedly distinctive form of explanation
in social science—structural explanation. This approach is divided into two
discrete paradigms of explanation. The first is a species of causal explanation
that focuses on social structures as prominent causes of social phenomena.
The second rejects the idea that explanation requires causal relations at all
and instead attempts to explain various aspects of social phenomena by
showing how they fit into abstract underlying structures. Here the paradigm
of explanation is derived from linguistic theory. Human language consists
of a perplexing range of verbal performances, but generative linguists (e.g.,
Chomsky 1965) show that there is a simple and abstract set of transformational

rules that generate all grammatical utterances. So it might then be held that the domain of language behavior is "explained" by the underlying grammar that generates sentences. Likewise, the structuralist social analyst attempts to find an underlying "grammar" of social phenomena that can be said to constitute the order underlying the phenomena.

Causal structural explanation

Causal structuralism asserts, first, that societies are complex systems that embody an indefinite range of social structures—for example, state forms, economic systems, or transportation networks. Second, it maintains that many important features of societies—patterns of stable organization as well as processes of change—can be explained as the causal consequence of the particular details of these structures. And, in line with the findings of Chapter 2, the causal powers of social structures are embodied in particular causal mechanisms mediated by individual action. Thus the tendency toward crises in capitalism, the occurrence of the French Revolution, and the technological stagnation of the Roman Empire have all been explained as the consequences of structural characteristics of capitalism, ancien régime France, and classical slavery. To evaluate this model of explanation, then, we must arrive at a clear understanding of what a "social structure" is, and we need to provide an account of how such things can have the causal properties they are thought to have.

What, then, is a social structure? Consider several examples:

- the system of land ownership and tenancy found in early-modern France,
- the political organization of the Chinese Communist party during the Sino-Japanese War,
- the local marketing system of South China,
- a peasant farming system,
- the internal organization of a modern corporation,
- the wage-labor system of industrial capitalism.

What constitutes a social structure? What is being asserted when a social scientist claims to identify a structure within a social unit? First, there is a claim of temporal continuity; a structure is a social system feature that persists over an extended period of time. Second, the properties of a structure are thought to be to some important degree independent of the particular persons who occupy roles within the structure. The causal properties of a bureaucracy, for example, depend on the features of organization and lines of command that are embodied in the bureau, not on the particular features of individual officeholders. Third, a structure is assumed to impose constraints on the actions of persons involved in it. Thus a bureaucracy is a complex organization involving large numbers of people and a set of rules. The rules determine the lines of authority within the bureaucracy and the rules of conduct that are intended to govern the behavior of persons in various offices. These points may be summarized in the following formulation: Social structures are enduring regulative systems that define opportunities and constraints that guide, limit, and inspire individual action.

Theda Skocpol's comparativist analysis of the causes of revolution in China, France, and Russia illustrates this model of social explanation (Example 2.5 in Chapter 2). Skocpol characterizes the state as an articulated social structure. "The state properly conceived is no mere arena in which socio-economic struggles are fought out. It is, rather, a set of administrative, policing, and military organizations headed, and more or less well coordinated, by an executive authority. Any state first and fundamentally extracts resources from society and deploys these to create and support coercive and administrative organizations" (Skocpol 1979:29). Here she asserts that the state is a temporally extended set of institutions that have long-term characteristics extending beyond the tenure of any particular individuals within them; these characteristics are variable from one state form to another. Further, Skocpol holds that the critical factors that determine whether or not rebellion will occur in an agrarian society are the structure of the state and the social and political arrangements that govern local life. In other words it is the specific political structures of agrarian societies that causally influence the outcome of rebellious protest.

How are social structures instantiated in a society? Consider the example of the land-tenure system at a particular time and place. The system is constituted by the conditions that tenants must satisfy to gain and retain access to land: payment of rent, provision of labor services, and the like. What stabilizes this structure, however? Legal institutions are part of the answer: Participants whose legal rights have been violated can appeal to legal authorities for redress. Local power arrangements are a second leg of stability for the institutions of land tenure: Landlords whose tenants withhold rent are often in a position to use force to gain redress. Thus a social structure is instantiated through a set of powers of enforcement and retaliation conferred on various agents within the social system.

Turn now to the question of how social structures acquire causal powers. Through what sorts of mechanisms do social structures exert their influence on social processes? Typically they serve as standing causal conditions within social explanations. A given system of land tenure, for example, may be identified as a causal condition for the occurrence of social unrest or a system of military governance may be identified as a cause of successful peasant rebellion. Here there is a close relationship between the topic at hand and the arguments advanced in Chapters 2 and 3 above: Structures exercise causal powers by providing an environment of incentives and prohibitions for various agents within a social system. Agents modulate their behavior accordingly, and specific social outcomes ensue. Suppose we are interested in understanding why English agriculture underwent a structural transformation toward capitalist farming, whereas French agriculture remained stagnant (Example 6.6 in Chapter 6). Robert Brenner argues that the key causal variable is differences in the social-property systems in the two countries: The English case embodied a system of landholding that gave landlords both the power and the incentive to modernize farming, whereas the French system gave peasants the power to effectively resist modernization. In this case, then, the different historical patterns are caused by the goal-directed activity of large numbers of rural people within the context of different structures of property ownership.

There is a tendency for causal structuralists to slight the importance of individual-level activity (agency), on the ground that the structures themselves are the critical causal variables. Thus Skocpol's attention to the structures of the state and her inattention to the local processes through which the state's constraints are translated into social action are representative. However, as Michael Taylor (1988) shows, this conflict between structure and agency is both unnecessary and undesirable. It is always desirable to have an account of the micromechanisms of social change, as I will argue at greater length in Chapter 9. So even if it were true that a given social structure uniquely determines a particular outcome, it would still be desirable to know how the structure affects individual behavior to bring about the outcome. In the more common case, however, structures do not plausibly determine outcomes; rather they make some outcomes more likely than others. And in these circumstances it is imperative to have further knowledge about the processes at work at the local level—the level of individual agency and choice—if we hope to say why one outcome occurred rather than another.

What sorts of mechanisms are relevant at the local level to convey structural causation? As indicated above social structures exert their influence by imposing incentives and constraints on individuals. Agents pursue their goals within particular social and political arrangements, and these arrangements limit their choices and provide opportunities for action. If we want to know how individuals will behave in a particular institutional environment of choice, we need to know what their beliefs and goals are and what choices are available to them through which they can pursue their goals. The incentives and constraints imposed by the social structure will have predictable consequences for the choices that individuals will make. In this light, then, there is no contradiction between rational choice theory and structural causation; instead the former describes one important family of mechanisms through which the causal powers of social structures are transmitted.[5]

Structural features of domestic and international politics have been said to have causal properties relevant to the occurrence of war and peace. In Examples 5.5 and 5.6 we find instances of such an account. Williamson is not suggesting that the alliance structure is the sole cause of World War I or even a supremely important one. Rather he is observing that the large-scale historical forces at work in 1912–1914 could have had a variety of alternative outcomes; the alliance structure that was in place made full-scale war more likely.

Consider now a second example—this one concerning peasant rebellion in early twentieth-century China. In this case Winston Hsieh explains features

---

Example 5.5   Alliance structure and the outbreak of war

In a review of recent thinking about the causes of World War I, Samuel
Williamson, Jr., distinguishes between the long-term conditions that have
traditionally been identified as causes of the war and the short-term political
circumstances in Europe between 1912 and the outbreak of war that have
received increased attention. "Recent studies . . . make clear the dramatic
changes that took place after 1911 in the relationships resulting from the
alliances and ententes, military planning, imperial attitudes, nationalism, and
confidence about the future of the governmental systems" (Williamson
1989:227). Particularly important among these short-term conditions are the
alliances and ententes that constrained the behavior of the major players—
Russia, France, Germany, Britain, Austria-Hungary, and Serbia. These were a
structural feature of the international political system in the decade prior to
World War I, and Williamson holds that they were an important causal factor in
the eventual outbreak of war because they locked various governments into
courses of action that were contrary to their own interests. "The alliances . . .
could also coerce a state into taking action simply for the sake of the alliance.
Strong, tight alliances may in fact be more dangerous to peace than loose,
ambiguous ones where the actors must negotiate among themselves before
taking action" (Williamson 1989:247). In this account the alliance structure was a
necessary condition for the outbreak of war in the particular circumstances of
central Europe in 1914. If the various governments had been unconstrained by
tight alliances, Williamson suggests, they would not have taken the actions that
made war inevitable.

Data: archival data on decisionmaking by the great powers; chronology of the
   events and decisions that led to war
Explanatory model: causal analysis identifying one significant necessary condition
   for a historical event (the outbreak of World War I)
Source: Samuel R. Williamson, Jr., "The Origins of World War I" (1989)

---

of the pattern of mobilization in Canton as the consequence of features of
the market structure embodied there.

In both Examples 5.5 and 5.6 the structures that are embodied in the
social environment—alliances in the first case and marketing hierarchies in
the second—have causal consequences for large-scale social phenomena.
This is because they alter the environment of choice for participants, either
by giving them different incentives or by making available opportunities
and strategies that they would otherwise not have.

It is also possible to offer causal explanations of the particular characteristics
of a given social structure. In this case the structure is an effect rather than
a cause. In Example 5.7 Linda Arrigo attempts to explain the structure of
land-tenure arrangements in traditional China on the basis of the carrying
capacity of land: High-income land supports tenancy, whereas low-income
land leads to poor peasant ownership. This is an effort to explain the fact
that a given structure obtains one context rather than another.

Example 5.6 Marketing hierarchies and patterns of rebellion

In 1911 large spontaneous armies of rural people converged on Canton intent on rebellion. However these armies were not drawn uniformly from the surrounding countryside; instead some villages were represented very heavily among the rebels and others not at all. Winston Hsieh uses G. William Skinner's analysis of marketing hierarchies to explain patterns of peasant mobilization in these events. "Using a recently unearthed daily chronicle on the uprising in conjunction with large-scale local maps, I have been able to demonstrate the central role of market towns in local uprisings and to delineate the pattern of revolutionary uprising. . . . Tracing the movements of insurrectionary armies on the map of local marketing systems helps to reveal the channels through which these bands were drawn to the centers of conflict and the patterns of mobilization at various levels of the marketing hierarchy" (Hsieh 1978:80). Hsieh finds that mobilization was highly successful in some market towns and highly unsuccessful in others, and he argues that this stems from differences in the processes of urbanization that overtook the different market towns. The most fully mobilized districts were those that had undergone the most rapid commercialization and urbanization (Hsieh 1978:89); these districts were the most vulnerable to the fluctuations in regional market economy that occurred in the first decade of the twentieth century. "The two dissident forces . . . came exclusively from marketing communities that had enjoyed prosperity for a significant period but had recently encountered sharp economic reversals. . . . Second, the local uprisings of 1911 clearly reflected the importance of natural marketing systems, and their independence of formal administrative boundaries" (Hsieh 1978:98–99).

Data: data on rebel group movements during 1911–1912 drawn from local gazettes and maps; data on economic change and urbanization in the preceding decades

Explanatory model: the patterns of mobilization result from the patterns of social contiguity created by market hierarchies, and differences across market towns reflect the different economic circumstances of each

Source: Winston Hsieh, "Peasant Insurrection and the Marketing Hierarchy in the Canton Delta, 1911–12" (1978)

Noncausal structural explanation

So far, then, it appears that structuralist explanation is simply a subspecies of causal explanation. But there is another form of structuralist explanation that rejects this line of thought altogether. Consider Claude Lévi-Strauss's treatment of kinship structures (Example 5.8). Lévi-Strauss's account represents a form of structuralism that derives as much from linguistics as it does from traditional social science. The guiding idea in this approach is that the goal of explanation is to identify an underlying order in the jumble of empirical experience. Therefore this approach represents a noncausal conception of explanation. It holds that there are underlying structures that possess an abstract order akin to a syntax in language that can be "decoded";

Example 5.7   Land-tenure systems and land yields

In prerevolutionary agrarian China there was a distinctive regional pattern in forms of land tenure. In the south there was a high proportion of tenancy with peasant farmers renting land from landlords, but in the North China plain small peasant ownership of land was typical. What accounts for this pattern? Linda Arrigo explains this outcome as the result of differences in the yield of land in given circumstances of cultivation. South China was rich rice paddy with high per-acre yields, whereas North China was dry wheat and millet cropland with low per-acre yields. In areas where the yield of an acre of land is only slightly greater than the subsistence needs of the cultivator, a rent relationship is impossible; in areas where the yield of land greatly exceeds the cultivator's needs, it is possible to extract a rent. Land with a substantial surplus thus gives powerful local agents an incentive to acquire ownership rights and to extract rents. Arrigo contends that the size of the feasible surplus establishes tenancy arrangements by determining whether a substantial rent can be collected over and above the subsistence needs of the cultivator. In South China this was possible, but in North China it generally was not. Arrigo writes, "In sum, the present article seeks a limited goal, to establish the relationship between land productivity and the percent of land on which landowners exploited the labor of others, through comparisons of regions of China" (Arrigo 1986:268).

Data: land-tenancy data for agrarian China
Explanatory model: social class relations explained as the result of the size of the surplus feasible for a given mode of technology
Source: Linda Arrigo, "Landownership Concentration in China: The Buck Survey Revisited" (1986)

---

such a decoding is explanatory of the phenomena described. Anthony Giddens describes this approach in these terms: "Structural linguistics . . . suggests the notion that society, like language, should be regarded as a 'virtual system' with recursive properties" (Giddens 1979:47). Society, by analogy, possesses an abstract "syntax," and a goal of social inquiry is to discover the rules that govern this syntax.

Let us consider a few examples of noncausal structuralist explanation. Nicos Poulantzas offers a reconstruction of Marx's theory of historical materialism (Example 5.9). Here Poulantzas argues for an antihistoricist conception of Marxism in which "the political must be located in the structure of a social formation" (Poulantzas 1973:30). The underlying assumption is that a proper scientific understanding of the capitalist state takes the form of a theory of the articulation of structures, economic and political, that constitute the capitalist mode of production and that this articulation has an abstract logic of its own. Questions about causal sequence (genetic questions, as Poulantzas calls them) are unnecessary. An extreme version of structuralist explanation within Marxism may be found in the writings of Barry Hindess and Paul Hirst (Example 5.10). The research described by Hindess and Hirst in Example 5.10 can be performed wholly at the level

---

Example 5.8 Kinship as an abstract structure

Claude Lévi-Strauss offers an abstract formulation of the system of kinship relations in several cultures. He then attempts to show that the structure of this system bears important abstract relations to other systems in these cultures. Particularly important in his view is the relation between kinship and language. "'Kinship systems,' like 'phonemic systems,' are built by the mind on the level of unconscious thought. Finally the recurrence of kinship patterns, marriage rules, similar prescribed attitudes between certain types of relatives, and so forth, in scattered regions of the globe and in fundamentally different societies, leads us to believe that, in the case of kinship as well as linguistics, the observable phenomena result from the action of laws which are general but implicit. . . . Although they belong to *another order of reality,* kinship phenomena are *of the same type* as linguistic phenomena" (Lévi-Strauss 1963:34). In this way Lévi-Strauss purports to *explain* the range of behavior and vocabulary pertaining to kinship relations in many different cultures by discerning an underlying "grammar": a set of abstract rules that generate the varieties of kinship patterns.

Data: study of kinship systems and vocabularies in a variety of cultures
Explanatory model: to explain a social structure is to identify its elements and
their abstract transformations
Source: Claude Lévi-Strauss, *Structural Anthropology* (1963)

---

of theory, without investigating the actual historical character of classical slavery or medieval feudalism; in fact Hindess and Hirst heap abuse on the uncritical empiricism of those who would make this effort.

Is noncausal structuralism a form of social explanation at all? This is a controversial question, and I will offer a controversial answer: It is not. At best noncausal structuralism represents an effort to discover unanticipated underlying regularities among a range of phenomena. At worst it represents the effort to provide an a priori conceptual reconstruction of social phenomena. The former is a legitimate research goal for social science, but it is not explanatory. The latter, by contrast, is more an exercise in speculative philosophy than social science. I will defend each of these judgments in turn.

Suppose that we are studying religious practices in the United States and have discovered that these practices conform to a "grammar" of behavior: There is a set of rules that permit us to comprehend all religious activity within their scope. Suppose, further, that we make the startling discovery that this grammar is formally identical with that underlying the behavior of traders on Wall Street. Believers interact with clergy, and traders interact with investment specialists; believers make contributions at their churches, and traders purchase commodity futures; and so forth. What, if anything, does this set of discoveries explain? Religious behavior is not explained by pointing out that it conforms to the underlying formal rules of religious practice—nor is the ensemble of a speaker's utterances in English explained by showing that they conform to the rules of English syntax. And neither

---

Example 5.9 Modes of production—I

Nicos Poulantzas offers a structuralist account of politics, locating political structures within Marx's conception of the mode of production. He defines a mode of production in these terms: "By *mode of production* we shall designate not what is generally marked out as the economic . . . but a specific combination of various structures which, in combination, appear as so many instances or levels, i.e., as so many regional structures of this mode. . . . The type of unity which characterizes a mode of production is that of a *complex whole* dominated, in the last instance, by the economic" (Poulantzas 1973:13–14). He distinguishes between the mode of production, which is a purely abstract theoretical notion, and the concrete social formation—the actually existing society. And he tries to show that the theory of the mode of production provides a basis for explaining capitalist society as an ensemble of social and political structures. "We arrive, then, at two results: 1. The state's global role as the cohesive factor in a social formation can, as such, be distinguished in particular modalities concerning the different levels of a formation. . . . 2. The state's various particular functions, even those which are not directly concerned with the political level in the strict sense (i.e., political class conflict) can only be grasped theoretically in their interrelation" (Poulantzas 1973:54). A feature of the state, then, can be explained by showing how it fits into the general theory of the state as an ordered set of political structures.

Data: Marxist theory; some historical data about the political arrangements found in particular capitalist societies

Explanatory model: explanation of particular historical features of society proceeds by showing how those features correspond to structures, conjunctures, and interrelationships within the general theory of the mode of production, superstructure, etc.

Source: Nicos Poulantzas, *Political Power and Social Classes* (1973)

---

the ensemble of religious practices nor the ensemble of trading practices is explained by the discovery that one is formally similar to the other. Instead, what we have arrived at is a set of perplexing empirical regularities that *now* demand explanation: How is it that the rules underlying religious practices are embodied in particular practitioners? What accounts for the stability of these rules? How are they transmitted from one generation to another? Answers could be produced for these questions, but the central point here is that it is these new answers that will be genuinely explanatory. And they will be causal: They will take the form of a specification of the social arrangements through which systems of rules are embodied and transmitted and through which individuals come to internalize these rules. Here the analogy with linguistics is revealing. Speech behavior is not explained merely by specification of the abstract syntax of the language. Rather it is necessary to have a theory of psycholinguistics—a causal theory that explains how knowledge of the rules of English are acquired and employed by typical speakers—if we are to find an explanation of linguistic competence.

Example 5.10 Modes of production—II

Extending some of the philosophical ideas of Louis Althusser, Hindess and Hirst argue that the structure of a mode of production—e.g., feudalism—determines a variety of the properties of the social systems that embody this mode. They characterize a mode of production as "an articulated combination of relations and forces of production structured by the dominance of the relations of production" (Hindess and Hirst 1975:9). They attempt to formulate an articulated theory of the alternative structures of precapitalist modes of production (they believe that there are only finitely many alternatives) and then work out the systemic dynamics of these alternatives. They write, "For each of the pre-capitalist modes of production . . . we may pose the following question: Is it possible to construct the rigorous concept of that mode of production as a distinct and determinate articulated combination of relations and forces of production?" (Hindess and Hirst 1975:18). And explanation is derived from a feature of a given type of precapitalist mode of production from the general theory of the mode of production. For example, Hindess and Hirst explain the tendency toward soil exhaustion within slavery in the United States as stemming from the elements of capitalist economic organization that were found in that system, not the essential features of the slave mode of production. "It is the specific conditions of commodity production and capitalist calculation in the absence of monopoly possession of the land which produce these tendencies toward soil exhaustion and expansion, and not slavery" (Hindess and Hirst 1975:170).

Data: some historical data on slave and feudal social-economic systems; Marxist theory
Explanatory model: derivation of structural features of various economic orders from an abstract theory of the mode of production
Source: Barry Hindess and Paul Q. Hirst, *Pre-capitalist Modes of Production* (1975)

Turn now to the claim that social structures have an abstract logic that can be unraveled by the social theorist. Here the work of Hindess and Hirst is the most glaring of the examples discussed above. This approach is profoundly antiscientific because it denies the inherent contingency of social phenomena. There are regularities that underlie social phenomena, to be sure, but these are contingent regularities that must be discovered through empirical investigation. The idea that a social formation—capitalism, for example—may be expected to unfold according to the underlying logic of the concept of the "mode of production" is preposterous. Theory is, of course, an essential part of social explanation. But theories must be constructed and evaluated in sober consideration of the complexity and underdetermination of social phenomena.[6]

These observations lead us to a pair of conclusions concerning structural explanation. Causal structuralism is unobjectionable, but it is a species of causal explanation. Here the chief caution is that identified in our discussion of functional explanation as well: the need to pay attention to the micro-processes that underlie structural causation. (This point will be further developed in Chapter 9.) Noncausal structuralism, by contrast, is not a model of social explanation at all. Either it is a method aimed at discovering complex empirical regularities that in turn require causal explanation or it is a quasi-philosophical method that takes us away from empirical social science altogether.

CONCLUSION

These arguments permit us to draw a conclusion: Functional and structural explanations are not distinctive forms of social explanation. Functional explanation is best understood as a complex form of causal explanation in which an item's current dispositional properties for future outcomes causally influence its behavior. Structural explanations can be understood as falling into two categories. First there are those that are genuinely explanatory but belong in the larger category of causal explanations. In these cases structural explanations identify units of social structure as causes of other social phenomena. The chief problem that must be addressed in considering such explanations is the microfoundational question: Through what individual-level processes does a social structure convey its influence? The other case of a structural explanation is spurious; either the structuralist interpretation of a set of social phenomena merely codifies a complex empirical regularity or it is an effort to derive social facts from a priori theory. Causal explanation based on regularities deriving from human agency thus underlies both functional and structural explanation.

NOTES

1. Jon Elster provides an interesting discussion of technical change in shipbuilding along these lines in *Explaining Technical Change* (1983).
2. See Schelling (1978) for several examples of such systems. And Herbert Simon draws numerous parallels between natural and artificial self-regulating systems in *The Sciences of the Artificial* (1969/81).
3. Richard Dawkins provides numerous accessible examples along these lines in *The Selfish Gene* (1976).
4. Jon Elster's critique of functionalism within Marxism provides a rigorous development of this position; these arguments are contained in "Marxism, Functionalism, and Game Theory" (1982).
5. For further discussion along these lines, see Michael Taylor's "Rationality and Revolutionary Collective Action" (1988).
6. E. P. Thompson subjects this form of structuralism to devastating criticism in *The Poverty of Theory* (1978).

SUGGESTIONS FOR FURTHER READING

Cohen, G. A. 1982. "Functional Explanation, Consequence Explanation, and Marxism."
Elster, Jon. 1983. *Explaining Technical Change.*

Giddens, Anthony. 1979. *Central Problems in Social Theory: Action, Structure and Contradiction in Social Analysis.*
Lévi-Strauss, Claude. 1963. *Structural Anthropology.*
Merton, Robert K. 1967. *On Theoretical Sociology.*
Simon, Herbert. 1969/81. *The Sciences of the Artificial.*
Skocpol, Theda. 1979. *States and Social Revolutions.*
Tilly, Charles. 1984. *Big Structures, Large Processes, Huge Comparisons.*

6
MATERIALISM

Materialism argues that important features of social life can be explained by analyzing the forms of technology and social arrangements governing production that are current at a particular time. We may refer to this ensemble of social and technological factors as a "material culture," an "economic base," or a "mode of production." According to materialism the fact that human beings satisfy their material needs through productive social labor creates a fundamental set of constraints and imperatives that strongly influence a variety of social phenomena—e.g., the character of political institutions, the occurrence of social conflict, the content of systems of norms and values or of a system of law.

In previous chapters we have seen that many social scientists attempt to discover social generalizations that exist across societies or cultures. Part of the attraction of materialism is the promise it holds for arriving at such generalizations. If there are important explanatory relations between the "material culture" of a civilization and its values, social institutions, and political arrangements, then it is promising to suppose that civilizations with similar material cultures will have similar political and social characteristics. And in fact various social scientists have made use of materialist arguments to account for such diverse phenomena as popular social conflict, forms of social consciousness, systems of law, and the occurrence of war and revolution.

A particularly important strand of materialist social science stems from classical Marxism. However, materialist arguments can be found within *non-*Marxist areas of social science as well. Consider a few examples of materialist explanations of social and historical developments:

- The diffusion of the metal stirrup into Western Europe in the eighth century caused the emergence of feudalism (White 1962).
- Food taboos result from ecological pressures and crises (Harris 1978).
- The simple material culture of the Nuer produces a characteristic form of social psychology in which "courage, generosity, patience, pride, loyalty, stubbornness, and independence, are the virtues the Nuer themselves extol" (Evans-Pritchard 1940:89–90).
- The technical imperatives of the medieval wheeled plow account for the characteristic long, narrow field shape of northern France (Bloch 1966).

- Differences in political attitudes among European workers stem from the technical characteristics of different industrial systems and occupations (Sabel 1982).
- Peasants have a distinctive sense of justice that is determined by the circumstances of material life associated with small-scale traditional agriculture (Scott 1976).
- Ideologies in capitalist societies emphasize atomized individualism because this conception of social life is most consistent with the needs of capitalist economic institutions (Marx 1848/1974).

What distinguishes Marxian materialism (usually referred to as *historical materialism*) from other varieties are a more articulated theory of the social structures associated with economic organization, a developed hypothesis about how these structures influence other social arrangements, and Marx's emphasis on class politics as the mechanism of social change. Facts about the economic basis of society determine a set of classes within society, and classes in turn shape and transform political and ideological institutions.

The classical application of historical materialism has focused on European history—the structure of feudalism, the transition from feudalism to capitalism, and the organization of capitalist society. But this model may also be applied to non-Western societies. An Asian agrarian society, for example, may be characterized in terms of the forms of land and water management that are current, the seed and fertilizer technologies that are available, and the forms of tools available for cultivation, food processing, and storage. The social relations of production in an agrarian society include the forms of land tenure that are current, the socially enforced organization of labor (wage labor or corvée labor, for example), and the social arrangements that extract surplus from the primary cultivators (rent, interest, profits, taxes, bandit predations). Historical materialism maintains that a number of peasant societies are quite similar in respect to these characteristics and that similar social processes in these societies result from this system of technological and social arrangements. Thus rent strikes, tax revolts, and rice riots are forms of collective action that emerge from the social structures described here.[1]

THE GUIDING THREAD

Materialism begins in the observation that all societies must have institutions through which the basic subsistence needs of the population are satisfied. Technology and labor must be organized to produce food, clothing, shelter, etc.; institutions must exist for the distribution of goods to individuals; and these institutions in turn must be rendered stable by higher-level institutions (e.g., systems of law). Moreover economic activity typically produces a surplus over and above the subsistence needs of the population, and contending groups may be expected to attempt to seize control of this surplus. (This is the substance of Marx's view that "all history is a history

Technology	Economic structure	Politics	Culture
Forces of production	*Relations of production*	*Superstructure*	
tools	property ownership	state	kinship
forms of agriculture	wage labor	legal system	religion
forms of manufacture	market system	police	ideology
water systems	slavery	parties	family
raw materials	serfdom		art
natural environment			
labor skills			

Fig. 6.1   Central concepts of materialism

of class struggle.") Materialism then moves to a second and more contestable view: that various features of a given society—for example, the organization and behavior of the state—can be understood in terms of their fittedness to the working of the production system. Materialism thus explains features of politics and culture by analyzing basic human needs and the production systems through which those needs are satisfied; these explanations potentially provide the basis for cross-cultural generalizations as well.

Karl Marx's theory of historical materialism, advanced schematically in his *Contribution to a Critique of Political Economy* (1859) and more fully in *The German Ideology* (1846/1970), holds that facts about the social and technical properties of the economic structure "determine" the properties of noneconomic institutions—political institutions, law, religion, ideology, etc. (Marx sometimes refers to the latter as the "superstructure" of society.) Here "determine" is in quotes to indicate that it is problematic; the term does *not* mean *uniquely determine* but rather "constrain" or "influence."

Historical materialism emphasizes two factors within the social process: the importance of the particular forms of *technology* in use within a given culture and the importance of the *social relations of power and authority* through which economic activity is organized (the social relations of production, in Marxist terms). The latter refers to the property relations governing the use and direction of the forces of production—land, capital, investment funds, raw materials, etc. Figure 6.1 identifies some of the main features of these concepts. Historical materialism generally maintains that factors to the left in this diagram exert explanatory primacy over factors to the right.

Consider a classic example of materialist explanation: Marx's explanation of the process of enclosure in early-modern England (Example 6.1). Here we find many of the main elements of a materialist explanation. Marx explains a change in the legal system and the organization of the rural property system as a response to the needs of the emerging capitalist mode of production. This example also raises some of the chief problems associated with this framework of explanation. The central problem is its implicit functionalism: the assumption that social relations will adjust to satisfy the needs of the emerging mode of production (capitalism). As we saw in Chapter 5, this assumption is untenable unless we can provide an account

---

Example 6.1 The expropriation of the agricultural population in England

English agriculture in the sixteenth century was largely dominated by smallholding peasant farmers. In the seventeenth century a series of legal enactments were undertaken (the Enclosure Acts) restricting and eventually abolishing peasant rights to land, and leading to the creation of capitalist farms. This process led in the following century to the large-scale expropriation of smallholders, expelling the majority from the farm economy and creating an influx of landless workers into towns and cities. Why did this change occur? Marx holds that the precondition for capitalist development is a plentiful supply of laborers who can be hired by capitalists. In a social system in which the bulk of ordinary people have easy access to the land, there is little incentive for them to hire themselves out to capitalists. Thus capitalist development is blocked by a smallholding peasant economy. Marx therefore interprets the process of enclosure as one through which English social arrangements were altered to create an adequate labor supply for capitalist development. "The theft of the common lands, the usurpation of feudal and clan property and this transformation into modern private property under circumstances of ruthless terrorism, all these things were just so many idyllic methods of primitive accumulation. They conquered the field for capitalist agriculture, incorporated the soil into capital, and created for the urban industries the necessary supplies of free and rightless proletarians" (Marx 1867/1977).

Data: historical data on the English rural economy
Explanatory model: materialist explanation interpreting social change as responsive to the needs of an emerging mode of production
Source: Karl Marx, *Capital*, vol. 1 (1867/1977)

---

of the mechanisms through which the needs of the mode of production stimulate the necessary adjustments in the social system. It is not impossible to provide an account of such mechanisms—for example, the relationship between the needs of the mode of production and the corresponding interests that are assigned to particular classes within society—but without such an account the explanation is faulty.

TECHNOLOGY AND CULTURE

Historical materialism maintains, then, that features of the "material basis" of society exert strong causal influence on other nonmaterial aspects of society. This claim raises a problem that was seen as central in Chapter 2: What are the mechanisms through which a given form of social causation is transmitted? Let us consider this question first in terms of a particular causal claim—the notion that a given form of material culture has distinctive effects on the forms of social consciousness characteristic of that culture. Technology and the material circumstances of production have been said to constrain or influence social consciousness in a variety of ways. First, it is sometimes held that an individual's experience of the dominant technologies

---

Example 6.2   Factories and social psychology

The world of the agricultural worker was dramatically different from that of the factory worker. How did these changes in the work environment affect the worker in the early period of the Industrial Revolution? Herbert Gutman chronicles some of the changes in social psychology that evolved with the transition from artisanal to factory production. For example, the experience of time was profoundly different in the two systems. The artisan could work at his own pace, both daily and seasonally, whereas the factory worker was forced to adjust to the regular hours of industrial production. A major task for industrialists was to create a new system of social control and discipline that would regularize workers' activity and prepare them for the routine, task-oriented labor of a factory. Gutman believes that the result was a new form of social psychology corresponding to the conditions of industrial production.

Data: historical data on the circumstances of labor in the early period of the
    Industrial Revolution in England and the United States.
Explanatory model: the circumstances of work shape a new social psychology
Source: Herbert Gutman, *Work, Culture, and Society in Industrializing America:
    Essays in American Working-class and Social History* (1976)

---

that appear in everyday life and the workplace directly influences his or her consciousness. Individuals acquire traits of personality, values, goals, aversions, and paradigms of social behavior from their life experience, and different technologies and economic settings produce characteristic patterns of social psychology. The subsistence peasant comes to have a risk-averse value scheme (Scott 1976); the hunter-gatherer develops a moral vision that emphasizes cooperation (Sahlins 1972); the factory worker or machine operator acquires a form of consciousness that prominently features social alienation and consumerism (Braverman 1974). Marx's own treatment of the French peasantry illustrates the same sort of point; he held that the material circumstances of peasant cultivation led quite directly to social conservatism.

Here the idea is that alternative technologies impose very different patterns of life on workers and that these differences lead to different forms of personality. Consider Examples 6.2 and 6.3. Gutman and Sabel both explain some characteristics of social consciousness—values, motives, political values—in terms of the work circumstances in which people find themselves. Similarly, various authors have argued for a characteristic form of "peasant mentality" that emerges from the technical characteristics of small-scale traditional agriculture. Thus Fei Hsiao Tung writes of Chinese peasants, "Peasantry . . . is a way of living, a complex of formal organization, individual behaviour, and social attitudes, closely knit together for the purpose of husbanding land with simple tools and human labour" (Fei 1987:57). Peasant cultivation involves intensive labor using traditional tools and techniques; it subjects the peasant farmer to the vagaries of weather and pest; it puts a premium on small-group cooperation; and it produces, according to Fei, a particular

---

Example 6.3 Working-class social attitudes

Is there a characteristic social psychology of the working class? Do working-class people share a common set of political attitudes? Charles Sabel argues that the conditions of the industrial working environment, conjoined with the social origins and aspirations of the work force, do produce characteristic "worldviews," but these worldviews vary sharply according to differences in the workplace and the social origins of the worker. It is not possible, therefore, to make general claims about workers' political and social ideas; instead it is necessary to consider in greater detail the particular circumstances in which workers find themselves. Sabel distinguishes among skilled craftsmen, workers with plant-specific technical skills, unskilled workers, peasant workers, and ghetto workers. He argues that each category has a substantially different ethos and worldview. Moreover these differences are of substantial import for the political behavior of various groups of workers. "Differences between world views of the 'same' situation are not unimportant. They lead to differing predictions about the significance of events that will occur in the future. . . . We can no more say that a world view is uniquely determined by, say, the technology of the part of society to which it refers than that a scientific theory is a mere extension of certain facts of nature" (Sabel 1982:13). He adds, "Many industrial conflicts arise from management's violation of the workers' expectations of propriety and justice" (Sabel 1982:15). Why do skilled craftsmen refrain from career progress to white-collar or management jobs? Because within the craftsman's ethos and the satisfactions that creative performance of the craft provides cannot be achieved in a management role (Sabel 1982:86–89).

Data: sociology of the industrial working classes of Western Europe and the United States
Explanatory model: explanation of political and economic behavior of working-class groups based on a hypothesis about their ethos and worldview
Source: Charles Sabel, *Work and Politics* (1982)

---

social psychology emphasizing family and mistrust of outsiders. Teodor Shanin provides a similar account of Russian peasants. "Russian peasant communities showed distinct *cultural patterns of cognition*—both the results and the determinants of other peasant characteristics. In this sense of specifically linked and mutually reinforcing political economy and consciousness, the description of peasanthood as a 'way of living' makes considerable sense" (Shanin 1985:84). He identifies the following elements as characteristic of Russian peasant mentality: traditionalism, conformism, egalitarianism (Shanin 1985:84). And his explanation of this common social psychology is that it emerges as a causal consequence of the social and technical features of Russian peasant life.

Closely related to this point about the technology itself is a parallel point about the technical organization of the process of production. Some forms of workplace organization have dramatically different effects on worker consciousness than others. Thus it is sometimes held that certain occupational

---

Example 6.4   Political attitudes in the Vendée

Charles Tilly explains political attitudes of peasants of the Vendée by analyzing the material culture in which they live. He writes, "The difference between the work of the traditional cultivator and that of the winegrower is important in itself. . . . The winegrower is a merchant by necessity and by inclination; he must calculate costs, prices, and the probable effects of distant decisions. He is inevitably sensitive to governmental policies affecting commerce. . . . He keeps up communication with the cities that consume or ship his output" (Tilly 1964:114–16). The subsistence peasants of the Mauges, by contrast, were insular and localistic and were concerned with satisfying subsistence needs rather than making a profit. Thus one group was oriented toward regional or national markets; the other attempted to avoid market involvement. And Tilly asserts that these differences lead to pronounced differences in political behavior as well: Winegrowers tended to be more cosmopolitan and to support the revolution, whereas the subsistence peasants tended to support the counterrevolution.

Data: historical data on the economy of eighteenth-century western France; data on political activity in various districts of the Vendée
Explanatory model: material culture strongly influences political attitudes and behavior
Source: Charles Tilly, *The Vendée* (1964)

---

groups—e.g., miners—have a higher level of group solidarity and militancy than others because of the shared features of their work—risk, dependency on fellow workers, and close working conditions. Harry Braverman (1974) explores some of the implications of this aspect of materialist explanation in his discussion of the labor process in capitalism, and Sabel and Zeitlin (1985) consider the differences between artisanal production versus factory production in this regard (Example 6.8).

Charles Tilly's (1964:113–45) treatment of the cropping patterns and political attitudes of the Vendée (the rural counterrevolution in France in the 1790s) illustrates both aspects of this form of materialism (Example 6.4).

This strand of materialist explanation hypothesizes a causal relation between the social and economic environment created by a particular level and character of technology and the forms of social psychology and political behavior that are cultivated in persons within that environment. This hypothesis depends on both an inductive generalization—it is possible to discern at least some important differences in the social psychologies of persons in alternative economic settings—and a theoretical argument based in social psychology. The latter argument comes in more or less a priori forms, but the heart of the argument is that human nature is not fixed by biology and that psychological traits of personality and behavior are influenced by factors in the individual's life experience—family, work, sport, and everyday politics. What materialism adds to this theory is the idea that facts about work experience are particularly central in the individual's psychological development, with the result that we should expect important causal consequences of the mode of production on individual psychology.

CLASS AND PROPERTY RELATIONS

The form of materialist explanation just described pays particular attention to the ways that important features of social life are influenced or constrained by the dominant technology and the forms of organization through which the technology is employed. At least as important, however, is the idea that an economy embodies a set of coercive institutions through which one group extracts economic surplus from other groups. These institutions are the property relations, which define a set of classes that have distinct and opposing material interests. Historical materialism maintains that the structure of the property relations has profound effects on higher-level social institutions. In this approach the social relations of production—the class and property relations—are the decisive factors within the process of social change. Thus historical materialism places primacy on the social relations of production through which the production process is organized and controlled and the classes that ensue, and it emphasizes the centrality of the system of *surplus-extraction* in place in a particular society.

In the classic Marxist view the social relations of production simultaneously organize the process of production *and* establish a division of society defined by access to the surplus product. That is, property relations define classes. Another way of characterizing this aspect of materialism is to say that it gives special attention to the system of surplus extraction in use in a given society and to the division into extractors and producers defined by that system. According to historical materialism the economic and political changes that follow upon the class conflict created by the system of surplus extraction have a central role in the process of historical change within a given society.[2] In particular, historical materialism regards class societies as systems of *exploitation*—the coercively enforced extraction of surplus from producers by an elite class. The property relations are the juridical embodiment of the system of exploitation; they establish the arrangements through which one group expropriates the surplus of another. Thus within feudalism the lord's right to the bonded labor of the serf was the mechanism of exploitation; in the capitalist system the fact that wage laborers have no access to means of production forces them to sell their labor power to capitalists for a wage that is less than the value added to the product by their labor. Workers are exploited by capitalists through the system of wage labor that creates a surplus, which is expropriated by capitalists in the form of profit, interest, and rent.

According to classical materialism the circumstances defining the institutions of production, including the class system, impress a dynamic of development on other aspects of social life. Marx maintains that the forces and relations of production impose a pattern of development on the rest of social life. In particular, Marx states that political institutions, some cultural phenomena, and various institutions of consciousness formation are strongly influenced by the "needs" of the economic structure and the property relations. Thus he holds that the forms of ideology that are current in a given social order have a functional relationship to the stability of existing property relations. As this description indicates there is a strongly functionalist strand of thinking in this explanatory model; in fact Gerald Cohen argues at length that Marxism postulates a functional relationship between such "superstructural" institutions and the economic structure (Cohen 1978:160–71).

The main elements of the materialist approach are summarized in the following ideas. (1) Various elements of social structure and ideology can be understood as functional adaptations to the needs of the economic structure and property system. (2) Members of classes will tend to perceive their common material interests, so class membership is a significant basis for explaining political behavior. (3) There is some correspondence between a class's political power and its rights within the property system and the relationship between that role and the expansion of the forces of production. (4) There are large-scale causal regularities at work among technological development, the social institutions of production, and the development of political, cultural, or ideological institutions. Hypotheses of these sorts constitute a program of research for social scientists. They lead the investigator to formulate questions about the material institutions of a given society, to pay attention to the particulars of local class relations, and to explore the causal relations between these material factors and other social developments.

Crucially important for the adequacy of materialist explanations is the answer to the question of what mechanisms establish the linkage between the economic structure and the evolution of various superstructural elements—for example, political forms. (This question reflects the central conclusions of Chapters 2 and 5: the need for an account of causal mechanisms in support of causal and functional claims in social science.) The most convincing answers involve several plausible social processes. Members of the elite class defined by the property relations are capable of perceiving the connection between their interests and the stability of the economic structure, and they typically have substantial political resources to expend on defending their interests. And there is a more anonymous process at work as well: Political institutions that are *not* consonant with the needs of the economic system will tend to give rise to adverse effects that are not desired by many or all segments of society, not merely the elite class (Przeworski 1985a). Thus a tax reform package that favors the poor over the rich may create strong disincentives to investment, leading to poor economic performance and in turn to widespread support for modification of the reform package.

Ralph Miliband provides a sophisticated development of the materialist program in application to the capitalist state (Example 6.5). Another important example of a class-based explanation of an important social phenomenon is Robert Brenner's treatment of the English agricultural revolution (Example

---

Example 6.5 The capitalist state

What factors propel the policies of the capitalist state? Ralph Miliband offers a sophisticated theoretical discussion of this issue from a Marxian point of view. His central thesis is that the behavior of the state in capitalist society—e.g., Great Britain, the United States, or France—is both propelled and constrained by features of the class system embodied in capitalism. The great classes are the bourgeoisie—owners of the means of production—and the proletariat—wage laborers. Rejecting the crude materialism that maintains that the state is nothing but the instrument of the dominant class, Miliband nonetheless attempts to establish some of the direct and indirect mechanisms through which class interests give rise to political power. He accepts the notion that the state's policies are to some degree autonomous from the economic structure—not every bit of state activity has its origins in some interest of the bourgeoisie—but he argues that there are constraints on state policy that force it to be broadly consistent with the interests of the dominant class. Direct mechanisms include the fact that state elites in the capitalist world are often drawn directly from economic elites, so their worldview and political attitudes are likely to reflect the interests of the dominant class (Miliband 1969:56ff.), and the fact that political parties in the capitalist world are heavily dependent on campaign financing that flows disproportionately from economic elites. Indirect mechanisms include the need of any government to avoid economic crisis—an outcome that is all too possible if it adopts policies fundamentally unacceptable to economic elites (Miliband 1969:96). The possibility of a "capital strike" (a policy of disinvestment and capital flight by displeased economic elites) is a towering deterrent to anticapitalist policies adopted even by a social democratic regime.

Data: political data concerning the state policies and organizations of capitalist democracies in the twentieth century

Explanatory model: the imperatives of class shape state policy in a way that serves the interests of the capitalist class

Source: Ralph Miliband, *The State in Capitalist Society* (1969)

6.6). Brenner's account represents an alternative materialist explanation of the same social processes considered by Marx in Example 6.1. Brenner's treatment, however, does not raise the problem of spurious functionalism that appears to threaten Marx's account. It does not presuppose the inevitability of the emergence of capitalism; on the contrary it begins with the recognition that capitalist agriculture was long delayed in France, while advancing rapidly in England. Moreover Brenner's explanation is forward-looking. He identifies features of early-modern English social life that were conducive to the emergence of capitalist agriculture, and he notes that the corresponding features were not present in the French case. This explanation yields a straightforward causal argument, then, from a description of the social-property system in England to an analysis of the effects of that system on later developments. At the same time the argument is a materialist one because it places features of the social organization of production—the

---

Example 6.6 The agricultural revolution in England

Sixteenth- and seventeenth-century England witnessed an agricultural revolution that involved massive changes in land tenure, the organization of production on farms, the techniques employed in farming, and the productivity of agriculture. French agriculture, by contrast, experienced a retrenchment of peasant cultivation and a century-long stagnation, in a rather similar macroeconomic environment. Robert Brenner asserts that the factors that led to these very different outcomes are the particular character of social-property relations in different regions of Europe (particularly the conditions of land tenure), the interests and incentives that these relations impose on the various actors, and the relative power of the classes defined by those relations in particular regions. Brenner's explanation of these developments is based on "microclass analysis" of the agrarian relations of particular regions of Europe. The processes of agricultural modernization unavoidably favored some class interests and harmed others. Capitalist agriculture required larger units of production (farms), the application of larger quantities of capital goods to agriculture, higher levels of education and scientific knowledge, etc. All of this required the expropriation of smallholders and the destruction of traditional communal forms of agrarian relations. Brenner holds that in those regions of Europe where peasant societies were best able to defend traditional arrangements—favorable rent levels, communal control of land, and patterns of smallholding—those arrangements persisted for centuries. In areas where peasants had been substantially deprived of tradition, organization, and power of resistance, capitalist agriculture was able (through an enlightened gentry and budding bourgeoisie) to restructure agrarian relations in the direction of profitable, scientific, rational (capitalist) agriculture. England satisfied these conditions, whereas France possessed a strong and militant peasantry. In the French case, then, the struggle over property relations and modernization was resolved in favor of the peasant cultivator rather than the modernizing managerial farmer, leading to agricultural stagnation.

Data: comparative data on the organization of the rural economies of France and England

Explanatory model: patterns of economic change can be explained as the outcome of local class struggles, determined by the powers and resources available to the several microclasses

Source: Robert Brenner, "Agrarian Class Structure and Economic Development in Pre-Industrial Europe" (1976); "The Agrarian Roots of European Capitalism" (1982). (See also Aston and Philpin, eds., *The Brenner Debate*, 1985.)

---

structure of the social-property system—at the center of the explanation and identifies class interests and powers as the critical causal factor.[3]

IDEOLOGY AND CLASS

An important component of materialist social science is the theory of ideology and social consciousness. The central claim of Marx's theory of ideology can be stated in these terms: Persons within class societies typically have false and distorted beliefs about themselves and the society in which they live; these beliefs, which systematically enhance the interests of existing ruling classes, may be explained causally as the result of the working of institutions through which consciousness is shaped. The theory of ideology plays a central role in Marx's system, resolving what appears to be a contradiction between his theory and the historical evidence. Marx maintains that "history is a history of class struggle"—a sequence of social systems based on exploitation and domination by ruling classes of direct producers. At the same time we know that rebellion and overt violent conflict between social groups are the rare exceptions, not the rule. But if exploitation and class opposition are ubiquitous, how can we account for the general social tranquility? If a given set of social institutions is exploitative, then it is irrational for the exploited group to knowingly accept its condition if it has the power to resist.

This means that an exploitative society can remain stable only on one of a pair of conditions. A class society typically contains substantial repressive institutions that intimidate the direct producers from taking action against their oppressors. That is, social stability may be secured through repressive means. We have many examples of regimes and classes that preserve their positions through largely repressive means (El Salvador, Romania, South Korea, etc.).

On the whole, however, the industrial democracies of the twentieth century have adopted institutions of ideological control rather than overtly repressive institutions as the chief instrument of social control. These societies feature extensive ideological institutions that beguile and mystify the oppressed, making them believe that they are not exploited after all. Through these means the exploited may be induced to fail to recognize their condition for what it is. The reality of social exploitation and control may be obscured or mystified by beliefs that existing social institutions are just, fair, divinely ordained, or inevitable. Given the reality of exploitation, these beliefs are a form of false consciousness, and, according to Marx, they are one of the central means by which social harmony is preserved in class society. Effective ideologies thus represent a possible alternative to violently repressive measures in support of a class-based regime.

An ideology thus represents a systematic division between the appearance and reality of a class society for the participants. The appearance—which is created by consciousness-shaping institutions—is one of fairness and mutuality, but the reality is one of exploitative and authoritarian social relations. The theory of ideology is therefore an empirical theory about the formation and function of consciousness within a class society. The core of the theory consists of three elements:

1. Beliefs and attitudes are causal factors within the social system; they affect the stability of society and its disposition toward change. Further, their characteristics are class-biased: One family of beliefs and attitudes

may favor the interests of one class, and another favors those of a different class. To give one relevant example, widespread belief in the legitimacy of private property favors a capitalist order, whereas widespread adherence to Proudhon's maxim ("property is theft!") threatens the stability of the order. The first belief therefore favors the interests of the property-owning class, and the second injures them.

2. Beliefs and attitudes are largely shaped, instilled, or extinguished through enduring social institutions. These range from the formal (school, church, military organization, political party organization) to the informal (mass media, folk literature and song, traditions of family life, traditions of sport and play, and the like). A class society embodies a wide range of institutions whose function is to conceal the exploitative character of its basic social relations.

3. These institutions are subject to the pressures and incentives that derive from class interest within class society. These channels of influence may be briefly indicated: Institutions that serve property relations will generally work more smoothly than those that upset such relations; the dominant class has the organizational, informational, and financial resources necessary to resist or subvert harmful institutions; and such institutions normally draw their personnel from the dominant class or its clients.

Given the threat to stability that the exploited would pose if they had clear perceptions of their dominant institutions, we would expect a class society to incorporate a wide range of institutions designed to conceal the exploitative character of its basic social relations. And in fact we can identify fairly clear examples of social institutions whose function is, among other things, the promulgation of an ideology. Educational institutions, church, family, media, and political processes all disseminate ideological commitments. (It goes without saying that they serve many other functions as well.) They effectively transmit a worldview and morality to most of the population that support existing relations of power and property. (Antonio Gramsci, the twentieth-century Italian Marxist, introduced the idea of *hegemony* to describe this phenomenon: Ruling classes retain their sway over subordinate classes by successfully dominating the system of ideas and values in terms of which social relations are understood; Gramsci 1971.)

The theory of ideology represents a clear example of materialist explanation in two respects. First, it illustrates the functionalist character of much materialist explanation; an economic system based on exploitation *needs* a set of institutions of consciousness-formation that create shared beliefs to conceal the exploitation from participants, and a system of ideology satisfies this need. The argument is that ideologies exist *in order to* stabilize a class society. Second, there are promising causal mechanisms available to undergird this functionalist explanation (as we found to be necessary in Chapter 5). Central among these is the theory of class politics—the idea that members of the dominant class have both the interest and the opportunity to bias social consciousness in the direction needed by the economic system. This process provides an individual-level mechanism through which the functional relation between the economic system and ideology is established.

MATERIALISM AND RATIONAL CHOICE THEORY

A central challenge for materialist explanation is the need to avoid spurious functionalism. We may go a good distance in answering this challenge by emphasizing the relations between historical materialism and rational choice theory for the tools of this theory offer an account of some of the mechanisms that underlie functional relations between levels of social organization. A materialist analysis of property relations and technology provides a framework in which to characterize the interests, opportunities, and limitations of various agents. Seen from this perspective, materialism incorporates the core elements of rational choice theory. It postulates that individuals will act to serve their material interests, and it devotes considerable effort to describing the salient features of the social environment. The ways in which a landless worker pursues his material interests are very different from those chosen by a poor peasant, let alone a lesser landlord. So by providing an extended description of the social environment, it is possible to make predictions about the forms of political and economic behavior that can be expected from participants within this environment. Using this analysis materialism postulates that it is possible to construct an explanation of the particulars of a given political occurrence by using information about the class interests and positions of the participants.

Consider an example that makes this connection explicit—Stephen Vlastos's analysis of Japanese peasant politics (Example 6.7). Vlastos's explanation of Japanese peasant politics illustrates a prominent feature of contemporary materialist explanation: the close relation between materialist explanation and rational choice analysis. Vlastos makes explicit the materialist idea that class identity has strong influence on political behavior, but he identifies class interests as the concrete material interests assigned to peasants in the particular social and economic arrangements of the Tokugawan peasant economy, and he explains their behavior as a rational effort to pursue and defend their interests within the political institutions in which they found themselves. Political action, then, is both class-inspired and individually rational in this account.

Analytical Marxism is an important new development in Marxist thought that takes this approach particularly seriously. It represents the marriage of some of the foundational ideas of classical Marxism with the methods and tools of rational choice theory.[4] As we have seen, Marxism is concerned with explaining a variety of large-scale processes of economic and political change—for example, the logic of development of capitalism, the transition from feudalism to capitalism, the evolution of the absolutist state, or the occurrence of peasant rebellion. Analytical Marxists have argued that the mechanisms that underlie these processes of change depend upon the rational

Example 6.7   Peasant uprisings in Tokugawa Japan

Tokugawa Japan witnessed substantial peasant protests and uprisings in spite of the extreme measures taken against protesters by the state. How were Japanese peasants able to achieve sustained collective action? Stephen Vlastos explains this phenomenon as the result of several factors: the rational decisionmaking calculations of individual peasants, the existence of deep and important shared material interests across the spectrum of peasant society, and a favorable social context in which tightly knit communities supported protest. Vlastos writes, "The first question to ask with respect to the political behavior of Tokugawa peasants is how to explain their demonstrated capacity to act collectively. Here structural features were paramount. The internal organization of the peasant class and its position within the Tokugawa polity were highly conducive to collective action" (Vlastos 1986:11). Vlastos finds that Tokugawa peasants had certain substantial advantages in achieving collective action. They were a genuine class, with "an essential similarity [in] the style, uses, and organization of each family's work force." Familial and village bonds promoted solidarity within the village, and the lord-peasant relation was particularly visible and exploitative. It was a single-stranded relation. Moreover villages rather than individuals were the tax unit (Vlastos 1986:11–13). "Finally . . . Japanese peasants constituted a racially, ethnically, and linguistically homogeneous population" (Vlastos 1986:14). He suggests that these contingent social circumstances, when conjoined with the substantial material interests shared by Japanese peasants, led to sustained rural protest and uprisings. He thus constructs peasant collective action in Japan as a rational, goal-directed, and interest-driven process. Peasants had certain goals and interests, they had a set of traditionally available instruments of protest, and they chose an appropriate instrument to accomplish a given end in a given set of circumstances.

Data: historical data on peasant collective action in Tokugawa Japan
Explanatory model: rational choice and class-interest analysis to explain patterns of collective protest in Japan
Source: Stephen Vlastos, *Peasant Protests and Uprisings in Tokugawa Japan* (1986)

---

actions of individuals, given the political and economic institutions in which they make choices and given their objective material interests. This approach therefore resorts to a handful of analytical tools based on the assumption that individuals make calculated choices in their economic and political behavior: theories of individual motivation and rationality, theories of organization and leadership, and theories of the logic of collective action. Jon Elster emphasizes primarily the pertinence of game theory for Marxism (Elster 1982), but collective action theory, social choice theory, and general equilibrium theory appear to be comparably important.

Consider, for example, Gerald Cohen's account of the social processes that underlie technological change in Marx's account. According to Cohen, Marx believes there is an endogenous tendency for the material forces available to a culture to expand over time. And in Cohen's account the rationale for this expectation depends on the following argument:

Men are, in a respect to be specified, somewhat rational.
The historical situation of men is one of scarcity.
Men possess intelligence of a kind and degree which enables them to improve
their situation. (Cohen 1978:152)

Essentially this argument embodies the idea of opportunistic rationality.
Cohen and Marx are assuming that, over time, human beings will notice
opportunities for improving existing technologies; that they have an interest
in implementing technological innovations because the resulting productive
forces will satisfy human needs more fully; and that as a result we should
anticipate a tendency toward technological development.

Many commentators now agree that Marx's economics are fundamentally
premised on the assumption of economic rationality: The laws of motion
of capitalism are the aggregate consequences of rational capitalist decisionmaking. However Marxism is not solely concerned with economic behavior.
It is also concerned with the politics of class: the success or failure of
working-class organizational efforts, the occurrence of collective action in
defense of class interests, the logic of working-class electoral politics, and
the occurrence of revolution. What assumptions underlie classic Marxist
analysis of the politics of class? To what extent does the rational choice
model carry over to Marx's *extra*-economic explanations—in particular his
explanations of political behavior?

It should first be noted that it is not difficult to extend the rational choice
model to a theory of political behavior. This is a much-employed model in
political science today, described under the umbrella of "public choice theory"
(to which we will return in Chapter 7). Such an approach postulates that
an individual's political behavior is a calculated attempt to further a given
set of individual interests—income, security, prestige, office, etc. One might
suppose that such an approach is unavoidably bourgeois, depending upon
a materialistic egoism characteristic of market society. However Marx's own
emphasis on class conflict based on material interests suggests a rational
choice model of political behavior: Classes have objective material interests
that are in opposition to one another, and members of classes are disposed
to act to defend and extend those interests. And in fact the rational choice
model has been effectively applied to political behavior from a Marxist
point of view in the work of Adam Przeworski. He analyzes workers'
political behavior in just these terms: "I assume, therefore, that workers
under capitalism have an interest in improving their material conditions.
The question is whether the pursuit of this interest, and only of this interest,
would necessarily lead workers to opt for socialism as a superior system
for satisfying material needs" (Przeworski 1985a:164.).

I maintain that Marx's theory of political behavior, like his theory of
capitalist behavior, is ultimately grounded in a theory of individual rationality.
But this theory is somewhat more comprehensive than public choice theory
in that it describes the resources needed to permit groups to overcome
atomization and privatization of action. Roughly stated:

- agents as members of classes behave in ways calculated to advance their perceived material interests;
- these interests are perceived as class interests (i.e., interests shared with other members of the class);
- class organizations and features of class consciousness permit classes to overcome implicit conflicts of interest between private and class interests.

This model is applied to political phenomena by analyzing the deliberate, calculated efforts of individuals to forward a set of shared material interests.

This analysis represents a Marxist political theory in terms quite compatible with public choice theory—a somewhat surprising discovery, given the proximity of that paradigm to neoclassical economic theory and a frequently conservative set of political views. However Marx's theory of political behavior is substantially richer than the public choice paradigm because it contains motivational resources over and above narrow calculation of self-interest. In addition to material class interests, Marx refers to two further elements of political motivation: ideology and class consciousness. The former concept is used to explain apparent failures to achieve rational collective action, and the latter explains how conflicts between private and group interests are surmounted. Ideologies sometimes lead individuals to act in ways that are contrary to their objective interests; while class consciousness leads individuals to act in ways that conform to their shared group interests at the possible expense of their individual interests.

Consider first the concept of ideology. How does the theory of ideology contribute to a Marxist theory of consciousness and political motivation? A clue may be found in the associated idea of "false consciousness": An ideology affects the worker's political behavior by instilling false *beliefs* and self-defeating *values* in the worker. An ideology may instill a set of values or preferences that propel individual behavior in ways that are contrary to the individual's objective material interests. Thus German and French workers were induced by appeals to patriotism and national identity to support their national governments in World War I, contrary to their objective shared class interests.[5] Such political behavior may be analyzed in this way: The French worker places a high value on the national interests of France, he believes that Germany is waging aggressive war against France, and he acts to support the French military effort against Germany. This behavior may be an example of rational action in pursuit of misguided ends—ends that are objectively contrary to the worker's class interests.

Ideologies may also modify rational individual action by instilling a set of false beliefs about the causal properties of the social world and about how existing arrangements affect one's objective interests. The belief that capitalism provides opportunities for advancement through education and individual initiative, for example, may lead workers to believe that a strategy of individual striving better serves their material interests than a strategy of collective action. The belief that inequalities in the United States in 1980 are less extensive than in 1940 may lead workers to assume that the direction of change within capitalism favors their interests. And the belief that the police powers of the capitalist state are overwhelmingly competent may lead them to assume that collective action is dangerous and ineffective. Each of these beliefs, when factored into a rational decisionmaking process in the circumstances in which the workers find themselves, inhibits militant collective action.

The theory of ideology, then, can be assimilated to a rational choice model of political action in a fairly direct manner. Ideologies modify the political behavior of individuals within a class society by instilling false beliefs about the environment of choice and by modifying the value system of the workers away from their objective material interests. Rational individuals, operating under the grip of an ideology, will undertake actions that are contrary to their objective material interests but are fully rational given the false beliefs they hold about the social world they inhabit and their mistaken assumptions about their real interests and values. An ideology is an effective instrument, then, in shaping political behavior within a class system; it induces members of exploited classes to refrain from political action directed at overthrowing the class system. And this is indeed Marx's use of the concept: An ideology functions as an instrument of class conflict, permitting a dominant class to manipulate the political behavior of subordinate classes.

The concept of class consciousness functions somewhat differently in Marx's writings. The term refers to a set of motivations, beliefs, values, and the like that are specific and distinctive for a given class (peasantry, proletariat, petty bourgeoisie). Marx holds that these motivational factors bind together the members of a class and facilitate their collective activities. Class consciousness can be expressed by such motives as loyalty to other members of one's class, solidarity with partners in a political struggle, and commitment to a future social order in which the interests of one's class are better served.[6] Thus a class is supposed to develop its own conscious identity of itself as a class. If a group of people who constitute a structurally defined class fails to acquire such attitudes, Marx denies that the group is a class in the full sense at all (a class-for-itself as well as a class-in-itself). Thus, in his famous view of peasants as a "sack of potatoes," Marx writes: "In so far as millions of families live under economic conditions of existence that separate their mode of life, their interests and their cultural formation from those of the other classes, they form a class. In so far as these small peasant proprietors are merely connected on a local basis, and the identity of their interests fails to produce a feeling of community, national links, or a political organization, they do not form a class." (Marx 1852/1974:239). Here Marx's point is *not* that the peasantry fails to constitute a class in the objective sense—a group of persons sharing a distinct position within the property and production relations—but rather that the conditions of life that characterize peasant existence systematically undermine the emergence of collective action and political consciousness. In other words peasants fail to arrive at a state of class consciousness.[7]

Marx does not provide an extensive analysis of the process through which class consciousness emerges, even within capitalism, but he suggests that it takes form through a historical process of class struggle. As workers or peasants come to identify their shared interests and as they gain experience working together to defend these interests, they develop concrete ties within their political groups that provide motivational resources for future collective action. Thus Marx writes in the *Communist Manifesto* that "this organization of the proletarians into a class, and consequently into a political party, is continually being upset again by the competition between the workers themselves. But it ever rises up again, stronger, firmer, mightier" (Marx and Engels 1848/1974:76). Finally a class's accurate perception of its material interests depends upon a crucial historical development: the more complete development of the economic structure that defines these interests and the disappearance of the vestiges of old systems of production. In *The Class Struggles in France* (Marx 1850/1974:45 ff.), Marx therefore diagnoses the Parisian proletariat in 1848 as immature and deceived about its true material interests.

This analysis of class consciousness suggests a model of political motivation that is somewhat richer than the theory of narrow self-interest associated with rational choice theory. In this view individuals are to some extent influenced in their political choices by strands of commitment deriving from class consciousness. However, as we saw in Chapter 3, there is now a perceived need within rational choice theory itself to make room for such commitments in the rational choice model. The concept of class consciousness thus has affinity with Sen's concept of commitments and other efforts to provide a more adequate conception of political rationality. We will return to this issue in Chapter 7.

Neither ideology nor class consciousness, then, requires that a rational choice analysis of Marx's central explanatory paradigm be abandoned. This paradigm represents an idealization of individual behavior, of course, but subject to the terms of the idealization, individual capitalists behave rationally within the context of the capitalist economy. And members of classes behave rationally in defense of their material interests, with two provisos: Dominant ideologies may give them false beliefs about both their objective interests and the causal properties of the social system they inhabit, and strands of class consciousness may give them the motivational resources needed to transcend implicit conflicts between individual and collective interests.

MARXISM AND LARGE-SCALE PREDICTIONS

The interpretation of materialism in rational choice terms offered in the previous section is highly localistic. It does not presume to offer a general recipe for interpreting social change at the level of epochal historical processes; rather it asserts only that we can better understand the perhaps unique sequence of developments under question if we analyze the confluence of class interests and actions that underlay it. Classical Marxism also makes large-scale predictions about the development of modes of production as a whole (the laws of motion of capitalism, the decline of feudalism) and about the "necessary" sequence of these modes of production. Such predictions derive loosely from the framework of class analysis described above, together with a highly abstract model of the various societies in question. It is entirely possible, however, that actual societies are too various, embodying too many conflicting tendencies and processes, to permit us to attach much weight to any of these macropredictions. In any complex system—social or natural—we may understand each of the causal factors in isolation. But because of their complex interactions and the sensitivity of the outcome to moment-by-moment particulars of the causal interaction, it may be impossible to derive any predictions at all about the final state of the system. However, we may still be able to explain various transitions within the evolution of the system appealing to the various factors. (We will return to this when we discuss the need for "microfoundations" for social explanations in Chapter 9.)

Example 6.8 illustrates that it is possible to remain sensitive to historical alternatives within the context of materialist explanations. In this example Sabel and Zeitlin show that factory production was not the inevitable result of technological change but resulted rather from strategies chosen by capitalists to control labor. The central hypothesis in Example 6.8 is that a system of production involving highly skilled, technologically flexible craftsmen may have comparable or even superior levels of efficiency within modern economic circumstances. The choice of factory production over artisanal production was, in this view, the result of strategies chosen by owners of capital in their struggles against workers; this struggle could have had a different outcome if workers and capitalists had chosen different strategies. The emergence of the factory system, then, does not reflect a process of economic determinism but rather the historically contingent choices of capitalists and workers.

Thus it is plausible that the development of capitalism itself contained substantially more historical contingency than Marx's own model recognized—with the result that the pattern of capitalist development might have been very different from that predicted by Marx. And even more skepticism may today greet the assumption that a necessary sequence of modes of production or even a short list of possible and discrete modes of production exists. Both these forms of skepticism are probably justified, but this does not invalidate materialism as an analysis of the causal importance of class, technology, and control of surpluses in the explanation of particular processes of social development.

If we take this perspective, the significance of materialism is *not* its claim to provide a basis for large-scale aggregative predictions about modes of production, revolutionary transitions, or sequences of modes of production. Rather it is the basis of analysis it offers for a cluster of important causal factors whose influence can be discerned at the local level and which contributes in important, but perhaps unpredictable, ways to the evolution of the system as a whole.

Example 6.8   Why factories?

A prominent feature of the changes brought on by the European Industrial Revolution was the emergence of a factory system. Large-scale production, making use of extensive division of labor, specialized machines, and unskilled labor, replaced artisanal production, employing small shops, skilled labor, and general-purpose technologies. Marx's explanation of this transition depends on the inherently superior efficiency of factory production. But Sabel and Zeitlin (1985) argue that factory production was *not* inherently more efficient than artisanal production and that it was possible to absorb technological innovation, including the application of new forms of power, within skilled artisanal shops. They contend that the true explanation of the emergence of factory production turns rather on the superior powers that this system confers on owners of capital over workers. By deskilling workers and reducing their dependence on expensive skilled artisans, capitalists were in a better position to realize maximum profits. Capitalists therefore selected factory organization over artisanal organization (on an individual basis); the result was an overwhelming balance in favor of factory over artisanal organization. The authors refer to the latter as "flexible specialization" (Sabel and Zeitlin 1985:142). If this form did not prevail, the reason should be sought in the political relations among classes rather than in the level of efficiency of one form or the other. Against the dominant interpretation—that factory production was technologically mandated—Sabel and Zeitlin ask: "Or was the breakthrough to mass production the result of some implicit collective choice, arrived at in the obscurity of uncountable small conflicts, to favour this form of mechanization over other, technologically viable ones? In that case, social struggles, not the technologies themselves, will decide the questions of future industrial organization" (Sabel and Zeitlin 1985:134).

Data: detailed studies of the history of technology in Western Europe and the United States
Explanatory model: the material interests and strategic behavior of participants determine which of the multiple possible lines of technology organization will prevail
Source: Charles F. Sabel and Jonathan Zeitlin, "Historical Alternatives to Mass Production: Politics, Markets and Technology in 19th Century Industrialization" (1985)

NOTES

1. Important contributions to the study of peasant societies may be found in Migdal (1974), Shanin (1985), Wolf (1966), Scott (1976), and Tilly (1964).

2. The chief sources for Marx's theory of historical materialism are *The German Ideology*, "Preface to a Contribution to a Critique of Political Economy," and scattered comments throughout *Capital*. For a pivotal contemporary exposition of Marx's theory of historical materialism, see G. A. Cohen (1978). The extensive literature that has developed on this topic is surveyed in Little (1986), Chapter 2.

3. Brenner's account is itself controversial, however; some economic historians now doubt that the contrast between English and French economic development was as sharp as Brenner asserts (O'Brien and Keyder 1978).

4. Some of the chief writings within analytical Marxism include G. A. Cohen, *Karl Marx's Theory of History: A Defence* (1978); John Roemer, *Analytical Foundations of Marxism* (1981); Jon Elster, *Making Sense of Marx* (1985); and Adam Przeworski, *Capitalism and Social Democracy* (1985a). Useful collections include Roemer, ed., *Analytical Marxism* (1986) and Ware and Nielsen, eds., *Analyzing Marxism* (1989).

5. See Marc Ferro's *The Great War 1914–1918* (1973) for an analysis of the role of patriotism in motivating European workers to support their national governments in their war policies.

6. Marx describes such a complex of psychological properties and their social foundation in *The Eighteenth Brumaire*: "A whole superstructure of different and specifically formed feelings, illusions, modes of thought and views of life arises on the basis of the different forms of property, of the social conditions of existence. The whole class creates and forms these out of its material foundations and the corresponding social relations. The single individual, who derives these feelings, etc. through tradition and upbringing, may well imagine that they form the real determinants and the starting-point of his activity" (Marx 1852/1974:173–74).

7. Michael Taylor argues that this conception of peasant politics is badly off the mark. "In all [peasant societies] there was cooperation amongst the peasants in the agricultural work which dominated their lives and usually communal regulation of the use of communal land" (M. Taylor 1986:7). He reminds us that peasants have historically been *more*, not less, capable of collective action in rebellion than workers.

SUGGESTIONS FOR FURTHER READING

Cohen, G. A. 1978. *Karl Marx's Theory of History: A Defence.*
Elster, Jon. 1985. *Making Sense of Marx.*
Harris, Marvin. 1980. *Cultural Materialism: The Struggle for a Science of Culture.*
Little, Daniel. 1986. *The Scientific Marx.*
McMurtry, John. 1977. *The Structure of Marx's World-view.*
Miliband, Ralph. 1977. *Marxism and Politics.*
Roemer, John. 1988. *Free to Lose: An Introduction to Marxist Economic Philosophy.*
Sabel, Charles F. 1982. *Work and Politics.*
Ste. Croix, G.E.M. de. 1981. *The Class Struggle in the Ancient Greek World from the Archaic Age to the Arab Conquests.*
Thompson, E. P. 1963. *The Making of the English Working Class.*

7
ECONOMIC
ANTHROPOLOGY

In this chapter I return to the question of the role and utility of the tools
of rational choice theory in applied social science. To what extent are these
tools applicable to non-Western societies? The rational choice paradigm has
been attractive to many social scientists in their efforts to arrive at explanations
of social and political behavior in various parts of the world. And this
model of explanation is simple yet powerful: We attempt to explain a pattern
of social behavior or an enduring social arrangement as the aggregate
outcome of the goal-directed choices of large numbers of rational agents.
Why did the Nian rebellion occur? It was the result of the individual-level
survival strategies of North China peasants (Example 2.4). Why did the
central places of late-imperial Sichuan conform to the hexagonal arrays
predicted by central place theory? Because participants—consumers, merchants, and officials—made rational decisions based on considerations of
transport cost (Example 5.4). Why was early-modern French agriculture
stagnant? Because none of the actors within the agricultural system had
both the incentive and the capacity to invest in agricultural innovation
(Example 6.6).

Let us begin with another example—Samuel Popkin's analysis of collective
action in traditional village society in Vietnam (Example 7.1). Popkin's
analysis implicitly abstracts from a number of factors that anthropologists
have usually taken as central in the explanation of a non-Western culture:
the specifics of religious beliefs (Buddhist, Catholic), the complexities of
kinship relations, the operation of culturally specific values and beliefs (for
example, magical beliefs or moral restrictions), and the possibility of a
radically non-Western worldview underlying individual action. Is this a
legitimate basis of social explanation in the context of traditional Vietnamese
village society?

This issue is complicated by recent arguments questioning the adequacy
of the concept of individual rationality itself. As we saw in Chapter 3, some
have argued that the concept of narrow economic rationality has no empirical
support and that a more complex theory of practical reason is needed if
we are to make inferences about the actual behavior of rational beings. In
Chapter 3 we also reviewed some of the proposals that have been offered

---

Example 7.1   Collective action and the traditional village

Many collective practices that would confer benefits on groups in traditional societies are not adopted; collective goods are not readily achieved in village society. Samuel Popkin asserts that the traditional Vietnamese village was conspicuously unable to secure collective action for shared interests, even when there were genuine and recognized shared interests (e.g., in large-scale water management projects, in deterring marauding tigers, etc.). "Many collective projects—such as law and order, firefighting, slaying marauding tigers—benefit an individual whether he contributes or not. I assume that the individual weighs his decision about participation in the supply of these public goods" (Popkin 1979:24). And the traditional village was not capable of creating effective subsistence insurance and welfare schemes because of free-rider problems, the problem of theft of collective resources, and the problem of mutual mistrust. Popkin explains the relatively low level of cooperative action for collective goods in traditional Vietnamese village society on the basis of Mancur Olson's analysis of collective action. On this basis villagers choose the free-riding option, and collective projects fail. This analysis presupposes that individual villagers make calculating decisions based on private interest, and it leads to the prediction that collective action will be difficult to attain.

Data: historical and sociological data on village life in Vietnam
Explanatory model: rational self-interest underlies the behavior of members of
    village society
Source: Samuel Popkin, *The Rational Peasant* (1979)

---

by recent economists and philosophers on this subject (including Sen, Harsanyi, Nagel, Parfit, and Regan). This literature has important consequences for the rational choice approach to traditional societies. For example, Mancur Olson's theorem of collective action is no longer derivable if we postulate a model of practical reasoning that gives weight both to self-interest and to collective welfare (conditional altruism).

The rational choice approach has much to recommend it in terms of scope and parsimony; it provides a basis for social explanation in a wide variety of cultural contexts and may support significant cross-cultural generalizations. Moreover much valuable recent work in area studies reflects this paradigm. However the rational choice model has encountered vigorous opposition from some social scientists on several grounds. A variety of authors have offered arguments to show that the rational choice approach to non-Western cultures is fundamentally flawed. Two principal positions have emerged in the social science literature on this topic: *formalism* and *substantivism*.[1] These positions disagree centrally over the legitimacy of the application of the tools of rational choice theory—markets, marginal utilities, profits—to premodern societies. Formalists believe that the assumption of rational self-interested behavior is crucial to understanding any social group in any historical circumstances and that the economies and societies of peasant cultures may be analyzed in terms of the familiar concepts of rational choice theory. Substantivists have maintained that the concept of private self-interest is culturally specific and inapplicable to much of the history of human social life. Instead, they contend, the culturally specific norms, values, worldviews, and forms of motivation for each traditional society must be studied. The contrast between the two positions, then, involves disagreement about what sort of knowledge is needed to provide an explanation of social phenomena. Formalists maintain that only minimal information is needed about agents' psychological states and that a thin description of interests and beliefs is sufficient to explain behavior. Substantivists, on the other hand, maintain that much more extensive information is needed about norms, values, and worldview before social behavior can be explained. Even more radically some substantivists hold that the notion of means-end rationality itself is culturally specific; the springs of social behavior are always culturally unique, and the notion of individual rationality is inapplicable to much of the history of human social life. (Note the resemblance between this view and interpretive social science, discussed in Chapter 4.)

In this chapter I will present the ideas of formalism and substantivism in somewhat fuller detail and then consider a number of specific challenges to the rational choice framework. Some have held that the notion of "interests" cannot be defined in a culture-neutral way. Others have criticized particular examples of rational choice explanation as resting on an overly schematic conception of interests and the social context of choice. Still others have argued that norms and values are central to social action and therefore the conception of maximizing goal-directed rationality is misleading. Finally and most radically some have held that the conception of individual rationality is inevitably ethnocentric and that interpretation of social action unavoidably requires a reconstruction of local conceptions of agency. Each of these criticisms has some force. But I will argue that none fundamentally discredits the rational choice approach; instead they impose valuable refinements on the rational choice paradigm. First, however, it is necessary to define the formalist and substantivist frameworks more explicitly.

THE FORMALIST FRAMEWORK

The formalist approach is sometimes described as *public choice theory*. Dennis Mueller describes public choice theory in these terms: "Public choice can be defined as the economic study of nonmarket decision-making, or, simply the application of economics to political science. The basic behavioral postulate of public choice, as for economics, is that man is an egoistic, rational, utility maximizer" (Mueller 1976:395). Public choice theory thus attributes to the agent a narrow calculation of self-interest. Samuel Popkin's important work, *The Rational Peasant* (1979), represents a careful study of Vietnamese rural society from this perspective. He describes his approach: "Economic theory (roughly equivalent to the political economy approach) is a method of analysis: the postulation of a number of actors with certain ends and a deductive attempt to work out how persons will act in situations which present certain alternatives, 'on the assumption that they pursue their goals rationally' " (Popkin 1979:30–31). And he defines rationality in these terms: "By rationality I mean that individuals evaluate the possible outcomes associated with their choices in accordance with their preferences and values. . . . I most emphatically deny that persons are self-interested in [a] narrow sense. . . . However, I do assume that a peasant is primarily concerned with the welfare and security of self and family" (Popkin 1979:31). He holds that many of the most important aspects of traditional village life can be explained on the basis of failures of collective action, village taxation policies, patterns of alliance between insiders and outsiders, policies towards newcomers to the village, cropping patterns, and readiness to support rebellious organizations. The tone of Popkin's analysis is captured in his observation about elite political behavior: "Village elites in [Cochinchina and Annam] responded to French policies quite differently because local economic incentives differed. . . . The French created new opportunities, options, and institutions; but much of the change in rural life occurred only because the village elites were willing to use these new possibilities in their own local, age-old power struggles" (Popkin 1979:139–40).

Manning Nash is another important exponent of the formalist approach. He describes the concept of economic rationality in these terms: "Economizing is a sort of strategy. The strategy needs the following components: (1) goods and services which can have multiple uses; (2) scarcity of these goods and services both in the cost to human beings of producing them and in respect to the many different ends they can implement; and (3) ends or goals, for which the actors strive, that are not on one dead level but differ in importance and value" (Nash 1966:4). And Nash maintains that this is a feature of social life that permits explanation of a wide variety of primitive and peasant economies.

Formalism thus rests upon a simple explanatory strategy—the model of aggregative explanation described in Chapter 3. To explain a social pattern we must show that it is the aggregate result of large numbers of goal-directed actors choosing their actions according to their interests and beliefs. When the tools of rational choice theory are applied to traditional social life, very specific and surprising consequences emerge. The field of public choice theory is concerned with deriving these specific consequences, and a number of paradoxes of group rationality have been developed in this field that seem relevant to empirical social science. These results include Mancur Olson's collective action theorem, the prisoners' dilemma of formal game theory, the suboptimalities created by asymmetric information costs in market transactions (the market for lemons discussed in the next example), the Arrow paradox, and many others. Many of these formal results show that action according to private rationality leads to paradoxes of collective rationality or that private rationality does not always aggregate to a collectively rational outcome. Consider one example—Popkin's analysis of the structure of rice and rubber markets in Southeast Asia (Example 7.2).

Example 7.2 Lemons, rice, and rubber

In Southeast Asia rice and rubber markets differ significantly.. Rice is purchased at auction by large middlemen from anonymous producers, whereas rubber is bought by middlemen from known sellers with whom they have ongoing relationships. What accounts for this difference? Samuel Popkin uses Akerlof's "market for lemons" analysis to explain the structure of these two markets. George Akerlof analyzes the market for used cars—a market in which there is a strong asymmetry in information between buyer and seller. The seller knows the hidden defects in the vehicle, and the buyer can only discover the defects through expensive investigation. The buyer therefore offers a price based on the "average" car of that year, with a typical number of defects. This means that owners of lemons are offered more than the true value of their car, and owners of "peaches" are offered less. The peach owner declines to accept this offer, and the average value of used cars falls further. Rubber and rice differ significantly in one important regard: It is possible to determine the quality of a quantity of rice easily and cheaply, but it is not easy to do so for rubber. Therefore rubber brings with it asymmetric information between buyer and seller. "A smallholder who produces high quality rubber . . . can get the 'peach bonus' for rubber quality by developing a reputation as a man who produces 'peachy' rubber as opposed to 'lemony' rubber (Popkin 1981:72). The model of a market for lemons thus explains the differences in the structure of rice and rubber markets.

Data: description of marketing arrangements for small producers of rice and rubber in Southeast Asia

Explanatory model: a microeconomic analysis is used to explain existing social arrangements in Southeast Asia

Source: Samuel L. Popkin, "Public Choice and Rural Development—Free Riders, Lemons, and Institutional Design" (1981)

In this analysis Popkin identifies an observed pattern in Southeast Asian society (differences in the ways that rice and rubber are marketed), and he deploys a piece of analysis from neoclassical economics to explain this pattern. This is a deductive explanation based on these premises: Buyers and sellers are rational profit-maximizers, the quality of bulk rice is easily ascertained, and the quality of bulk rubber is not easily ascertained. These premises can now be fitted to Akerlof's general analysis of markets with information asymmetry: The rubber market should have the characteristics of a "market for lemons," but the rice market should not. And this is precisely the outcome that was to be explained.

Formalists have made use of these "theorems" of economic rationality as explanatory tools in their various disciplines to explain otherwise puzzling social phenomena. Consider a pair of examples—Burton Pasternak's explanation of changes in family structure in rural Taiwan in the 1930s (Example 7.3) and Susan Hanley's interpretation of family behavior in Tokugawa Japan (Example 7.4).

Example 7.3   Family structure and household economy

Rural society in pre-1930 Taiwan featured a "joint-family" system, in which a parent and married sons would continue to live together and farm their holdings together rather than dividing into two or more nuclear families. After the 1930s, however, a trend toward divided families began and has continued until the present. Why did this change in family structure occur? It is often believed that family structure is a deeply idiosyncratic feature of culture. But Burton Pasternak attempts to show that the joint-family system in the Taiwan rice economy is a prudent arrangement for the organization of farm labor, given the uncertainties of rainfall. Pasternak offers this model of the domestic economy. Rice must be transplanted within 20 days and can only be transplanted if there is enough water. The model family contains two married brothers (A and B) and A's son. The family owns 2 hectares (5 acres) and two water buffalo. As a joint family the unit can manage field preparation and transplanting in 19 to 22 days. As two divided units A and his son can manage 1 hectare in 17 to 20 days, but B needs 22 to 25 days. This means that his rice crop will often fail. If there are fewer than 10 days of rain, both families will lose the crop. If there are fewer than 15 days of rain, A will survive and B will not. In times of water crisis, the joint family has enough labor to plant a crisis crop (sweet potatoes), but the divided families do not. Therefore, if cropping depends on rainfall, the joint family is substantially more secure. After the Japanese removed this uncertainty by creating a large irrigation system in the 1930s, the joint-family practice began to disappear. With irrigation the water supplies are much more secure, and crisis is therefore less likely. Under these circumstances there are incentives for dividing the family and fewer economic reasons not to do so. Once the imperative to protect against catastrophic crop failure due to inadequate labor supply was diminished, the normal frictions of social life (between sisters-in-law, for example) led to a division of families. Thus Pasternak explains the change in family structure as the effect of changing circumstances of the rural economy— the availability of reliable irrigation water.

Data: field work in two Taiwanese villages, providing detailed information about the farming system and family structure
Explanatory model: family structure is a prudent adaptation to the needs of the domestic economy, given the circumstances of agriculture; when those circumstances change drastically, family structure changes as well
Source: Burton Pasternak, "The Sociology of Irrigation: Two Taiwanese Villages" (1978)

Both these examples represent attempts to explain important cultural characteristics of Asian societies as the result of individual-level efforts to protect individual and family interests within specific ecological and insti-tutional circumstances. Pasternak's analysis (Example 7.3) represents a fairly straightforward causal explanation of a change in family patterns: The Japanese establishment of large-scale irrigation projects in the 1930s caused the decline in the joint-family system. The mechanism that mediated this causal relation, however, was a process of rational decisionmaking by large

---

Example 7.4 Family and fertility in Tokugawa Japan

What determines the behavior of the chief demographic variables (age of marriage, marital fertility, and absolute fertility) for a given culture? The chief cultural variables that potentially influence these are marriage customs, norms governing abortion and infanticide, and the effects of poverty on infant and child mortality. To what extent are these norms explicable as the result of economic pressures on the family? Susan Hanley treats this question in the context of rural Tokugawa Japan. She argues that Japanese families were highly sensitive to their economic needs in deciding whether or not to raise a child. "On the one hand, people had to have children to provide labor for their farm, to care for them in their old age, and to carry on their line of descent. On the other hand, they had to make the family fit its resources" (Hanley 1985:197). Further Hanley holds that this economically rational decisionmaking about family structure was strongly reinforced by powerful local norms. These norms of family practices, finally, were sensitive to varying economic circumstances. "All evidence suggests that the Japanese achieved their relatively low birth rates through conscious population control, using methods that not only limited the number of children born, but limited the composition of families to the stem type" (Hanley 1985:212–13). This explanation depends *both* on rational decisionmaking by family decisionmakers *and* powerful cultural norms "designed" to keep population growth to sustainable levels given available economic resources. "Families not only responded to their own economic situation and goals, they were extremely responsive to economic conditions in the community and region" (Hanley 1985:227). "[Family decisionmakers] were constrained from behaving as if their own family was all that mattered by strong, concerted pressure from their fellow villagers" (Hanley 1985:228).

Data: vital statistics from four Tokugawa Japanese villages
Explanatory model: family practices and social norms governing family growth were highly sensitive to economic circumstances in Tokugawa Japan
Source: Susan B. Hanley, "Family and Fertility in Four Tokugawa Villages" (1985)

---

numbers of Taiwanese rice cultivators. The new opportunities made available by large-scale irrigation induced changes in the choices made by individuals, and these new forms of behavior led in the aggregate to a decline in the joint-family system. This account is a clear example of an aggregative explanation (described in Chapter 3).

Hanley's explanation of demographic behavior in Japan (Example 7.4) is somewhat more complex. She shares Pasternak's assumption that a central variable in the process is the rational decisionmaker who chooses among options according to a calculating assessment of the interests of the family. The demographic patterns characteristic of Tokugawa Japan are, in this account, the expression of individual-level choices about family size and composition. However Hanley adds a new variable as well: the working of powerful cultural norms concerning demographic behavior that worked to offset free-riding behavior (for example, families choosing to have more children than the village economy could sustain if universalized). And she suggests but does not explore extensively that these norms themselves are controlled by economic interests—in this case the interests of the group as opposed to the interests of the individual family. (This latter suggestion is vulnerable to the criticism that it depends on functionalist assumptions; as we saw in Chapter 5, we must have an account of how individual-level processes work to establish and reproduce a set of norms that are adjusted to the needs of the group rather than to the interests of individuals.) In Hanley's account, then, demographic patterns in Tokugawa Japan are the result of rational individual behavior within a constrained context of choice, and the constraints on individual choice include both limits on available strategies and the working of socially enforced norms.

THE SUBSTANTIVIST PARADIGM

Turn now to the substantivist approach. The substantivists maintain that traditions and norms are fundamental social factors and that individual behavior is almost always modulated through powerful, traditional and motivational constraints. It is therefore futile to look for explanations of individual behavior couched only in terms of a thin description of interests and beliefs; rather we must provide a more extensive—and culturally specific—description of the norms, values, and worldviews that define and structure the arena of action for individuals. Traditional societies are *communities*—tightly cohesive groups of persons sharing a distinctive set of values in stable, continuing relations to one another (M. Taylor 1982:25 ff.). The central threats to security and welfare are well known to such groups— excessive or deficient rainfall, attacks by bandits, predatory tax policies by the central government, etc. And village societies have evolved *schemes of shared values* and *cooperative practices and institutions* that are well adapted to handling these problems of risk and welfare in ways that protect the subsistence needs of all villagers adequately in all but the most extreme circumstances. One consequence of this modulation of behavior by norms is that many societies do not display a sharp distinction between group interest and individual interest. James Scott discusses this position. "[A strictly materialist view] risks treating the peasant purely as a kind of marketplace individualist who amorally ransacks his environment so as to reach his personal goal. . . . The individual and society are set apart from this perspective and society is simply the milieu in which he must act. . . . To stop there is to miss the critical social context of peasant action. It is to miss the central fact that the peasant is born into a society and culture that provide him with a fund of moral values, a set of concrete social relationships, a pattern of expectations about the behavior of others, and a sense of how those in his culture have proceeded to similar goals in the past. . . . We are thus in the presence of cultural values and forms in all peasant social action" (Scott 1976:166).

Karl Polanyi's *The Great Transformation* represents a classic statement of one form of the substantivist paradigm. Polanyi argues against the validity of applying the concepts of economic rationality, profit maximization, exchange relations, and the like to premarket societies. "The outstanding discovery of recent historical and anthropological research is that man's economy, as a rule, is submerged in his social relationships. He does not act so as to safeguard his individual interest in the possession of material goods; he acts so as to safeguard his social standing, his social claims, his social assets. He values material goods only in so far as they serve this end" (Polanyi 1957:46). Instead of economic calculation, Polanyi holds that we need to pay primary attention to patterns of reciprocity and redistribution, shared values, traditions, and the determining role of community and politics. Polanyi thus maintains that the concept of economic rationality is a very specific historical construct that applies to the forms of market society that emerged in Western Europe in the early-modern period. Market behavior came to replace other forms of motivation within European society in this period, and individuals came to act more and more on the basis of a calculation of self-interest. However, Polanyi holds that this form of behavior, like the economic institutions of the market within which it emerged, is highly specific to a particular time and place. To make use of this model of action as though it were a universal feature and determinant of human behavior is as unjustified as it would be to extend medieval chivalry to all times and places.

Thus Polanyi maintains that it is socially motivated behavior—behavior motivated toward the interests of one's family, clan, or village—rather than self-interested behavior that is "natural" for human beings. Rational self-interest is instead a feature of a highly specific society—market society. In place of economic rationality and the market mechanism providing the basis for organization of the premarket economy, Polanyi argues that communitarian patterns of organization are found: "The premium set on generosity is so great when measured in terms of social prestige as to make any other behavior than that of utter self-forgetfulness simply not pay" (Polanyi 1957:46–47).

A more recent exponent of the substantivist analysis of traditional societies is Clifford Geertz. He offers scathing criticism of what he calls "economism"—a term that captures the same approach as "formalism." "[Economism] is the view that the moving forces in individual behaviour (and thus in society, which is taken to be an aggregate of individual behaviours or some stratificational arrangement of them) are those of a need-driven utility seeker manoeuvring for advantage within the context of material possibilities and normative constraints" (Geertz 1984:516). Against such an approach Geertz insists that we can only understand a given society within a framework of analysis that gives full attention to the distinctive cultural features of that society—its religious views, its moral and normative context, and the categories of the worldview of its members.

Only the recontextualisation of Javanese and Indonesian economic processes within Javanese and Indonesian life as concretely enacted, the de-externalisation of culture, can reduce this indeterminacy, however slightly, and deliver answers we can have some faith in, however modest. It is not economic analysis itself that is the problem, any more than it is quantification. It is economism: the notion . . . that a determinate picture of social change can be obtained in the absence of an understanding of the passions and imaginings that provoke and inform it. Such understanding is inevitably limited. . . . But without it there is nothing but polemic, schematicism and endless measurement of amorphous magnitudes: history without temper, sociology without tone. (Geertz 1984:523)

Substantivists acknowledge that premodern societies possess economies, to be sure, but they hold that traditional economies are determined by substantive and culturally specific social norms shaping the process of production and exchange. Thus George Dalton maintains that there are severe limits to the relevance of technical economic concepts in the description and analysis of premodern market economies and that it is necessary to consider primarily the social and cultural relations within the context of which production, consumption, distribution, etc., take place. These relations, however, are highly specific to the society being studied. Dalton writes, "To put interesting questions about the organization of traditional, primitive economies, and primitive and peasant economies undergoing change, growth, and development, requires conceptual categories different from those used in conventional economics" (Dalton 1969:68). And once we turn our attention to the particular features of traditional economies, Dalton believes that we will find features of social cohesion and group-oriented behavior that operates in the place of calculations of self-interest: "Low-level technology combined with small size and relative isolation results in ingrained mutual dependence among people sharing many relationships: those with whom one is economically involved are the same as those with whom one is involved through neighborhood, religion, kinship and polity" (Dalton 1969:72–73). Against the assumption of economic rationality, Dalton argues that premodern societies are fundamentally regulated by a set of shared values and forms of social consciousness.

Marshall Sahlins pursues a substantivist approach in his study of hunter-gatherer societies, *Stone Age Economics* (Example 7.5). Sahlins's central methodological point is this: It is impossible to separate economic activity from the dense web of values, assumptions, and social relationships that make up a particular culture. "A material transaction is usually a momentary episode in a continuous social relation" (Sahlins 1972:185–86). So the formalist approach is defective in its most basic assumptions.

A second important example of a substantivist approach to a traditional economy is Clifford Geertz's influential concept of agricultural involution (Example 7.6). Here again we find an analysis of the social and economic institutions defining the structure of a particular agrarian economy that emphasizes the ability of a set of norms and expectations to bind individual behavior. Whereas Popkin explains Vietnamese social arrangements as the aggregate outcome of the prudent strategies of large numbers of Vietnamese villagers and farmers, Geertz presupposes a level of social causation—a set of shared norms of reciprocity—that effectively constrains individual action

---

Example 7.5   Stone Age economics

What was daily life like for neolithic and hunter-gatherer peoples? Marshall
Sahlins attempts to reconstruct the "domestic mode of production" of hunter-
gatherer groups, not on the basis of the abstract concepts of marginalist
economic theory but on concepts that conform to the specific cultural
worldviews of these societies—reciprocity, kinship, prestige, and a thick
conception of property and labor. "This book is substantivist. It thus takes on a
familiar structure, as provided by traditional substantive categories. . . .
'Economy' becomes a category of culture rather than behavior, in a class with
politics or religion rather than rationality or prudence: not the need-serving
activities of individuals, but the material life process of society" (Sahlins
1972:xii). He finds that hunter-gatherer societies were the original "affluent
society" (Sahlins 1972:1) because hunter-gatherer groups could satisfy their
subsistence needs in only a few hours a day (Sahlins 1972:21). He argues that
the hunter-gatherer economy is organized around domestic groups and kinship
relations, that it embodies a structure of "underproduction"—a consistent
underutilization of resources and labor power—and that there are complex
exchange and gift relations (reciprocity) that effectively distribute resources
across families. Such institutions succeed in regulating individual activity that
would undermine the long-term viability of the group.

Data: data describing labor usage, caloric consumption, family structure, etc.,
     drawn from a range of hunter-gatherer societies described in the ethnographic
     literature
Explanatory model: examination of many-sided causal relations among social
     variables—kinship and family structure, use of labor time, nutritional levels,
     economic intensity
Source: Marshall Sahlins, *Stone Age Economics* (1972)

---

and imposes a distinctive pattern of social organization on Javanese society.
As with Hanley's analysis in Example 7.4 above, Geertz's explanation requires
further elaboration if it is to avoid the charge of spurious functionalism.
We need some idea of the social mechanisms at work in local society at
the level of individual activity that select, enforce, and reproduce this system
of norms. Without an answer to this question, we must groundlessly
presuppose that social arrangements will emerge to satisfy the needs of the
group. We will return to this topic in Chapter 9, where I will argue that
social explanations require *microfoundations*—accounts of the individual-level
mechanisms through which postulated social causation occurs.

CRITICISMS OF THE RATIONAL CHOICE APPROACH

Let us now evaluate the criticisms of the rational choice approach inspired
by substantivist and interpretivist social science.

Example 7.6   Agricultural involution

Clifford Geertz carefully surveys the agricultural and ecological basis of traditional Java and the consequences of colonial agriculture (coffee and sugar) on Javanese society. He considers the response of Javanese social arrangements to the pressure on subsistence created by Dutch colonialism and capitalist markets, and he concludes that the response was a process of "agricultural involution"—the subdivision and refinement of economic positions within the village economy so that all villagers would continue to have a precarious basis of subsistence. Geertz's account thus emphasizes village institutions of leveling and subsistence insurance (Geertz 1963:99). Moreover, he notes, this process was propelled by a set of norms emphasizing the right of each villager to a viable economic niche. Geertz writes, "The involution of the productive process in Javanese agriculture was matched and supported by a similar involution in rural family life, social stratification, political organization, religious practice, as well as in the 'folk-culture' value system . . . in terms of which it was normatively regulated and ethically justified" (Geertz 1963:101–2). Thus, in Geertz's account, agricultural involution is a social response to population pressure and resource scarcity; instead of declaring part of the rural population "surplus," work roles and entitlements are redefined to permit each villager a continuing position within the local economy. Involution is a complex result of "increasing tenacity of basic pattern; internal elaboration and ornateness; technical hairsplitting, and unending virtuosity. . . . Tenure systems grew more intricate; tenancy relationships more complicated; cooperative labor arrangements more complex—all in an effort to provide everyone with some niche, however small, in the over-all system" (Geertz 1963:82). "The productive system of the post-traditional village developed, therefore, into a dense web of finely spun work rights and work responsibilities spread, like the reticulate veins of the hand, throughout the whole body of the village lands" (Geertz 1963:99).

Data: historical and ethnographic data on the organization of Javanese agriculture and village life

Explanatory model: norms of reciprocity lead village society to agricultural involution when subjected to the strains of increasingly commercialized agriculture

Source: Clifford Geertz, *Agricultural Involution* (1963)

"Interests and beliefs are culturally variable"

We may begin with one basic objection to the rational choice approach: the view that the central assumption of this approach—that individuals have interests they seek to further—cannot be employed without detailed ethnographic information about the particulars of those interests. The rational choice approach tacitly assumes that we can uncontroversially reconstruct goals and beliefs in terms of material interests and causal beliefs. However critics contend that there is radical diversity across cultures in the definition of both goals and beliefs. Clifford Geertz, for example, argues that the concept of need is itself a cultural particular; there is no culture-independent way of characterizing the needs that persons, in theory, seek to satisfy. This claim may be put in the following terms: Needs and interests are always culturally defined, so to apply the rational choice framework to a particular society, we must engage in the hermeneutic project in order to discover what local standards of need are. Two common assumptions are particularly suspect: that the agent's *goals* centrally include material well-being and that his *beliefs* are grounded on factual-scientific procedures of inquiry. Against the first point it is sometimes maintained that the agent's goals depend on a culturally unique set of values; against the second, that magical, "irrational" beliefs play a crucial role in determining action. (This point will be pursued further in Chapter 10.) Therefore we cannot apply a rational choice model to Chinese peasant rebellions unless we undertake a detailed ethnographic investigation of the worldview of Chinese peasants—what their culturally specific values and beliefs are. This also entails that we will not be able to produce cross-cultural theories of rebellion based on the assumption of rational political behavior because a critical component of such an explanation varies radically across cultures. This position thus expresses fundamental skepticism about the project of explaining social phenomena on the basis of an abstract theory of means-end rationality and an abstract, materialistic account of goals and beliefs.

How compelling is this objection? This much can be said in its support: It is plainly true that there are cross-cultural variations in both goals and beliefs. The question is, however, whether variation is the rule or whether, on the contrary, there is a core set of *human* interests and beliefs that constitute the basis for much behavior, around which cultural variations rotate. And in fact it is possible to motivate a materialistic assumption about goals in a cross-cultural sense. This position consists of the following points: All persons have the cognitive capacity to acquire true beliefs about their material environment, they have a set of objective material needs (subsistence and security), and they act deliberately in relation to their material and social environments to satisfy those needs. These beliefs and interests constitute a core upon which culture, meanings, values, religious experience, etc., are added in various settings. Finally it is stipulated that culture and significance have interactive effects on the core. We may use the term "welfare" to refer to the individuals' means of satisfying basic subsistence and consumption needs—food, clothing, shelter, education, and health care—and the conditions of security that permit them to rely on their ability to continue to satisfy those needs.

Why should we suppose that there is such a core of cognitive capacities and goals underlying behavior in all cultures? Begin with causal beliefs. Anyone who has observed the finely tuned relationships between agricultural techniques and local ecological variation cannot but be impressed with the capacity of peasants and pastoralists to observe their natural environment and determine the properties of various plants, fertilizers, and water resources. Likewise the impressive ability of ordinary rural people to identify and exploit the blind spots of the extractive mechanisms in their social and economic environment (taxation, rent, corvée labor systems) suggests that a capacity for learning the workings of the social environment is equally well developed. It appears that one inescapable feature of human nature (shaped by the evolutionary history of the species) is that people are able to learn about their environment and exploit the opportunities it affords. Modern scientific reasoning develops this capacity to a highly sophisticated level, but the discovery of the causal properties of ordinary elements of the environment is a common feature of human life across cultures and historical periods.

Consider now the notion that the material requirements of everyday life— needs, in short—define a set of goals with substantial cross-cultural relevance. All human beings require food, shelter, and clothing; they therefore require access to the social instruments, whatever they are, through which such goods are acquired. We may expand this list fairly quickly: Health care, education, and old-age security are goods that all human beings are likely to care about. These concerns are not culturally specific (though the ways in which they are pursued are); rather they are *species*-specific. Given the natural characteristics of the human organism and the cognitive and motivational resources that we have acquired through our evolutionary history, we may infer that human beings are motivated by the pursuit of goals defined by basic human needs. In short, Aristotle and Marx were right: Humans are rational, goal-directed beings whose goals include the satisfaction of material needs.

In many social contexts these basic material needs can only be pursued through a small number of instruments: income, political power, access to land, patron-client relations, and the like. This circumstance permits us to hypothesize, then, that individuals will act to pursue income, power, and security. The following, then, is a tolerable generalization about human motivation: Persons are concerned about their material welfare, they are aware of the factors in their social and natural environment that influence their welfare, and they are disposed to act in such a way as to protect and, if possible, enhance their welfare in the future. Several observations about this thesis are in order. Note that it encompasses both a minimal materialism and an assumption about belief rationality. The materialism component assumes that the goal of satisfying minimal welfare needs is a central one in all human social environments; the rational belief assumption is that persons are able to form reasonably accurate beliefs about the causal properties of the environment they occupy, both natural and social. Note finally that this thesis does not assume that action is always oriented toward *maximizing* welfare or exclusively motivated by welfare concerns. Thus risk-aversive behavior is fully compatible with this assumption about welfare as a fundamental interest; satisficing behavior likewise counts as rational. The hypothesis only postulates that welfare concerns are motivationally important.

If this fairly innocuous assumption is accepted, then there is a good theoretical justification for applying rational choice analysis to important aspects of social life in every culture. In particular, given the close connection between the institutions defining traditional agriculture, rural politics, and the material needs of peasants, this thesis would lead us to expect that peasants will act in a calculated and rational way in the context of those institutions. Similarly, given the proximity of surplus-extraction systems—taxation, credit, rent, corvée labor—to the material needs of peasants, this hypothesis would lead us to expect that peasant behavior in relation to these institutions will be calculated and prudent.

These points suggest that it *is* legitimate to apply the concept of individual rationality cross-culturally and that it is reasonable for social scientists to postulate that a great deal of social phenomena may be understood as the aggregate consequence of individuals acting out of a prudent regard for self- or family-welfare. This rational choice framework is not suited for every topic of social inquiry, to be sure, but for many problems in social research—technological change, rebellion, social cooperation, and economic decision-making—the rational choice framework is a defensible one. If this is conceded, it follows that these constitute important areas of social science where the central problem is *not* to discover culturally specific meanings and values but rather to identify the specific social arrangements and institutions that constrain individual activity into certain channels and that, in the aggregate, produce a given pattern of social life.

"Rational choice approaches are overly schematic"

Other critics believe that the rational choice approach is flawed by a tendency to provide an overly abstract characterization of agency and structure in its concrete applications. Although the idea that human beings are goal-directed is acceptable to these critics, they note that action always takes place in a concrete social, normative, and political environment, and the environment makes a difference to the behavior. Their objection has two parts. At the level of individual agency, they claim that an adequate analysis of behavior must provide more detail about the various sources of motivation at work. The assumption that individuals act on the basis of calculations of self-interest abstracts from other crucial features of motivation—love, friendship, loyalty, habit, anger—so predictions made on this basis are unreliable. Calculations based on self-interest are part of the explanation, in this view, but only part; therefore theories that only represent this feature of behavior will misunderstand social action. And at the level of social structure, they claim that rational choice theorists tend to abstract from too much of the social environment of choice in their description of action. One form of this defect is the use of a competitive market concept to replace more particular descriptions of institutional arrangements. (Gary Becker's efforts to extend economic analysis to family relations represent an extreme example of this tendency [Becker 1976].)

It should be noted that this is an objection to the level of detail in terms of which a rational choice analysis is provided, not to the rational choice approach itself. Recall James Tong's analysis of the rational underpinnings of peasant rebellion in the Ming dynasty (Example 2.2). Tong argues that the incidence of rebellion and banditry throughout this period can be explained by considering variations in two of the variables: the severity of subsistence hardship and the likelihood of survival as an outlaw. Peasants turn to banditry when the severity of hardship outweighs the likelihood of capture and punishment. This account incorporates a very high level of abstraction, and it may be argued that the adequacy of the account could be much improved by including more specific detail about the social and political arrangements found in various parts of China throughout this period. In areas where effective redistributive mechanisms existed, for example, it may turn out that the same level of food availability results in substantially lower levels of starvation—thus fundamentally altering the costs and benefits confronting the potential outlaw. And in areas where there was a well-developed tradition and organization of banditry, it may be that substantially lower levels of deprivation are sufficient to bring marginal rural people into rebellion and banditry (as Perry suggests in her treatment of the Nian rebellions of the nineteenth century—Example 2.4).

This line of criticism has a good deal of merit. Rational choice analysis *is* often guilty of schematism regarding agency and structure. The paradigm of narrow economic rationality is particularly vulnerable to this criticism. However this does not mean that the rational choice framework should therefore be avoided; instead it suggests that researchers employing this framework should pay more attention to the institutional setting within which choice takes place. There are substantial variations, both within a culture and across cultures, in the institutional environment of choice, and these variations have significant effects on the best choice available to the individual. But this is perfectly compatible with a rational choice approach; it suggests only that additional detail about the institutional context of action may be needed before it is possible to work out the optimal strategy for a given decisionmaker. And in fact there are numerous examples of rational choice approaches that satisfy this caution—for example, Perry's analysis of the context of choice in rural North China leading to strategies of predation (banditry and rebellion). Moreover the rapprochement between rational choice analysis and analytical Marxism has increased the adequacy of the rational choice framework in this dimension for Marxism places a high premium on analysis of the specific institutional arrangements within which action takes place.

In this context it is reasonable to ask what relationship should obtain between the commonsense categories that participants use and social scientific categories. Should the theoretical concepts of social science correspond to the participants' commonsense categories of action and social organization? That is, should social scientists couch their theories in terms of the "folk psychology" and "folk sociology" of members of a society?[2]

Consider the concept of class. This is a social science concept based on an individual's position within the property relations of a given economy. It gives rise to a scheme of classification of individuals into groups in a given society. However we can also ask how members of that society classify themselves—what distinctions they make in everyday speech and judgment. And it may emerge that there is no close correspondence between the classification provided by the economic theory of class and that in use in the culture. Thus Chinese peasants may classify their local society in terms of kinship and status, producing groupings that cut across the class categories of "landless worker," "tenant farmer," or "landlord." What is the significance of such a discovery? Does it indicate that the theoretical concept of class is defective?

The reason that some social scientists argue for the priority of commonsense concepts over scientific concepts stems from the interpretive doctrine of the intrinsic meaningfulness of social phenomena. If we maintain that social phenomena are constituted by the understandings implicit in the minds of the participants, then it seems unavoidable that they should be characterized in those terms as well. If social relations in the North China village are conceived by participants in terms of kinship rather than class, how can it be legitimate for the social scientist to use class rather than kinship to explain events in the village?

This argument is less compelling than it initially appears to be, however— even on its own terms. It is clear on reflection that there are social circumstances that influence individual action and belief without themselves being the object of belief. The fact that Li is landlord to Chen imposes a set of interests on both parties that are properly characterized as the landlord-tenant relation. And both Li and Chen may well be induced by circumstance to behave in ways consonant with this relation—even if they do not formally conceive of their relation in this way. So it is legitimate and explanatory for the social scientist to assert that the landlord-tenant relation structures behavior in the village, even though this is not a relation that figures prominently in the commonsense conception of village social life.

"Rational choice approaches neglect norms and values"

A distinct strand of criticism of the rational choice framework involves the role of norms in action. Here the objection is that the rational choice approach, by attending solely to calculations of self-interest, is blind to the workings of normative frameworks, although such frameworks are powerful factors underlying behavior in most traditional contexts. This objection has some validity but probably overstates the import of normative constraints on action. There is a substantial literature suggesting that the moral economy school overstates the effectiveness of redistributive norms within traditional societies (Popkin 1979:1–31). As a matter of empirical fact, there appear to be strong reasons to doubt the level of communitarian redistribution that occurred in peasant Russia, traditional China, or English working-class communities. Thus Popkin charges the moral economy tradition with romanticizing traditional village institutions, reading into them an egalitarianism and communitarianism that the historical record does not bear out (Popkin 1979:6–8).

Moreover there are theoretical reasons to doubt that normative systems could profoundly and permanently interfere with the individual pursuit of private interests. Normative systems are inherently ambiguous and subject to revision over time. Consequently we should expect that opportunistic agents will find ways of adapting given social norms more comfortably to the pursuit of self-interest. Consider the requirement that elites should provide for the subsistence needs of the poor in times of dearth. There are some grounds for supposing that such a requirement is in the long-term interest of elites—for example, by promoting social stability and establishing bonds of reciprocity with other members of an interdependent society. But it seems reasonable to expect that elites—who, with their superior economic position, are already able to exercise political and social power as well—will find ways of limiting the effect of such norms on their behavior.

These points notwithstanding, there remains a credible line of criticism of the rational choice paradigm based on the role of norms in behavior. Clearly individuals pay some attention to normative constraints within the process of rational deliberation. The model of simple maximizing goal-directedness is overly abstract; instead we need a conception of rational action that permits us to incorporate some consideration of normative requirements as well as purposes and goals. A number of authors on the rational choice paradigm have taken this point seriously. Particularly important among these is A. K. Sen (discussed in Chapter 3). Their arguments are telling; the model of narrow economic rationality makes overly restrictive assumptions about the role of norms in rational behavior. Human behavior is the resultant of several different forms of motive—such as self-interest and altruism—and several different types of decisionmaking processes—such as maximizing and side-constraint testing. The model of broadened practical rationality therefore needs to incorporate a decision rule that represents the workings of moral constraints and commitments as well as goal-directed calculation. This is not a small problem, however, for one of the chief merits of the paradigm of narrow economic rationality is its parsimony—the fact that it reduces rational choice to a single dimension of deliberation. Once we require that rational choice take normative constraints and commitments into account as well as interests, it is much more difficult to provide formal rational choice models. (See Margolis 1982 for an attempt to formalize some of these contrasts.)

"Rational choice approaches impose an ethnocentric conception of rationality"

Let us turn finally to the most radical challenge to the rational choice analysis of traditional societies: the claim that the model of behavior driven by calculation of self-interest is itself a culturally specific mode of behavior, present in some cultures (e.g., ours) and absent in others. Individual rationality is a cultural construct, and rational choice analysis is unavoidably ethnocentric. In this view there are alternative modes of action fundamentally and radically distinct from means-end rationality. This is the most basic charge against the rational choice framework because it casts doubt on the means-end model of agency altogether and maintains that there are radically distinct forms of agency in different cultures.

This charge is associated with the paradigm of interpretive social science, discussed in Chapter 4 above. To give an interpretation of an action or a practice is to describe the cultural context and state of mind of the agent in such a way that his or her action becomes intelligible to us. In this approach, social inquiry is bound to be culturally specific. There is no antecedent framework—whether instrumental rationality, materialism, or anything else—that will provide an explanatory key to a given society; rather the values, meanings, practices, and modes of behavior that make up the given culture must be explored without presupposition about the sorts of processes that will be found. This preference for cultural specificity is connected with the primary emphasis on social meanings for this reason: If social phenomena are constituted by the workings of human consciousness and if human creativity is diverse, then there is no reason to suppose that different cultures will produce similar social processes and structures.

The interpretive approach to social phenomena amounts to the general claim that all social action is framed by a meaningful social world. To understand, explain, or predict patterns of human behavior, we must first penetrate the social world of individuals: the meanings they attribute to their environment (social and natural), the values and goals they possess, the choices they perceive, and the way they interpret other individuals' social action. Only then will we be able to analyze, interpret, and explain their behavior. But now their actions are thickly described in terms of the meanings, values, assumptions, and interpretive principles they employ in their own understanding of their world.

I hold that this perspective on social action is legitimate but that it does not have the radical consequences that some have attributed to it. The interpretive approach requires that we consider the character of human agency when analyzing and explaining social phenomena. However, the rational choice paradigm of explanation does not deny the importance and variability of human agency. Instead, it provides explanations based on more abstract characterizations of agency—beliefs, norms, motives, and purposes—than ethnographers offer, and it postulates that it is possible to explain a wide range of human social behavior on the basis of these more abstract descriptions.

This position can be defended in at least two ways. First, there are good theoretical grounds for supposing that instrumental rationality is a common human mode of behavior and that goals and beliefs can be characterized abstractly in terms of material needs and causal beliefs. These arguments have been sketched in previous sections. Second, we may return to the most basic touchstone of the validity of any scientific research program: the fruitfulness of the perspective when applied to a range of empirical problems. And here the evidence from area studies is rather clear. There is a solid and growing volume of insightful work in Asian studies that proceeds on the basis of the central assumptions of the rational choice framework. The interpretive challenger is thus in a position akin to that of the skeptic who denies that bumblebees can fly; the evidence is that the rational choice paradigm has produced a volume of convincing explanations of Asian social and political behavior. And this in turn strongly supports the idea that participants in Asian societies are rational agents (on a suitably developed conception of rationality—e.g., broadened practical rationality).

Further, it should be noted that the interpretive paradigm drastically reduces the scope of social generalization and explanation. If each social phenomenon is sui generis—that is, if each society works according to forces that are unique to it—then generalizations are impossible in social science. But if the interpretive methodological principle above is accepted—with the result that all social relations and behavior must be explained on the basis of a culturally specific mentality—then social science is condemned to a purely descriptive chronicling of concrete phenomena. If, on the other hand, the rational choice approach is legitimate, then we have a basis for cross-cultural generalizations for there will be patterns of social behavior, stemming from the general features of human rationality in environments of choice, that are appropriately similar. Thus free-riding phenomena, prisoners' dilemmas, and the instability of cooperation among groups of powerholders are phenomena that may be identified in a variety of cultures and explained on the basis of fairly thin assumptions about what participants want and how they deliberate about the choices before them. And the rational choice framework maintains that explanation requires this sort of generalization; if generalizations are unavailable, then explanation is impossible. It might turn out that this is the case, but there is enough prima facie support for the assumption of rationality across cultures to make this a viable research program.

Thus the radical interpretive challenge to the rational choice framework fails. Certainly there are some research topics that require the sort of hermeneutic, culturally specific investigation recommended by interpretation theory. But there are many others that do not require this level of detail. And employing the concept of prudential rationality allows us to construct parsimonious explanations of a wide variety of social phenomena in various non-Western cultures—for example, patterns of peasant rebellion, the stagnation of traditional agriculture, the stability of patron-client relations, the pattern of distribution of bureaucratic resources across space, or the appeal of Catholicism in rural colonial Vietnam.

CONCLUSION

Several important criticisms of the standard conception of economic rationality emerge in this chapter. The standard conception has historically been inclined toward an assumption of egoistic self-interest; in fact prisoners' dilemma situations, game theoretical reasoning, and the like depend upon this assumption. However, it is possible to introduce the assumption that decisionmakers take the interests or welfare of others into account (with or without a discount function) and preserve the main outlines of the thin theory of rationality. More fundamentally we found that telling objections have been put forward against the maximizing structure of narrow economic rationality; philosophers and economists alike have argued that a full theory of rationality needs to consider the operation of moral principle in the decisionmaking process.

Another important issue that has arisen in this chapter concerns the definition of the environment of choice within which we assume that agents deliberate. This environment may be described more or less thickly. On the paradigm of narrow economic rationality, the environment is defined abstractly in terms of the prices and incomes associated with various alternatives. This approach abstractly describes concrete social arrangements in terms of the notion of a market. But, once again, arguments in previous sections show that a more plausible interpretation of the rational choice framework results if we provide a thicker description of the context of action. At the least we need to take into account the natural and social environment within which deliberation occurs—not merely price and profit. The environment defines the opportunities through which individuals may pursue their interests and the constraints and powers that are assigned to various agents in pursuit of their purposes. In particular the social environment consists of a large set of political, economic, and social institutions that both constrain and motivate individual choices. Such institutions identify the interests that guide various actors within society and the prohibitions and incentives that influence deliberation. They thus represent a highly structured system within which individuals act, and they impose a pattern of development and organization on society as a whole. For example, a share-tenancy land-tenure arrangement imposes a different set of incentives on the cultivator than a fixed-rent tenancy system. We should therefore expect different patterns of behavior to emerge from rational actors situated in the two different tenancy systems. So it is reasonable to conclude that we must provide concrete information about the natural and social environment of choice within the context of which the agent deliberates.

A third topic of concern is the role of norms and values in shaping individual behavior. The paradigm of narrow economic rationality minimizes their role, either by supposing that a person's normative system is highly flexible in response to changes in his or her interests—thus being only a secondary variable—or by supposing that norms may be represented as preferences. By insisting on a thin theory of individual rationality, rational choice theorists tend to conclude that norms and values cannot have much influence on decisionmaking in traditional societies. But this conclusion is overly strong. As we saw in Chapter 3, a persuasive case has been made by Sen, Nagel, Rawls, and others that the notion of narrow economic rationality should be broadened if it is to successfully serve as a theory of practical rationality. Rational choice theories must give some place to norms, commitments, and moral constraints. These considerations are not "extra"-

rational; instead, they are among the parameters within which an individual calculates a choice. A number of authors have tried to formulate a conception of rational decisionmaking that takes into account *both* preferences and norms.[3] With such an approach, a rational decisionmaker surveys options with an eye both to the costs and benefits of the various alternatives and to the possible relevance of accepted norms to available choices. He or she then selects the highest ranked option that remains. (A decisionmaker who respects the norm of solidarity to one's fellows, for example, will exclude those high-utility options that involve betrayal.)

Finally it should be understood that the rational choice approach must be understood as a single perspective among several and that it corresponds to a form of social behavior that is widespread but not exhaustive. There are some research tasks for which this approach is well suited, and others for which it is not. Formalism, substantivism, and interpretive social science are complementary approaches to social explanation, each identifying genuine and compatible features of the social world. Thus these frameworks are not logical contraries but rather alternative perspectives that are more or less pertinent to particular research questions. So researchers are not forced to decide, once and for all, whether to pursue the one or the other; instead, they may legitimately make use of each of these approaches in studying the various domains of social research.

These qualifications noted, arguments in this chapter indicate that the central assumptions of the rational choice framework are plausible: Human beings are goal-directed, they are concerned about personal and familial welfare, they are capable of acquiring well-grounded beliefs about their natural and social environment, and they are capable of comparing the costs and benefits of various possible actions. If these premises are accepted, there is a wide range of potential applications for the rational choice framework within area studies; it is possible to employ the models and analytical techniques of microeconomics, game theory, collective action theory, Marxist social analysis, and the like to explain patterns of social behavior and social arrangements in a variety of social settings.

There is another rather intriguing possibility as well: The distance between the two paradigms may not be as great as it appears. The substantivist approach need not deny the workings of means-end rationality in traditional societies; it is enough that it insists on the essential importance of norms, values, and worldview in constraining and propelling individual action. Seen from this perspective, substantivism requires a richer and more culturally detailed conception of individual agency—not a thin but a thick theory of agency. But this description is compatible with the possibility that individual conduct in, say, Balinese village life is rational when we take into account the beliefs and values that influence choice. Moreover it is also possible that there are areas of Balinese life—for example, farm management—where culturally specific values and beliefs do not come into play, so that we can explain Balinese farmers' choices on the basis of a microeconomic theory of profit maximization. This suggests that substantivism can absorb many of the analytical insights of formalism, while at the same time holding out the proviso that meaningful explanations of important Balinese social phenomena will require detailed description of the culturally specific norms, values, and worldviews that formalism overlooks.

NOTES

1. The infelicitous terms apparently come from Max Weber. "Formalism" denotes the idea that explanation can proceed on the basis of an abstract (formal) description of the environment of choice of participants, whereas "substantivism" denotes the idea that social explanation requires concrete (substantive) knowledge of participants' norms and values over and above the circumstances of choice in which they find themselves. See Weber's discussion in *Economy and Society* (1978:85). Formalists include Samuel Popkin, Manning Nash, Theodore Schultz, Ramon Myers, and Kang Chao; substantivists include James Scott, Karl Polanyi, George Dalton, Marshall Sahlins, and Clifford Geertz.

2. See Stephen Stich (1983) for a discussion of the role of folk psychology within scientific psychological theory.

3. Recent economists and philosophers have offered a number of proposals on this subject, including A. K. Sen, John Harsanyi, Howard Margolis, and Donald Regan.

SUGGESTIONS FOR FURTHER READING

Dalton, George. 1971. *Economic Anthropology and Development.*
Hardin, Russell. 1982. *Collective Action.*
Little, Daniel. 1989. *Understanding Peasant China: Case Studies in the Philosophy of Social Science.*
Nash, Manning. 1966. *Primitive and Peasant Economic Systems.*
Polanyi, Karl. 1957. *The Great Transformation.*
Popkin, Samuel L. 1979. *The Rational Peasant.*
Russell, Clifford S., and Norman K. Nicholson, eds. 1981. *Public Choice and Rural Development.*
Sahlins, Marshall. 1972. *Stone Age Economics.*
Scott, James C. 1976. *The Moral Economy of the Peasant.*
Shanin, Teodor. 1985. *Russia as a 'Developing Society.'*
Taylor, Michael. 1982. *Community, Anarchy and Liberty.*

8
STATISTICAL ANALYSIS

A common mode of explanation in social science is *statistical*, wherein the scientist explains a phenomenon in terms of its correlation with other variables. Why has Korean economic growth been so remarkable since 1965? Because that nation has had a stable political environment, a relatively equal distribution of assets, and an educated labor force—variables that are positively correlated with economic growth in the countries of the less-developed world. But what sort of explanation is this? This chapter will attempt to answer this question more fully, but a brief reply may be presented in advance. Statistical correlation is *explanatory* to the extent that it provides evidence of a credible causal process underlying the variables being analyzed. Statistical explanations, that is, must be accompanied by a *causal story* indicating the mechanisms through which observed correlations evolve, if the analysis is to be explanatory at all. (The causal story may be provided in greater or lesser detail.)

The explanation of Korean economic growth in the previous paragraph is couched in terms of correlations between a dependent variable (growth) and several independent variables (political stability, equality, and education levels), but this claim is intended to show that there is a *causal* relation between the latter factors and economic growth. In this case the causal story is not difficult to construct. Political stability is causally relevant to growth because growth requires investment and investors are more likely to invest if they are confident that existing institutions will continue. Equality is causally relevant to growth because it stimulates smooth structural change (by creating strong consumer demand for commodities). And education levels are causally relevant to growth because they are a measure of the human capital available to a society.[1] The correlations identified here are explanatory, then, because they identify causal factors that influence the rate of economic growth through credible causal mechanisms.

Thus statistical explanation is a form of causal explanation, and the conclusion of Chapter 2—that causal explanations require hypotheses about underlying causal mechanisms—is equally pertinent here as well. Mere evidence of statistical correlation between a pair of variables does not constitute an explanation of the behavior of either. Instead we can properly rest our explanatory inquiries only when we have established in a credible way the causal relation between the variables.

Consider some of the following research topics in the social sciences:

- What factors stimulate rapid economic growth in the less-developed world?
- What explains the distribution of earnings in the U.S. economy?
- Is the religious identity of a population relevant to the presence or absence of democratic institutions?

Each topic involves the search for an association between two or more variables. In the first instance the researcher aims to discover one or more factors—social, political, or economic—that are positively associated with rapid economic growth. In the second the researcher hopes to discover features of individuals that correlate positively with variations of earnings— for example, gender, skill level, race, or education level. And in the third the researcher aims at evaluating a simple causal hypothesis about regime types—that religious identity (Catholic, Protestant, Islamic) is a causal variable in the development and stability of democratic political institutions.

Statistical explanations raise two sorts of problems that are relevant to the concerns of this book. First, we must have at least a rudimentary understanding of the statistical concepts on which such explanations depend— for example, correlation, regression, association, and conditional probabilities. But second, we must ask a more philosophical set of questions. What have we learned when we have uncovered a statistical relationship between several variables? Is this discovery itself explanatory or is it an empirical circumstance that demands theoretical explanation (hypothesis formation about causal relations)? How do statistical findings support causal inferences? And what are the limitations of statistical analysis in social science?

An attractive example of a causal argument that combines statistical analysis with a hypothesis about the underlying causal mechanisms is a recent study of English demographic history (Example 8.1). Wrigley and Schofield's argument supports a causal hypothesis about economic and demographic change on the basis of a statistical correlation over time between demographic variables and the standard of living. The hypothesis is that growing real wages will result in a rise in the rate of population increase, both through higher fertility and lower mortality, and falling trends in real wages will bring a slowing of the rate of population increase. The greatest difficulty in evaluating this hypothesis empirically is the need for detailed time-series data on real income and fertility and mortality rates; the large data set compiled through parish registers permits such an evaluation. If we graph real wages and rate of population increase over time, the results resemble Figure 8.1, and the correlation between the two variables is evident. Real wages fall between 1577 and 1617; with a short lag the population growth rate begins to fall in the late 1670s. Real wages begin to rise again in the 1630s, and, with a 30- to 40-year lag, the rate of population increase begins to rise as well.

Example 8.1   Historical demography

What factors influence demographic change—fertility rates, age of marriage, rise and fall of population, or age structure of the population? A major effort to answer this family of questions is the recent study of English population (1541–1871) by Wrigley and Schofield and the Cambridge Group for the History of Population and Social Structure. The study provides a detailed description of the year-to-year state of the English population over a three-hundred-year period, based on data drawn from hundreds of Anglican parish registers that record baptisms (births), burials (deaths), and marriages. Using the statistical summary of this data, the authors attempt to empirically evaluate the Malthusian hypothesis that European demography is highly sensitive to economic variations (rising and falling real incomes). "We, therefore, preferred to follow Malthus in taking a wider view of economic opportunity in relation to the preventive check and to consider marriage to have been responsive to the level of real incomes rather than determined solely by access to a niche" (Schofield 1986:15). To evaluate this hypothesis Wrigley and Schofield provide a time series for real-wage levels for the period 1500–1912 and compare the results with the patterns of fluctuation in demographic variables over the same period. Their analysis shows that fertility varied substantially over long periods of time and that fertility fluctuations were approximately twice as important in population change as fluctuations in mortality rates (Schofield 1986:27). And their analysis also corroborates Malthus's general hypothesis that preventive checks (behavioral limitations on fertility), dependent on movements of the real wage, were of primary importance in controlling the English population increase.

Data: population data (births, deaths, and marriages) from English parish registers, 1541–1871

Explanatory model: evaluation of causal hypotheses about demographic change based on analysis of large-scale quantitative analysis of demographic data

Sources: E. Anthony Wrigley and Roger S. Schofield, *The Population History of England, 1541–1871: A Reconstruction* (1981); Roger S. Schofield, "Through a Glass Darkly: *The Population History of England* as an Experiment in History" (1986); Robert I. Rotberg and Theodore K. Rabb, eds., *Population and Economy Population and History from the Traditional to the Modern World* (1986)

QUANTITATIVE REASONING IN SOCIAL ANALYSIS

In this section I will provide an abstract account of statistical reasoning in social science. This discussion is not intended to replace detailed mathematical study of the subject, but it is possible to present enough of the elements of statistical reasoning in this context to identify some of the problems of social explanation in this area.

A *data set* involves the following structure:

• a domain of items, events, or individuals (persons, countries, riots, crimes, suicides);

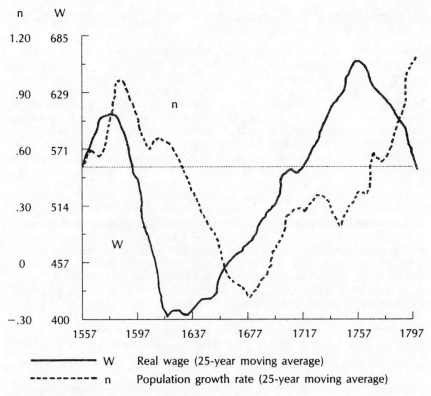

Fig. 8.1   Real wage and population growth rate

Source: Adapted from Lee 1986:89

- a set of properties of these items that are of interest to the researcher (variables);
- a specification of the state of each item with respect to each property.

We may think of a data set as a table listing individuals in the rows and the properties in the columns. Figure 8.2 is an example of a data set providing economic and social data for twenty-two less-developed countries. This table gives information on ten variables for the countries under study.

There is an implicit temporal structure in empirical studies; data may be collected either to capture change over time or to characterize the state of a set of individuals at a given time. The data provided in Figure 8.2 is a *cross-sectional* data set—one providing a "snapshot" of the state of the items at a moment in time with respect to the properties. A *time-series* data set is a study organized over a time sequence, involving data points for one item at successive moments in time. It is possible to design a study that

Country	GNP per capita* ($)	Energy use per capita*	Labor force in agric.* (%)	Life expectancy at birth* (years)	Adult literacy* (%)	Growth rate in GNP per capita* (%)	Gini coef.*	Ratio of top 20% to bottom 40% of income*	PQLI**	Infant mortality /1000 live births**
Ethiopia	120	19	80	43	15	0.50			20	181
Bangladesh	130	36	74	50	26	0.50	0.389	2.74	35	132
Mali	160	22	73	45	10	1.20			15	188
Tanzania	240	38	83	51	79	0.90			31	162
India	260	182	71	55	36	1.50	0.42	3.15	43	122
China	300	455	74	67	66	4.40	0.407	3.05	69	78
Ghana	310	111	53	59		-2.10			35	156
Sri Lanka	330	143	54	69	85	2.90	0.345	2.26	82	45
Kenya	340	109	78	57	47	2.30	0.55	6.79	39	119
Pakistan	390	197	57	50	24	2.50			38	121
Senegal	440	151	77	46	10	-0.50			25	159
Bolivia	510	292	50	51	63	0.60			43	108
Indonesia	560	204	58	54	62	5.00	0.43	3.43	48	137
Egypt	700	532	50	58	44	4.20	0.403	2.91	43	116
Philippines	760	252	46	64	75	2.90	0.459	3.80	71	74
Nigeria	770	150	54	49	34	3.20			25	180
Guatemala	1120	178	55	60		2.10			54	80
Colombia	1430	786	26	64	81	3.20	0.53	6.32	71	97
Malaysia	1860	702	50	67	60	4.50	0.5	5.01	66	75
Brazil	1880	745	30	64	76	5.00	0.605	9.51	68	82
South Korea	2010	1168	34	67	93	6.70	0.378	2.68	82	47
Mexico	2240	1332	36	66	83	3.20	0.52	5.83	73	66

Fig. 8.2 Third World country data set

Sources: *Adapted from Gillis et al. 1987:9, 10, 76; **Morris 1979:138–144

incorporates both cross-sectional and temporal dimensions, consisting of coordinated time-series studies for a group of items.

How do social scientists collect data? A great volume of statistical data is gathered by national governments and governmental institutions, available for analysis by social scientists. For example, much of the data in Figure 8.2 was compiled by the World Bank. But many social science research topics require that the investigator collect data that has not been previously gathered by formal reporting agencies. A *survey* is a study designed to elicit information concerning the properties of items within the universe of items (or a sample of them), keeping certain hypotheses in mind. The designer must have some idea about what factors are potentially relevant to the occurrence of the phenomena of interest—that is, a range of causal factors. The goal of the study is to collect data indicating the strength (or absence) of correlation among the factors.

A central problem in designing an empirical study is that of *sampling*. Many social features can only be determined through studies that single out a subset (sample) of the whole population and then draw inferences about the population properties. And two problems arise in sampling: size and randomness. If the sample is too small, then there is no reason to expect that the features of the sample correspond to those of the population. For example, if we were interested in the party affiliation of steelworkers in Pennsylvania but interviewed only twenty workers, we would not be able to draw a statistically significant inference from our study.

Sample bias is a different sort of problem. For a sample to be a good indicator of the population as a whole, the individuals selected must be randomly drawn from the population. A survey rests upon a *biased* sample if the individuals studied were chosen according to criteria that make it likely they will share features that are not representative of the population as a whole. Age, gender, place of residence, social class, type of employment, or ethnic identity can all lead to a biased sample. The problem of bias often arises not because the researcher favors one hypothesis over another but because collecting information is difficult and costly, and it will sometimes be possible to collect data from a subpopulation that is conveniently at hand. This subpopulation, however, is not randomly drawn from the whole population. An example of this possibility is found in the important land surveys of China conducted by John Lossing Buck in the 1930s. Buck sent Chinese investigators into a number of different regions of China with a detailed survey to complete concerning land ownership. However the investigators had no easy access to absentee landlords—landlords who owned property in a village but lived elsewhere. So the survey excluded these individuals. Absentee landlords, however, owned larger-than-average pieces of land, and their exclusion led to a downward bias in estimates of the average size of landholdings (Esherick 1981).

The variables defining the information collected in the data set may be either discrete or continuous. Discrete variables include religion, marital status, and class membership. Continuous variables include income, population size, and unemployment rates. (The latter examples make it plain that continuous variables may include quantities for which only integer values are possible.) This distinction is important because the techniques of data analysis are different in the two cases. Continuous variables may be analyzed using regression techniques, whereas associations among discrete variables require different tools.

Once we have a data set we need some way of aggregating the data. The distinction between discrete and continuous variables is particularly important here for the techniques available for aggregating and analyzing discrete data are different from those available for continuous data. Discrete data primarily involves the use of probability tools (discussed in Chapter 2). We can count individuals having a certain property or set of properties, and we can use that information to derive incidence rates (for example, the suicide rate among Protestant widowers). The concept of conditional probabilities is the central tool in this type of case. Continuous variables, on the other hand, permit more extensive forms of mathematical analysis, including particularly the attempt to identify functional relations between variables (discussed below). Several types of *descriptive statistics* are particularly useful in characterizing such a data set. We can calculate mean (average) values for a set of individuals with respect to a given property— for example, the average life expectancy in Figure 8.2 is 57 years. And it is useful to provide measures of the variance of each variable—that is, a measure of the amount that the variable changes over the population. (The *variance* of a set of values is the average squared deviation of each value around the mean of all the values; the *standard deviation* is the square root of the variance.)

Once we have a data set[2] we must try to extract some order from it. At this point our interest becomes explicitly *explanatory*. We want to know whether the data is patterned and whether there are unexpected probability distributions, correlations, or functional relations between variables. A tool of general utility in science is the *null hypothesis*—the hypothesis that there is no relationship between two or more variables. The null hypothesis concerning smoking and cancer, for example, is that smoking is not causally involved in the production of cancer. The null hypothesis concerning economic growth and political stability is that the processes of economic growth do not affect political stability, either positively or negatively. The null hypothesis converts rather directly into various mathematical expectations deriving from the expectation of randomness in the behavior of the variables with respect to each other. In the case of probabilities, it implies that the conditional probability of an event in the presence of a specified condition will be equal to the absolute probability of the event. And in the case of continuous variables, it implies that the *correlation coefficient* of two variables will be 0—that is, there will be no observable pattern in the values of the two variables. (Correlation is the subject of the next section.)

If we find that the null hypothesis is not borne out—that is, that there is a nonzero correlation between two or more variables or that the conditional probability of an event given a condition is different from the absolute probability of the event—then we may consider whether there is some causal process underlying the behavior of the variables. It may be a case of direct causation—smoking does cause cancer; rising per capita GNP does cause a fall in infant mortality. Or it may be indirect—a common set of factors may be influencing the behavior of the variables under observation, without the variables causally interacting. An example of this possibility is seen in the fact that energy use per capita is negatively correlated with the infant mortality rate. The best explanation of this fact is *not* that more energy use is good for infant health; it is rather that rising per capita income in a society gives rise to *both* rising energy use and falling infant mortality, thus inducing a correlation between the latter variables.

CORRELATION AND REGRESSION

The central idea underlying statistical explanation is the notion of a *correlation* between two or more variables. This concept describes covariance among variables: The variables in question take different values in different circumstances, and there is a tendency for the variables to vary together. A positive correlation means that an increase in one variable is associated with an increase in the other; a negative correlation means that an increase in one variable is associated with a decrease in the other. Two central questions must be posed in considering whether specific variables are correlated. What is the functional relationship between the variables? And how strong is the correlation between them—that is, how much dispersion is there in the data set? The first question asks how the dependent variable behaves in relation to changes in the independent variable(s); the second asks how much the dependent variable varies from what we would expect assuming a strict correlation between the variables.

Turn once more to the country data set in Figure 8.2. The variable describing energy use per capita is positively correlated with per capita incomes across countries; that is, the higher a country's per capita income, the greater the amount of energy used per capita. (Conversely the greater the energy use per capita, the greater the country's per capita income is likely to be.) An example of a negative correlation is found in the relation between infant mortality rates and per capita income; countries with higher per capita incomes generally have lower infant mortality rates.

There is a simple test for correlation between continuous variables. We can construct a *scatterplot* of the data—a graph that represents each variable along an axis and plots each data point in terms of the values of the variables for that point. (This can be done for two or more variables, but the most common application is the two-variable case.) Then we can inspect the resulting chart for an orderly progression among the data points. If the points are randomly scattered over the field, we may conclude that there is no correlation among the variables; if the points fall along a *trend-line*, we may conclude that a correlation does exist.

The statistical technique of *regression analysis* provides a quantitative method for analyzing covariance among two or more variables. Regression analysis, which underlies much quantitative reasoning in social science, is a mathematical technique designed to assess the claim that two continuous variables **x** and **y** are correlated. This means that each variation in the independent variable leads to a regular alteration in the dependent variable. There is, then, a functional relationship between these variables:

$$y_i = f(x_i) + e_i$$

Here we have broken down the behavior of the dependent variable **y** into a functional component $f(x_i)$ and an error component e_i. In principle the function may take any form whatsoever, but there are several simple functions that suggest themselves. The function may be *linear*, representing a straight-line relationship between the variables. Or it may be *curvilinear*—for example, logarithmic, exponential, or quadratic. Linear and logarithmic functions are the most common forms for representing relations among social variables. A linear function represents the dependent variable as rising or falling at a constant rate with respect to the independent variable, and a logarithmic function represents a declining rate of change as the independent variable increases. Linear functions have the form "**y = a + bx**," while logarithmic functions have the form "**y = a + b∗log(x)**."

Linear regression on two values is the simplest form of regression analysis; this technique finds a straight-line function that passes through the data set and minimizes the variance around the line.[3] That is, the regression analysis provides a "best-fit" curve (a straight-line, in this case) that passes through the data points. (The regression curve is constructed according to the "least-squares" rule: It is the function that minimizes the sum of the squares of the distance off the trend-line of all points.) Figure 8.3 provides linear and logarithmic regressions on six pairs of variables drawn from the country study. Each panel represents a scatterplot of the data, along with the regression line for each data set. And each panel provides the computed correlation coefficient **r** (explained below), measuring the strength of the correlation of the data for this regression line.

Once we have performed a regression on our data, we have answered one of the questions posed above—what is the functional relationship between the variables? But we have not addressed the second question: How well does this functional relation characterize the data set? That is, how much scatter is there in the data around the regression line? Here we need an indicator of the closeness of fit between the data set and the regression equation—a measure of the degree of variance of the data around the function. There are several statistical measures of this variance, but the simplest is the coefficient of variation R^2. R^2 is defined as:

$$R^2 = 1 - \Sigma e_i^2 / \Sigma v_i^2,$$

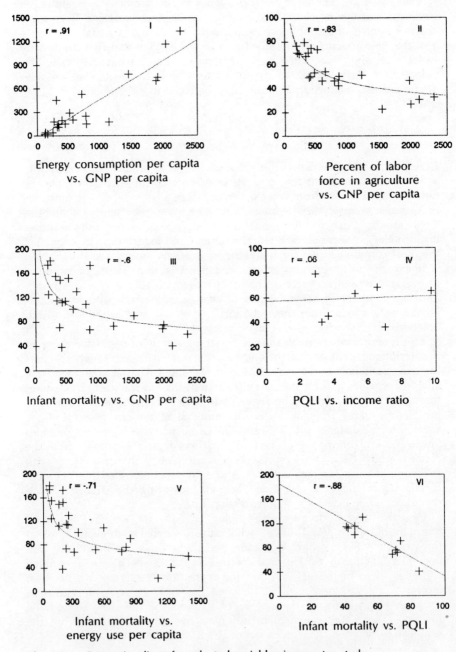

Fig. 8.3   Regression lines for selected variables in country study

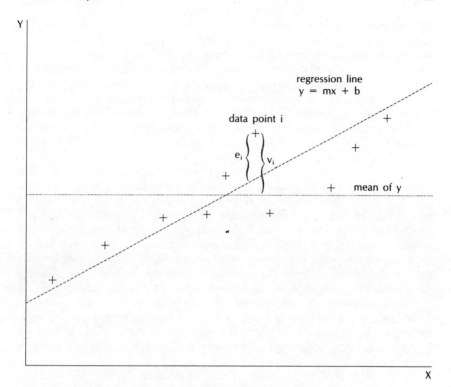

Fig. 8.4   Computation of R^2 for linear regression

where e_i are the error terms for each data point (deviations from the value predicted by the regression equation) and v_i are the variations of each data point around the mean value of **y** (Figure 8.4). R^2 is a *proportional reduction of error* statistic; it measures the percentage of variation in the dependent variable that can be explained by the regression function. Related to R^2 is the correlation coefficient **r**, the square root of the coefficient of determination. The correlation coefficient indicates the direction and strength of the relationship between the two variables, and it can vary between 1 and -1. A value of 1 corresponds to the case where the dependent variable always falls on the regression line; a value of 0 corresponds to the case where the dependent variable is randomly scattered around the regression line; and a negative value indicates that the regression line has negative slope (in other words there is a negative correlation between the two variables).

Figure 8.3 shows that there are significant correlations between various pairs of variables in the country study. Which, if any, of these correlations provide the basis for an explanatory relation between two variables? Panel I shows that there is a positive linear relation between gross national product (GNP) per capita and energy consumption; that is, economies with higher GNP per capita strongly tend to consume more energy per capita. The regression shows that the relation between these variables is linear, and the correlation is high ($r = .91$). (In other words, 83 percent of the variation in per capita energy consumption can be accounted for on the basis of per capita GNP.) But how should we account for this correlation? Does growth in GNP cause growth in energy consumption (in the way that it plainly causes growth in luxury good consumption)? The causal story in this case is more complex. Growth in GNP unavoidably involves industrialization, and industrialization is energy intensive. Therefore rising energy consumption per capita is a necessary condition for rising per capita income. What panel I identifies, then, is the behavior of two variables within a complex causal process of economic growth, neither of which is the cause of the other. Much the same may be said about panel II. In this case we find a negative logarithmic correlation between GNP and the percent of the labor force in agriculture. Here again the correlation between the variables is high ($r = -.83$). The curve fits the data well. And the relationship between these variables is explanatory, reflecting the generalization that economic growth involves the structural transformation of an economy away from agriculture and toward industrial expansion. But once again it would be most plausible to construe this correlation as one between collateral effects within a complex process of economic growth: Industrialization leads both to rising per capita GNP and a structural transformation from a rural economy to an increasingly industrial one. In each case, then, the correlations we have discovered are best understood as correlations between collateral effects within a complex causal process.

Panels III and IV, by contrast, attempt to evaluate direct causal relations between pairs of variables. In panel III we find that there is a negative logarithmic relationship between GNP per capita and infant mortality rates, with a moderate correlation coefficient ($r = -.6$). Countries with higher income generally have lower infant mortality rates. And a simple causal hypothesis can account for this correlation: Both household and public health care expenditures rise quickly as incomes rise, and rising health care expenditures have major effects on infant mortality at low income levels. (This effect falls off as health care expenditures rise; there is a falling marginal effect of health care dollars on health status.) This analysis permits us to assert that rising income levels cause falling infant mortality levels. (However only 36 percent of the variance in infant mortality can be explained on this basis, so there must be other causes of variance that exercise influence as well.) Panel IV, however, may be construed as a refutation of a causal hypothesis concerning the relation between inequalities and physical quality of life. The measure of inequalities used in this panel is the ratio of the share of income going to the top 20 percent of income earners to that going to the bottom 40 percent. Physical quality of life is measured here by PQLI— an index that incorporates data about infant mortality, life expectancy at age one, and literacy (Morris 1979). One might reason that greater inequalities imply greater poverty, which in turn implies lower average physical quality of life. Thus one might entertain the following hypothesis: Greater inequalities will cause lower PQLI. However panel IV shows that there is little significant relationship between these variables; the correlation coefficient is low (.17) and trends in the opposite direction to that predicted by the hypothesis. Greater inequality is therefore weakly associated with higher physical quality of life (presumably because both are correlated with per capita GNP).

Finally, consider panels V and VI. These panels identify two strong correlations: the first between infant mortality and energy use per capita and the second between infant mortality and PQLI. In each case we find a high degree of correlation between the variables. However, these correlations are spurious. Panel V shows that infant mortality falls with rising energy use per capita, but this correlation is induced by the common correlation between these factors and rising GNP per capita. In fact there is no direct causal connection between these variables at all. And the correlation between PQLI and infant mortality is purely artifactual: The PQLI index is defined in terms of the infant mortality level (along with two other factors). So it is a matter of definition rather than contingent association that these two factors are correlated.

Let us return now to an example discussed in several contexts above—James Tong's analysis of banditry in the Ming dynasty (Example 2.2). Tong believes his data set supports the hypothesis that the incidence of rebellion is correlated with the circumstances of risk found in various places and times. His own analysis rests on the observation that the incidence of banditry reported in Figure 2.2 varies in the direction predicted by the rational choice model. In this chapter, however, we have seen that it is desirable to ask two sorts of questions that Tong does not raise. What is the functional relation between risk and rebellion? And how high is the correlation between incidence of banditry and the two variables? The first question parallels the problem of determining how the incidence of rebellion should be expected to vary in response to an alteration in the level of risk; the latter involves determining how much of the variation of the dependent variable (incidence of banditry) is explained by the two independent variables.

We can use the technique of multiple regression to assess the degree of correlation in this analysis. Consider Tong's original table (Figure 2.2). Here we have two independent variables (hardship survival and outlaw survival) and one continuous dependent variable (incidence of banditry per 100 county-years). The dependent variable rests on observations of 630 cases and 303,869 county-years covered by the survey. It is reasonable to construe the survival levels as continuous variables measured discretely. Let us then assign a value of 3 for maximum survival, 2 for moderate survival, and 1 for minimum survival and perform a multiple regression analysis on the resulting data set. This produces the following functional relation between the risk variables (PEASANT and BANDIT) and the incidence of banditry (INCID):

$$INCID = -.48 \text{ PEASANT} + .39 \text{ BANDIT} + .86$$

This equation indicates that the incidence of rebellion rises as the prospects of survival as a peasant fall and the prospects of survival as a bandit rise.

Example 8.2   Sources of economic growth

What factors influence the rate of economic growth in various countries in the less-developed world? Adelman and Morris consider a list of 41 features of the social and economic organization that are potentially relevant to economic growth. They then construct a large study of 74 countries with respect to these features. Once the data is collected they make use of a statistical technique similar to regression analysis (factor analysis) designed to determine (1) the correlations among these variables across countries and (2) the correlations among groups of these variables (factors) and the rate of economic growth in the countries studied. Adelman and Morris conclude that two clusters of economic and social variables are significantly correlated with economic growth: variables that reflect processes of change in attitudes and institutions and variables corresponding to political regime type (Adelman and Morris 1967:153, 155). This analysis provides a basis for explaining why Korea experienced a very rapid rate of growth, India an intermediate rate, and Kenya a slow one.

Data: 74-country data set including 48 socioeconomic, political, and economic variables

Explanatory model: Statistical analysis of a large number of variables causally relevant to economic growth, based on data from 74 countries

Source: Irma Adelman and Cynthia Taft Morris, *Society, Politics, and Economic Development: A Quantitative Approach* (1967)

Moreover this function succeeds in explaining a high percentage of the variation in the dependent variable; there is a high multiple correlation between incidence of banditry and the two risk variables (multiple $R = .93$). (Multiple R is the multivariate equivalent to the correlation coefficient r discussed above.) This analysis gives us a more adequate way to estimate the degree to which Tong's data supports the rational choice hypothesis about banditry and rebellion than he himself provides. It shows that his data implies a correlation coefficient greater than .90 between the independent variables and the incidence of banditry, explaining over 80 percent of the variance in the data.

Consider an example that illustrates many features of the statistical analysis of a complex social phenomenon—an analysis by Adelman and Morris of the factors that influence economic growth in the less-developed world (Example 8.2). This study by Adelman and Morris is a major statistical undertaking, involving as it does the identification of a large number of potentially relevant variables, the collection of a vast quantity of data, and the application of a powerful computational method to sort the sources of variation within the data set. They arrive at a set of statistically significant correlations between a number of the variables and economic growth. What precisely is the significance of this effort, however? It should be noted that there is enormous variation across the countries surveyed. To make sense of this argument, we must postulate that economic growth is a structured process that is responsive to a variety of social, political, and economic factors. And here we encounter a serious shortcoming in the Adelman-Morris study: Their analysis attempts to identify causally relevant variables without using a theory of the mechanisms through which various factors influence the growth rate.

Turn now to a more pervasive problem—the quality and comparability of the data on which a statistical argument depends. The Adelman-Morris study raises several problems in this regard. First, in some cases there are conceptual problems in the measurements that they attempt to collect. (They try to classify political regimes on the basis of the types and varieties of political parties that are active, although it is not clear that this is a useful comparative framework.) Second, some measures are conceptually clear but difficult to collect, and as a result there is little correspondence between the measure and the real value of the variable in the population. (Infant mortality figures, for example, are poorly collected in impoverished countries, implying that these figures may underestimate the extent of infant mortality.) Finally, some important economic variables that are monitored by national governments—e.g., the savings rate—may be defined differently by different national statistical agencies, resulting in a meaningless cross-country comparison.

This study thus illustrates both the strength and some of the shortcomings of a purely inductive approach to social causation. It succeeds in identifying some causal factors that influence the phenomenon to be explained, but at the same time further causal analysis is required to distinguish between genuine and spurious correlational data. We must identify the causal mechanisms that are at work among the various factors.

PHILOSOPHICAL GROUNDS OF STATISTICAL EXPLANATION

The preceding discussion provides a basic knowledge of some of the statistical concepts used in the social sciences to analyze and explain social phenomena. We may begin a more philosophical discussion of statistical reasoning by asking a fundamental question: What is the role of statistical arguments in social science? There are several general answers to this question. First, statistical tools may be used to empirically evaluate causal hypotheses—that is, statistical analysis can be a method of *hypothesis testing*. Suppose that we hold, on theoretical grounds, that rapid social change is a cause of third-world civil unrest. If this hypothesis is true, there should be a correlation between rapid social change and civil unrest. A statistical study of a sample of countries is a particularly direct way to test if this theoretical expectation is borne out.

Rapid social change and civil unrest are not directly observable, however, so to conduct such a study we need observable variables that correspond to these concepts. We need, that is, to *operationalize* the theoretical hypothesis in terms of observable variables. We can empirically evaluate the hypothesis that **A** is a cause of **B** through a study that operationalizes **A** and **B** in terms of observable variables **A*** and **B*** and then determines whether **B***

is correlated with **A***. Suppose, then, that we take "rate of population movement from rural to urban residence" as a measure of the rapidity of social change and "violent incidents involving five or more participants" as a measure of civil unrest. If we find that there is a correlation between the variables and if we judge that these are plausible measures of the causal factors in question, then we have some confirmation for the causal hypothesis. (Note, however, that such a finding does not establish the truth of the causal hypothesis for it is possible that both variables are the collateral effects of some third causal factor.)

Suppose, however, that we find that **A*** and **B*** are not correlated; it is not true that societies with a higher value for **A*** also have a higher value for **B***. Does this refute the claim that **A** is a cause of **B**? It does not for there are several other possible explanations of this null discovery. It may be that we have not chosen appropriate measures of the causal variables; **A*** and **B*** may not be good surrogates for **A** and **B**. Or there may be a causal relation between **A** and **B**, but it is one that is highly context-dependent: There is a third factor **C** that, if present, facilitates the causal process from **A** to **B** and, if absent, prevents this causal process. Now, suppose that **C** is present in about half the cases under study. If this is true we will not find that countries with high values for **A*** will tend to have high values for **B***; there will be a low correlation between **A*** and **B***. A new study incorporating **C** would, on these assumptions, show that **A** in the presence of **C** is highly correlated with **B**, and **A** absent **C** is not. But if we happen not to identify **C** as a causally relevant variable, our statistical analysis will produce a false inference of no causal relation between **A** and **B**.

The lesson of this example is an important one: A statistical study can provide empirical grounds for accepting or rejecting a causal hypothesis, but the statistical findings themselves are not final or conclusive. Study of covariance among factors is a useful tool for investigating causal hypotheses, but it is always possible that the causal hypothesis is true although the corresponding statistical test is negative.

Consider a second common use of statistical analysis—as a preliminary way of probing a complex range of social phenomena for underlying regularities. Here the goal is to discover regularities as a first step in establishing causal relations. The Adelman and Morris study (Example 8.2) represents a good illustration of this use of statistical analysis; they cast a wide net over a range of potentially relevant social, economic, and political variables and then attempt to see which of these are significantly correlated with the dependent variable under scrutiny (the rate of economic growth per capita). Their discovery that a small handful of features is highly correlated with economic growth then indicates where further theoretical analysis should be conducted. The next task is to formulate a theory of the causal processes through which these social variables influence the rate of economic growth. In this approach a statistical study may be seen as an exploratory work aimed at uncovering the patterns present in the empirical phenomena. The resulting patterns can then serve as the basis for hypothesis formation about underlying causal processes.

STATISTICAL ANALYSIS AND COMPARATIVE STUDIES

We have now examined causal investigations in a range of levels of concreteness. In Chapter 2 we examined the case-study method and the comparative method. In the case-study method the investigator considers a particular event or process—for example, the occurrence of the Chinese revolution—and examines the history of this event in detail, attempting to identify the causally significant factors that led to the occurrence and particular character of the event. The comparative method, we found, is a common and powerful technique through which social scientists attempt to identify social causes. This method isolates a small number of cases—for example, the Chinese, Russian, and German revolutionary movements—and then tries to identify the causal processes that lead to different outcomes in these cases. The statistical method, by contrast, involves a large number of cases— perhaps a hundred countries—and a set of abstract variables designed to apply across the highly diverse settings of the various cases. What is the relation between case studies, comparative studies, and statistical studies?

The general perspective I adopt here—in line with the methodological pluralism urged throughout—is that each approach has its own strengths and weaknesses, each is strengthened by the resources of the other, and each has a range of research topics to which it is best suited. At the same time I will hold that the comparative method is in one sense more fundamental than either the case-study or the statistical method. It permits the investigator to identify causal processes that are basic to explanation without unavoidable reference to either case or statistical studies. Case studies, by contrast, require background theoretical beliefs that could only come through knowledge of a number of different social settings, implying either comparative or statistical studies. And statistical studies require knowledge of particular cases in order to sort out the causal mechanisms that are in play, underlying the regularities discovered by statistical analysis. Either explicitly or implicitly, then, statistical studies must be supplemented by hypotheses about causal mechanisms that can only come from case or comparative studies.

We can best study the relation between statistical and comparative studies by considering an example of each. Recall Atul Kohli's comparative study of poverty reform in India (Example 2.6). Kohli tries to identify one or more variables that account for the varying successes of poverty reform in the context of a theory of the politics of reform in India. His work, based on a detailed comparative examination of the politics of reform in three Indian states, reflects a high level of detailed knowledge about the economic arrangements in each state, the political organizations active in each state, the ways in which state bureaucracies function in each state, and the official policies of each state government. In other words this is a very detailed study of the particulars of the politics of poverty in these three settings.

Using this analysis, Kohli comes to the conclusion that the governing variable in determining whether state poverty policies are successful is tied to the ideology of the regime in power, its internal coherence and discipline, and its organizational reach and competence.

Now contrast this study with that of Adelman and Morris (1973). (This is the sequel to the study presented in Example 8.2.) Adelman and Morris are concerned with a problem that is closely related to Kohli's: What are the economic and social features that determine the distributive characteristics of economic development processes across countries? They employ a large country study, involving 74 nations and 48 indicators. And, using a statistical technique (discriminant analysis), they determine that a small cluster of these indicators are closely correlated with distributive consequences—rate of improvement in human resources, direct government economic activity, socioeconomic dualism, potential for economic development, per capita GNP, and strength of the labor movement (Adelman and Morris 1973:184). This conclusion is clearly related to that reached by Kohli, who finds that the regimes that exert disciplined policy attention to the problem of the poor have the greatest effect on poverty alleviation. The first two factors listed by Adelman and Morris are associated with this feature of regime policy choice. And the final factor listed by them (the strength of the labor movement) is consistent with the idea that regimes that take power in the environment of a significant labor movement will be more prone to poverty reduction than others.

So there is a substantial degree of coherence between Kohli's findings and those of Adelman and Morris. However, there are several important shortcomings to the second study that can best be addressed through the comparative method. First, there is the problem of the coarseness of the analytical net that Adelman and Morris throw over the data: Their study ranges over several decades and dozens of countries. It may be, however, that there are regionally or temporally specific processes that must be identified if we are to understand the mechanisms of economic growth and distribution but that operate more finely than the factors measured by their study. Second, their study unavoidably employs highly abstract descriptive categories, although there is little reason to expect that these will capture the causally relevant factors. Finally, at its best their study identifies causally relevant variables without determining the causal mechanisms that connect them. Take their first factor (rate of improvement in human resources). Their study shows that countries that effectively direct social efforts toward improving human resources have more equal distributive outcomes than those that do not. But this finding sheds no light on the underlying question: Why do some countries in fact exert this sort of effort toward improving human resources? By contrast, Kohli's conclusions, if true, do provide an answer to this question: The regimes that make poverty reduction a high-priority goal select improvement in human resources as an instrument to reach this goal.

The two approaches also differ in their treatment of the causal field as related to distributive justice. The relevant factors may be impossible to discern without in-depth study of a small number of cases. Kohli's investigation does not presuppose that we can identify the causally relevant variables in advance; instead, they emerge as findings. He brings with him a set of theoretical hypotheses about political processes and economic change, but the set of causal factors that he arrives at—leftist ideology, political competence, leadership, intraparty coherence—emerges from his study of the data. Adelman and Morris, however, are forced to identify the causal field in advance because their study requires that they collect data in predefined categories. Consider the following thought experiment: If Kohli's hypothesis is correct, how would Adelman and Morris's analysis come out? They cast their net widely, but if they have not identified left-right regimes as a variable, they will have missed a strong correlation that is present among the phenomena. Indeed, if Kohli is right, it is the decisive correlation. The variables that they consider do not include what turn out to be the causally salient factors: regime type, ideology, and organizational competence. None of the variables used by Adelman and Morris correspond closely enough to these features of state activity to allow them to arrive at the most fundamental causal relations. In general, then, it is unjustified to suppose that we can identify the causal field a priori for a particular circumstance, which suggests that large statistical studies must be supplemented by smaller-grain comparative studies that shed light on the social and political mechanisms underlying the large-scale processes identified through statistical analysis.

ARE THERE AUTONOMOUS STATISTICAL EXPLANATIONS?

It is sometimes held that the discovery of statistical regularities is the beginning and end of explanation. In other words to explain a phenomenon is to show that its occurrence in observed circumstances conforms to an underlying statistical regularity. This view differs sharply from the one argued in this book because it denies the importance of identifying underlying causal mechanisms. So let us confront this position head on. Are there autonomous statistical explanations—that is, explanations that do not depend on a causal story? Is the discovery of a strong statistical correlation ever an explanation of an event or pattern? Is it ever reasonable to say that we have explained an event or regularity by showing that it is a member of a class that has different conditional probabilities from absolute probabilities? Sickle cell anemia is relatively rare among the general U.S. population but substantially more common among Afro-Americans. We find that Tony has this illness, but have we explained this circumstance by discovering that he is Afro-American? Or suppose we find that GNP per capita is strongly correlated with the proportion of college-educated adults in the society. Does this finding constitute an explanation of *either* the fact that France has a high proportion of college-educated adults *or* the fact that it has (by international standards) high GNP per capita? In each case it is most reasonable to suggest that the discovery of the correlation or abnormal probability distribution is the beginning of an explanation but almost never the final explanation. In general I propose the following principle on probabilistic and statistical explanation: A discovery that refutes the null hypothesis is explanatory only if it leads us to a plausible causal mechanism producing the significant relationship between the variables. When we have discovered a pattern in a data set, we have laid the basis for an explanation of the phenomena in question. But to have a satisfactory explanation we must be able to identify, at least approximately, the causal mechanisms that underlie the statistical regularities.

To begin with, there is the problem of spurious correlation. Some statistical techniques can help to exclude this possibility (by collecting data for other conditional probabilities—for example, the incidence of cancer among non-smokers with nicotine stains).[4] But the most direct way of excluding the possibility of a spurious correlation is to discover the causal mechanism connecting the variables. Correlation between x and y is prima facie evidence of causal connection, but to establish a causal connection it is necessary to exclude the possibility that both are the effects of some third condition. Analysis of the mechanism of causation is an effective way of supporting judgments of causation based on correlational data for once we have a theory of the process by which condition x produces condition y in typical circumstances, we also have a theoretical basis for judging that the correlation is genuinely causal rather than spurious.

There is a deeper consideration as well that militates against rock-bottom statistical explanations. Recall the discussion in Chapter 1 about "why-necessary" questions. The demand for an explanation of an event or regularity typically involves this question: Why did this event come about, given the circumstances at the time of its occurrence? This is a demand for a causal story, which in turn requires an account of the laws and mechanisms through which antecedent conditions brought about the explanandum. We are satisfied with an explanation when we are confident that we have identified the antecedent conditions C_i and laws L_i that brought it about. An adequate causal story permits us to make counterfactual judgments—if conditions C_i had not been present, E would not have occurred. And it provides the basis for making judgments of causal irrelevance about other factors: If condition D was present or not, E would still have occurred.

Whether there are autonomous statistical explanations, then, reduces to this question: Does a well-established statistical association between two variables yield a causal story? It does not. The statistical association does not establish the presence or character of a set of causal mechanisms connecting the variables. There may be no causal mechanism leading from one variable to the other; each may be the effect of some third variable (as was the case in panel I, Figure 8.3) or the association between them may be artifactual (panel VI, Figure 8.3). The statistical association also does not establish the basis for counterfactual judgments because collateral effects are not necessary or sufficient conditions for the occurrence of one another. Finally the statistical result does not establish the causal irrelevance of other factors. On these grounds, then, it is reasonable to conclude, as I do, that statements of statistical regularities are not in themselves explanatory. The discovery of a statistical regularity among variables rather constitutes an empirical description of social phenomena that itself demands explanation. As we have seen above it is possible that the correlations reflect experimental artifact or collateral causation, so the statistical findings themselves do not permit us to conclude what explanatory relations obtain among the variables. (Note the similarity between this conclusion and the parallel findings concerning functional and structural explanation in Chapter 5.)

NOTES

1. For discussion of Korean development along these lines, see Mason et al. (1980).

2. This is not to imply that the data comes before the theorizing for it is plain that the researcher has had to employ some set of provisional hypotheses about the causal structure of the domain he is working with in order to identify appropriate features to study.

3. It is also possible to perform regressions on three or more variables; the task is more computationally demanding but in principle the same. *Multivariate regression analysis* for n variables involves constructing an n-dimensional plane (corresponding to the two-dimensional line in the two-variable case) that best fits the n-dimensional scatterplot of data. And it is possible to perform nonlinear regressions on two or more variables. Nonlinear regression finds a curvilinear function of specified form (e.g., exponential, quadratic, or logarithmic) that best fits the data set (once again by minimizing the variance around the function).

4. Herbert Simon addresses this problem in "Spurious Correlation: A Causal Interpretation" (1971).

SUGGESTIONS FOR FURTHER READING

Blalock, H. M., Jr., ed. 1971. *Causal Models in the Social Sciences.*

Bohrnstedt, George W., and David Knoke. 1988. 2d ed. *Statistics for Social Data Analysis.*

Suppes, Patrick. 1984. *Probabilistic Metaphysics.*

Tufte, Edward. 1974. *Data Analysis for Politics and Policy.*

PART III
CURRENT
CONTROVERSIES

In the final three chapters I will discuss a number of philosophical issues concerning social explanation that have arisen over the previous pages. The emphasis throughout this book on causal explanations of social phenomena raises the important topic of methodological individualism: What is the relation between social causation and individual-level processes? Chapter 9 explores the issues tied to this topic and argues that the concept of supervenience provides the best formulation of the doctrine of methodological individualism. It concludes that social explanations require microfoundations. A second topic that has arisen stems from the observation that there are profound differences in social behavior and values across cultures. This diversity leads to the question of cultural relativism: Is there a common human core of values and motives that persists across cultures, or is each culture a unique complex of values and forms of social behavior? Chapter 10 considers this question from three perspectives: conceptual relativism, the relativity of rationality, and moral relativism. Finally I turn to a particularly vexing problem in the philosophy of social science—the relation between social science and natural science. It is sometimes maintained that all sciences should emulate the methods of the natural sciences; this is called the doctrine of "naturalism." Others hold, by contrast, that the social sciences depend on radically different methods and metaphysics. Chapter 11 considers arguments on both sides of this debate and concludes that both are incorrect. The social sciences have some elements in common with the natural sciences and some elements that are more distinctive, which is true of biology, psychology, and other special sciences as well. Chapter 11 suggests that social science methods are diverse and eclectic and that it is a mistake to attempt to formulate a single unitary description of social science methodology.

9
METHODOLOGICAL
INDIVIDUALISM

Many social explanations purport to explain a social phenomenon—the occurrence of rebellion, the spatial distribution of cities and towns, or the tendency toward crisis within late capitalism—as the effect of other social phenomena, such as millenarianism, a commercialized economic system, or the workings of the capitalist mode of production. That is, one social pattern, structure, or entity is explained by reference to other social phenomena. Such explanations may be called *macroexplanations*, and they have long been an object of criticism within the philosophy of social science. Social scientists and philosophers of science alike have often argued that social science must be subject to the principle of *methodological individualism*—the view that social explanations and descriptions must be grounded in facts about individuals. This doctrine consists of several related but distinct claims: a thesis about social entities, a thesis about the meaning of social concepts, and a thesis about explanation. And, as we will see, the several versions of the doctrine are not equivalent. The ontological thesis is true but fairly trivial; the meaning thesis is entirely unpersuasive; and the explanatory thesis, with qualification, is a legitimate restriction on social explanation, but not for the reasons usually given.

INDIVIDUALS AND SOCIAL REGULARITIES

The ontological thesis of methodological individualism (MI) holds that all social entities are reducible without remainder to logical compounds of individuals. On this account, social entities are *nothing but* ensembles of individuals in various relations to one another. A university is nothing but the individuals who are involved in university activities—professors, students, trustees, deans, and custodians. This version of the thesis is a claim about the composition of social phenomena, asserting that every social phenomenon is composed of ensembles of individuals and their behavior. (By analogy the mind-brain identity thesis holds that all mental events are composed of some set of brain events.) J.W.N. Watkins represents this view in an influential essay about methodological individualism: "The ultimate constituents of the social world are individual people who act more or less

184 Current Controversies

appropriately in the light of their dispositions and understanding of their situation. Every complex social situation or event is the result of a particular configuration of individuals, their dispositions, situations, beliefs, and physical resources and environment" (Watkins 1968:270–71).

The ontological thesis is manifestly true—social entities are no more independent of individuals than biological entities are independent of atoms and molecules. Even Emile Durkheim, who is a committed social holist (that is, a critic of methodological individualism), insists only that there are nonreducible social *facts*, not nonreducible social entities. He describes social facts as "a type of conduct or thought [that is] not only external to the individual but, moreover, endowed with coercive power, by virtue of which they impose themselves upon him, independent of his individual will" (Durkheim 1938:2). His insight here is that social behavior is constrained by social norms that are external to the individual and authoritative. But such norms are enforced on the individual only through the direct and indirect effects of the behavior of other persons toward that individual. So the working of a set of social norms is compatible with the ontological thesis: Social norms are embodied in the behavioral dispositions of individuals.

It is reasonable, then, to accept the ontological thesis and agree that all social entities—states, economies, contracts, legal systems, religions, artistic traditions, wars, strikes, trade regimes, and revolutions—are constituted by the ensemble of individuals and the behaviors that underlie them. Social structures and institutions, systems of norms, and patterns of social relationship are all made up of human beings engaged in various kinds of meaningful and intentional activity. What flows from this conclusion, however? Less than might seem to be the case. In particular we will see that neither the meaning thesis nor the explanation thesis follows.

The meaning thesis is a claim about social concepts, stating that they must be *definable* in terms of concepts that refer only to individuals and their relations and behavior. According to this doctrine it should be possible to define social concepts—e.g., the university—in terms of the ensemble of individuals and their actions that contribute to the social phenomenon. This claim is much more problematic. To begin with, which facts about individuals can be employed? Certainly there are many properties of individuals that presuppose social properties and arrangements. Consider the following true descriptions of Albert's behavior:

Albert is waving his hands;
Albert is gesturing to Fred;
Albert is insulting Fred;
Albert is committing a breach of diplomatic protocol.

These various levels of description of facts about Albert differ in terms of the assumptions about social facts that we are forced to make in order to interpret them. The meaning thesis only has bite if we require that the admissible facts be those that refer only to individuals and their psychological properties. But there is no reason to think that such a reduction is possible. Instead it is plausible to suppose that we are forced to make reference to social institutions, rules, and meanings in order to characterize the facts about individuals to which we must refer. (Stephen Lukes develops arguments of this sort [Lukes 1973].)

Thus the sentence "Jones is an astute politician" presupposes that we understand what a politician is, which brings with it an ensemble of beliefs about political institutions, parties, elections, logrolling, and use of the media. If this sentence expresses a fact about individuals that can be used to define social concepts, then the task is an easy one. But it seems unlikely that a defender of methodological individualism would be willing to accept it. The other alternative is to require a narrow criterion of individual-level properties and restrict the available facts about individuals to those that do *not* presuppose social relations—narrow psychological facts summarizing behavioral dispositions. If we impose this restriction, we are prohibited from referring to social relations within which individuals find themselves; we are also prohibited from referring to many beliefs that individuals have— beliefs about social institutions and social relations.

The narrow requirement on individual-level facts makes it highly implausible that definitions of social concepts exist. Consider the difficulties involved in defining the game of baseball. Baseball is a social activity, and it is constituted by the meaningful activities of countless human beings who orient their behavior according to their understanding of the game. Can we define the game and its chief elements in terms that refer only to individuals, however? It would appear that we cannot. The central difficulty is that the concept of a game is irreducibly social in at least this sense: Each player's actions are oriented around his or her understanding that other players share central assumptions on the rules of the game and will behave accordingly. In other words, a proper understanding of baseball requires that we recognize that it is a *game* with multiple players, each oriented to the actions of the others. The system of rules that govern baseball thus cannot be defined simply as a complex system of behavioral dispositions on the part of baseball players; instead it is essential that each player's understanding of the rules must refer to the other-directedness of his or her own play and that of others. If we attempt to eliminate this aspect from our characterization of each player's behavior, we no longer have enough structure to interpret the complex interactions among players.

This irreducibly social character of the concept of baseball does not conflict with the ontological thesis. The rules of baseball are embodied in the actions and understandings of the various participants; when the batter takes a third strike he and everyone else know that he is out. Thus the rules depend on the actions and dispositions of individuals, as the ontological thesis requires. However, a system of rules cannot be defined in terms of concepts that refer only to individuals and their narrow psychological properties; rather it is necessary to attribute to the individual a system of concepts that make reference to other persons and their interrelations.

This argument suggests that there are logical impediments to carrying out the meaning reduction associated with methodological individualism. But even if such definition were possible, there is no reason to require that it be performed in order to have a satisfactory scientific theory of the phenomena as described at the social level. A baseball consists of hundreds of billions of molecules, and it might be possible to introduce a definition of "baseball" that refers only to molecules and makes no reference to ordinary-sized objects. However, such a definition would be a perverse step back from scientific explanation because baseballs and other ordinary-sized objects conform to lawlike regularities that permit explanation at that level of description. Reasoning along these lines suggests the following requirements on scientific concept formation in place of methodological individualism: Scientific concepts should (1) provide clear criteria of application so that we can be rigorous in applying the concept to the phenomena, and (2) permit us to discover regularities among phenomena. A level of description of phenomena—that is, a scheme of concepts identifying entities at a given level of abstraction—is acceptable if it satisfies these requirements. Our concepts should facilitate analysis and explanation of phenomena at the level in which we are interested. And if a system of concepts functions adequately at that level, then arguments requiring conceptual reduction are unsuccessful. (Garfinkel 1981 provides extensive arguments about the pragmatic features of social explanation along these lines.)

I conclude, then, that the MI thesis about the meaning of social concepts is entirely unpersuasive. We have good reason to doubt that such a reduction is possible; even if it were possible, we have good reason to doubt that it is scientifically desirable. I will therefore hold that typical social science concepts—capitalist economic system, bourgeoisie, rice riot, rate of inflation, anomie, ethical system, and so on—are legitimate and do not require reduction to a lower level of description (in particular to individual-level concepts). What determines the adequacy of a system of concepts in science is its ultimate utility in analyzing and explaining the range of phenomena to which it is applied—not its "foundations" in a supposedly rock-bottom level of ontology.

The MI thesis about explanation contends that there are no autonomous social explanations; instead all social facts and regularities must ultimately be explicable in terms of facts about individuals—their motives, powers, beliefs, and capacities. If we say that a high rate of inflation causes political instability, this is a shorthand explanation that should, ideally, be replaceable by an account of the origins of instability in the economic circumstances of individual actors. In particular, all social regularities must be derivable from laws describing individual activity. Watkins writes, "There may be unfinished or half-way explanations of large-scale social phenomena (say, inflation) in terms of other large-scale phenomena (say, full employment); but we shall not have arrived at rock-bottom explanations of such large-scale phenomena until we have deduced an account of them from statements about the dispositions, beliefs, resources, and inter-relations of individuals" (Watkins 1968:271).

What grounds support the explanatory dictum? The most common is an argument from ontology to methodology. Because social phenomena are constituted by individual-level activity, they must be explained by individual-level activity. This is not a valid inference, however. We have already accepted the ontological point—the obvious truth about social entities that they are ultimately constituted by individual agents and their behavior. It is a short step to this inference: If **B** is *constituted* by things of type **A**, then the behavior of **B** is wholly *determined* by the properties of things of type **A**. Clouds are composed of water droplets, and the dynamics of clouds are in principle determined by the mechanical properties of water droplets in large ensembles. There are no "emergent" properties of clouds—properties that cannot be reduced to the dynamics of water droplets. It does not follow from these putative truths, however, that satisfactory explanations of higher-level phenomena must be ultimately grounded in the laws governing the behavior of lower-level constituents.

To draw this conclusion we would have to assume that an explanation is satisfactory only if it shows how the explanandum is determined by the properties of its lowest-level constituents. This is a wholly unreasonable constraint on explanation, however; it would require, for example, that the only satisfactory explanation of the trajectory of a cannonball is a derivation of the path of the constituent molecules, given their initial positions and momenta. There are two possibilities that are incompatible with the explanatory thesis, each of which has some basis of support in social explanation. First, it might be that there *are* emergent properties in some domains of phenomena—that is, laws might exist among phenomena at the higher level of description that are not derivable from laws at the lower level. And second, it might be that all regularities at the higher level are in fact determined by regularities at the lower level, but pragmatic features of explanation make it preferable *not* to perform the reduction.

To support the first possibility we must consider the distinction between token-identity and type-identity. A token is a single individual within a kind; a type is a "natural kind" or a whole class of tokens sharing important properties. An identity thesis claims the following:

All As are composed of Bs.

For example, all pains are identical with patterns of stimulated neurons, all clouds are identical with sets of water droplets, and all universities are identical with an ensemble of individuals. A token-identity thesis may be formulated as:

Each A-thing is identical with some B-thing.

A type-identity claim is stronger:

Each A-type is identical with some B-type.

In the case of a cloud, the first claim asserts only that there is an instance of water droplets with which the cloud is identical. The second claim is stronger because it asserts that the natural kinds at the higher level can be mapped onto natural kinds at the lower level. Thus the class of clouds is identical with a class of items at the level of water droplet description (ensembles of water droplets). The type-identity thesis implies the token-identity thesis, but the reverse is not true. (See Boyd 1980 for a discussion of this distinction as applied to mind-brain identity theory.)

Now consider an example of a pair of levels of description in which token-identity obtains but type-identity fails. Suppose that all pains (P) are identical with neural-activity events (N) but that there are many different kinds of neural-activity events that correspond to pains—N_1, N_2, N_3. When a pain occurs it is sometimes identical with an N_1 event, sometimes an N_2 event, and so on. Finally, suppose that there are some instances of N_1, N_2, N_3 events that are not pain events—that is, not all N events are P events. Now we have a case of token-identity without type-identity for P is not extensionally equivalent to any of N_1, N_2, N_3, or the union of N_1, N_2, N_3. Now, finally, suppose that there are regularities at the level of pain descriptions. These regularities will *not* necessarily correspond to regularities among N_1, N_2, N_3 events and will not necessarily be derivable from regularities at the level of N.

This is a highly abstract argument, but the application to social phenomena is suggestive. It might well be true that each instance of a social kind— for example, a state structure—is identical with an ensemble of individual actors having certain properties although there are no regularities among these ensembles at the individual level of description. In this case the regularities that characterize states would not be derivable from regularities about "state-constituting ensembles of individuals."

The other way in which the MI explanatory dictum might err is a pragmatic one. It might be that all the laws among the higher-level phenomena are in principle derivable from the laws of the lower-level phenomena, but the derivations would be extremely difficult or impossible to construct. It is possible in principle to derive the orbits of a tightly packed solar system with twenty planets from information about the initial positions and momenta of the stars and planets, but such a derivation is vastly beyond current computational abilities. Likewise, simple regularities like "hyperinflation in Argentina causes political instability" might be derivable from facts about the psychological states of tens of millions of Argentines, but such a derivation is practically impossible. Further, even if it were possible, we might well maintain that the simple explanation at the level of social factors like inflation, economic security, and voter behavior is preferable to the plethora of singular statements about millions of Argentines. This is the appropriate level of description and explanation—if it is possible to arrive at empirically sup-portable explanations at this level.

Instead of this strong requirement of explanatory reductionism, consider an alternative constraint: An explanation is satisfactory if and only if the regularities and structures that it postulates are sufficiently well established on empirical grounds to permit confidence that they fall within a causal system.

This criterion allows explanatory autonomy for higher-level domains. It is possible (and in a variety of higher-level disciplines it is true) that there are sufficiently strong regularities and causal relations discernible among structures at the higher level to permit us to frame an explanation of higher-level phenomena strictly in terms of higher-level causes and regularities. Meteorology treats weather phenomena—fronts, high and low pressure areas, tornadoes and thunderstorms, and so forth—as elements in a causal system. And it is credible that meteorology arrives at satisfactory explanations of weather phenomena on the basis of causal models that refer to these elements, without the need for a more fine-grained description of the microstructure of weather phenomena. It is certainly true that the terms of such causal explanations—elevated ocean temperature, the direction of the Gulf Stream, and the occurrence of severe coastal storms—can be reduced to facts about ensembles of constituent factors (water molecules). But there is no scientific need to do so, and no explanatory purposes would be served in this process.

This argument suggests that the a priori basis for the explanatory doctrine of methodological individualism fails. It is perfectly possible that social phenomena might constitute a causal system with strong causal laws; if so, the fact that social phenomena are constituted by individual actions would not mandate that social *explanations* should be reduced to facts about individuals. Thus if methodological individualism is sustainable, it must be supported by considerations specific to social and individual phenomena— not general arguments about intertheoretical reduction.

A second ground of methodological individualism is specific to social science—the skeptical observation that social phenomena are not strongly law-governed and that there do not appear to be extensive examples of strong causal systems of social variables. If there were, this argument goes, it would be reasonable to regard social explanations as autonomous. But because there are not, it is necessary to drop down a level to the constituent elements of social phenomena in order to identify satisfactory explanatory regularities. In this approach, then, methodological individualism is mandated by the paucity of strong social regularities. I will return to this argument below.

Let us consider an example: Durkheim's analysis of suicide rates in different communities (1897/1951). Durkheim's explanation is based on the assumption of *methodological holism*. He holds that individual psychological states can only be explained through reference to facts about the societies in which they find themselves. So psychological states are not more fundamental than social facts but less so. Is it possible to provide an individualistic basis for Durkheim's theory of suicide? Yes. At one level of description, Durkheim asserts a causal relation between a social fact (the community's degree of cohesiveness) with an individual fact (suicide proneness of the

---

Example 9.1 Suicide and anomie

Emile Durkheim analyzes rates of suicide in different communities and finds that they vary over time and space in different social groups. He attempts to explain this difference on the basis of different normative systems that provide cohesion in different societies—religion, family obligations, nationalist ideals—and that provide the individual with his or her social identity. Different social groups possess such systems in varying degrees, and Durkheim introduces the collective property of "anomie" to refer to the state of groups with low levels of shared norms. Such groups lack cohesiveness, and anomie is a measure of the moral disorder of the group. It is a collective property in that it attaches to the group rather than the individual. Durkheim offers a causal hypothesis: A prominent cause of variation in suicide patterns across social groups is the level of anomie that characterizes the group; those with higher levels of anomie will be more prone to suicide. Anomic suicide "results from man's activity's lacking regulation and his consequent sufferings" (Durkheim 1897/1951:258). The level of anomie varies across social groups, according to Durkheim—for example, Protestant groups have higher anomie than Catholic, and professionals higher than farmers. Therefore we should expect higher suicide rates in those groups with higher anomie.

Data: Statistics on rates of suicides in a variety of social groups—Catholics and Protestants, urban and rural groups, married and single people, military and civilian populations

Explanatory model: A causal hypothesis postulating that a collective property of groups (the level of social cohesion) explains differences in suicide rates across groups

Source: Emile Durkheim, *Suicide: A Study in Sociology* (1897/1951)

---

individual). But this social fact does not influence the individual directly; rather it should be understood as a statistical generalization about typical social interactions within the given society—i.e., most such interactions provide the individual with a high degree of psychological satisfaction and a feeling of cohesiveness. A given individual, however, is not influenced by the statistical fact but rather by his or her own personal history of social interactions. In a society with high cohesion, it is likely that most of these social interactions will be positive, thus leading to a positive psychological state. The individual's positive psychological state, however, is caused by the particular interactions in his or her own history. Moreover it is possible (but unlikely) that any given individual may encounter only the infrequent curmudgeons and grouches in the cohesive society. This person will have a less positive psychological state and will be more prone to suicide. This explanation is thus fully consistent with methodological individualism.

REDUCTIONISM AND SUPERVENIENCE

Methodological individualism is related to a more general position in the philosophy of science that concerns itself with relations between adjacent areas of scientific research: the program of reductionism. According to reductionism all lawlike regularities and all types of entities and structures fall in a hierarchy ranging from the most fundamental—subatomic physics— to higher-level domains. (Boyd 1980 and Fodor 1980 provide useful discussions of the doctrine of reductionism in application to cognitive science.) The relation between methodological individualism and reductionism is straight- forward. The ontological thesis requires the reduction of higher-level entities to lower-level entities, the meaning thesis requires the reduction of higher- level concepts to lower-level concepts, and the explanatory thesis requires the reduction of higher-level regularities to lower-level regularities. Thus methodological individualism may be construed as the application of re- ductionism to social science.

Reductionism is a more general doctrine, however. It requires that we conceive of science in terms of strict hierarchies of entities, laws, and explanations in which less fundamental areas of science are to be grounded in more fundamental sciences, leading eventually to physical science. Con- sider, for example, the following domains and sciences:

sociology
social psychology
cognitive science
neurophysiology
cell biology
molecular biology
molecular physics
subatomic physics and quantum mechanics

Each of these domains identifies a class of entities and structures, and each seeks to discern a set of lawlike regularities among these entities and structures. Reductionism maintains (1) that it is possible to provide a rigorous specification of the dimension underlying such a hierarchy and therefore to unambiguously rank any pair of domains and (2) that the entities and laws of higher levels can be reduced to facts about entities and laws at lower levels.

The underlying rationale for reductionism so defined is a view of expla- nation—it is always desirable to explain more complex structures in terms of less complex ones—along with the idea that physical phenomena are the most fundamental. David Lewis describes the doctrine of physicalism in these terms: "Roughly speaking, Materialism is the thesis that physics— something not too different from present-day physics, though presumably somewhat improved—is a comprehensive theory of the world, complete as well as correct" (Lewis 1983:127). According to physicalism, then, a general aim of scientific explanation is to show how higher levels of phenomena are ultimately determined by the physical structures of the world.

Consider an example drawn from twentieth-century biology. Mendelian gene theory postulates a genetic factor that controls heritable traits; molecular biology provides a description of the molecular structures that contain and transmit genetic information. Molecular genetics advances a theory of the molecular composition of the gene and the mechanisms through which genetic information is used in the process of cell specialization, and it permits us to derive the laws of Mendelian genetics. Classical genetics is a higher-level science, and molecular genetics is a lower-level one. The former describes a level of biological structure farther out on the spectrum, ranging from atomic structures to social institutions; the latter describes structures that are closer to the physical basis. The program of reductionism postulates, in this case, that it should be possible to reduce the entities and laws of classical genetics to logical constructs of entities and laws within molecular biology. Genes are chains of proteins on a DNA molecule, and the laws of classical genetics are to be derived from the laws of molecular biology. This is a classic example of intertheoretic reduction: The terms of the higher-level science have been reduced to entities at the lower-level (genes to complex DNA molecules), and the laws of the higher-level science have been derived from the laws of the lower-level science. (See Hull 1974 for an extensive analysis of the successes and failures of this program.)

One way of viewing reductionism is as an explanatory strategy; we can often explain a range of phenomena by showing that they derive from the properties of entities at a lower level of organization. And seen from this point of view, reductionism is an acceptable research strategy. Usually, however, reductionism is put forward in a stronger form, asserting that it is *necessary* to provide such reductions if explanations at the higher level are to be validated. In application to the social sciences, this would mean that social explanations must be couched in terms of the laws of individual psychology. This constraint on explanation is undoubtedly too strong—a conclusion that we can justify by returning to biology. In the case of Mendelian genetic theory, it is plain that Mendel's explanations were genuine scientific explanations of the phenomena of the transmission of traits from parent to offspring. It is also explanatory, and perhaps more deeply so, to know what the molecular-level processes are that underlie genetic transmission of traits, but the latter is not necessary in order to validate the former.

Most philosophers of science now agree that reductionism is not a plausible requirement on scientific concept formation and explanation when we look at specific areas of science. In a variety of examples of intertheory boundaries, it has proved difficult to provide the sorts of reductions of entities and laws that reductionism requires. And pragmatic arguments suggest that explanations couched at higher levels of description are superior to those at lower levels under certain circumstances: (1) when the higher-level explanations are supported by strong empirical regularities at that level and (2) when the prospective lower-level explanation imposes computational costs that make prediction impossible and explanation difficult.

A somewhat weaker requirement has emerged as an attractive alternative to intertheoretic reductionism: the idea of *supervenience*.[1] Supervenience is a doctrine about the relations that obtain between the systems of regularities and facts in a pair of domains. It absorbs the truth of the ontological thesis (that higher-level entities are constituted by lower-level entities) but rejects the doctrines of meaning reduction or explanatory reduction. To say that one level of description supervenes on another is to assert that all distinctions and variations among phenomena at the higher level depend upon distinctions and variations among phenomena at the lower level. David Lewis describes the view in these terms: "A supervenience thesis is a denial of independent variation. . . . To say that so-and-so supervenes on such-and-such is to say that there can be no difference in respect of so-and-so without difference in respect of such-and-such" (Lewis 1983:124).

For example, consider the relation between computation and machine states in computer science. We can describe the performance of a computer at two levels: in terms of the particular sequences of hardware states that the machine goes through and in terms of the computations that it performs. Suppose that we assert that "the computer is calculating the millionth digit of pi." This is a computational description. Then the computer engineer informs us that "the computer is going through a sequence of machine states $S_1, S_2, \ldots$, and finishes in state S_n." This is a machine-state description. The computational-state description supervenes upon the machine-state description: It is impossible for two machines to be in different computational states while being in the same machine state, that is, there can be no difference at the level of computational-state description without a difference at the level of machine-state description. Note, however, that the reverse is not true; a given computational state can be realized in alternative machine states (since different programs may be written that perform the same computation and different types of machines can embody the same program). In other words, a given functional capacity can be realized in a variety of nonequivalent ways. (Call this the feature of functional multiple realizability.) Furthermore, the supervenience thesis does not require that we explain the sequence of computational states by referring only to the sequence of machine states. Such an account would be possible but uninformative; if we want to know how the computer arrived at a solution to the problem, we need to know the process of computation that it embodied, not the sequence of the machine's physical states. In addition, the fact that the same computation can be embodied in many different kinds of machines (computers based on pneumatic tubes, for example) means that an explanation of this computation in terms of this machine will exclude all the alternative machines that are functionally equivalent and perform the same computation.

The supervenience thesis also does not imply that it is possible or desirable to derive regularities at the higher level from regularities at the lower level. The machine example makes this clear: The regularities of behavior of a device that computes arithmetic functions are best described in terms of algorithms (rules of computation) rather than the physical processes that embody these algorithms, and various bits of the device's behavior can be satisfactorily explained by relating it to the stage of computation that the device has reached. Suppose that we have programmed the computer to print out the prime factors of the integers beginning with 100 and we notice that it takes longer and longer on average to print the next number. We might ask why the program is slowing down. And an appropriate and explanatory reply is this: because the algorithm for finding prime factors takes more time for larger numbers.

How does the idea of supervenience help us to analyze the relation between social phenomena and individual action? We may formulate the thesis in these terms: Social phenomena supervene upon individual action and belief. This thesis allows us to incorporate the truth of the MI ontological thesis above; the supervenience claim establishes that social phenomena are wholly dependent on ensembles of individuals. Consider next the concept of multiple realizability, however. Suppose that we conceive of a "bureaucracy" as a hierarchical social organization in which officeholders perform tasks in accord with plans established by a centralized decisionmaker. This is a functional description in that it characterizes individual behavior in terms of functions defined within the organization. A particular bureaucracy is realized in a particular set of individuals at a given time, but it is obvious that a given bureaucracy can be realized in infinitely many different sets of particular individuals without losing its identity. (Similarly the same physical machine can be realized in infinitely many different ensembles of silicon chips.) More significantly, though, there are alternative systems of incentives that could be established to induce officeholders to perform their tasks as described. For example, some implementations might emphasize sticks over carrots, and others carrots over sticks. (This is the problem of institutional design.) So the fact that a particular bureaucracy supervenes upon a particular set of individuals and individual-level incentives does not imply that *only* these individual-level arrangements could implement the same bureaucratic organization. If we are interested in the regularities that can be found among human bureaucracies, then, we should not restrict our attention to the particular realizations of bureaucracies but rather to the social characteristics that bureaucracies share.

Turn now to explanatory adequacy. Suppose that we have arrived at an empirical generalization about bureaucracies—for example, that bureaucracies tend to be conservative in adopting innovations in procedures. How should we explain this regularity? The fact that bureaucracies supervene on particular individuals might suggest that we should look for features in these individuals (or sets of individuals realizing a number of bureaucracies) for explanation of this tendency. However, this effort would be misguided for it is a fact about *bureaucracies*, not about ensembles of individuals, that explains this conservativism concerning innovation. An explanation might go along these lines: Once a set of procedures is established, it is costly to change them even where alternative procedures are more efficient. Or we might hypothesize that the authority of superior to subordinate within a bureaucracy is always less than absolute, so that a significant degree of slippage unavoidably occurs when large-scale changes are mandated from the top; officeholders are able to resist change without penalty. Each of these explanations is set in terms of the concepts used to characterize a bureaucracy as a social organization, and each is superior to what we might call the "fallacy of particularism"— the effort to explain bureaucratic conservativism in terms of the particular characteristics of the men and women who constitute a specific conservative bureaucracy.

These arguments suggest that it is reasonable to hold that social phenomena supervene upon individual phenomena but that this does not imply that social concepts or social explanations need to be reduced to individual-level concepts and explanations. Rather, social analysis needs to be made at the level that provides the basis for the most general and most empirically well-grounded explanations of social phenomena; this may be the level of social institutions, rules, and practices rather than particular patterns of individual behavior.

These conclusions give some support for the position that may be described as maintaining the "autonomy of the social." Most critics of methodological individualism concede that social phenomena are composed of individual agents acting purposively: Armies, social structures, market economies, and wars are all made up of vast numbers of agents engaged in purposive activity. However, a number of anti-individualist positions are possible, even on this assumption. First, it might be held that social structures and entities, though composed of individual agents, cannot be defined exhaustively in strictly individualist terms. Second, it might be held that statements of social regularities may be viewed as genuinely explanatory without even a sketch of a set of regularities of individual behavior that underlie them. And third, it might be held that there are social regularities that are "emergent": They cannot be derived from underlying facts about individual activity at all. In the next section I will consider a line of argument that to some extent reduces this indeterminacy.

THE MICROFOUNDATIONS DEBATE

The issue of the relation between social processes and individual actions has arisen in a somewhat different context within contemporary Marxism, and this discussion has provided more telling reasons for adopting an individualist restriction on social explanation. So let us turn briefly to the issue of the "microfoundations" of Marxist social science.[2] Marxism commonly has advanced macroexplanations of social phenomena in which the object of investigation is a large-scale feature of society and the explanans a description of some other set of macrophenomena. Thus Marxist economists are interested in discovering and explaining the large-scale patterns of economic development based on features of the capitalist economic structure; Marxist political scientists are interested in the ways in which state policy in a capitalist democracy serves the needs of the capitalist economic structure; Marxist sociologists are interested in analyzing patterns of class activity in terms of objective interests (for example, labor organization, mass protest, or organized revolutionary activity) and so forth. In each case the object of investigation is a large-scale characteristic of capitalist society or a supraindividual entity (for example, a social class or a state), and the explanans is a description of some other set of macrophenomena.

Some Marxist theorists have recently argued, however, that macroexplanations need *microfoundations*—detailed accounts of the pathways by which macro-level social patterns evolve. Thus John Roemer writes that "class analysis must have individualist foundations. . . . Class analysis requires microfoundations at the level of the individual to explain why and when classes are the relevant unit of analysis" (Roemer 1982b:513). This doctrine maintains that macroexplanations of social phenomena must be supported by an account of the mechanisms at the individual level through which the postulated social processes work. These theorists have held that it is necessary to describe the circumstances of individual choice and action that give rise to aggregate patterns if macroexplanations are to be adequate. Thus, in explaining the policies of the capitalist state it is not sufficient to observe that this state tends to serve capitalist interests; we also need an account of the processes through which state policies are shaped and controlled so as to produce this outcome.

More specifically, the microfoundations thesis holds that an assertion of an explanatory relationship at the social level (causal, functional, structural) must be supplemented by two things: knowledge of what it is about the local circumstances of the typical individual that leads him or her to act in such a way as to bring about this relationship and knowledge of the aggregative processes that lead from individual actions of that sort to an explanatory social relationship of this sort. (In Chapter 3 we referred to explanations of this type as "aggregative explanations.") This doctrine may be put in both a weak and a strong version. Weakly social explanations must be *compatible* with the existence of microfoundations of the postulated social regularities, which may, however, be entirely unknown. More strongly social explanations must be explicitly grounded on an account of the microfoundations that produce them. I will argue for an intermediate form— that we must have at least an approximate idea of the underlying mechanisms at the individual level if we are to have a credible hypothesis about explanatory social regularities at all. A putative explanation couched in terms of high-level social factors whose underlying individual-level mechanisms are entirely unknown is no explanation at all.

The arguments for the microfoundations thesis stem from specific features of macroexplanation of social phenomena rather than general, a priori arguments about social explanation. The justification for the microfoundations thesis is *not* simply a general preference for intertheoretical reductionism— a preference sometimes found within the philosophy of biology and the philosophy of psychology as well. The microfoundational requirement depends instead on several specific problems that arise in common forms of macroexplanation—problems with functional and collective-interest explanations and the typical weakness of social regularities. One consequence of this is that there may be legitimate forms of macroexplanations in social science that are not subject to these specific criticisms, and in that case microfoundational arguments would be silent.

The problems of collective rationality were discussed in Chapter 3, and the defects of functional explanations were considered in Chapter 5. In each case it was concluded that we need to have an account of the individual-level processes through which the macro-level outcomes emerge—a conclusion equivalent to the microfoundations requirement. A particularly telling argument for the need for microfoundations for macroexplanations stems from the character of social regularities. It was argued above that autonomous explanations in a higher-level discipline depend on the existence of strong empirical regularities among phenomena at this level. Consider by analogy the relation between cognitive psychology and neurophysiology. In cognitive psychology there are strong regularities among cognitive phenomena, so it is credible to hold that various elements of the cognitive system are causally related to others without having specific knowledge about the neurophysiological mechanisms that underlie them.[3]

In the social sciences, however, we often do *not* find the strong types of regularities and laws that would make us confident in the causal connectedness of social phenomena. Instead, we find laws of tendency and exception-laden regularities. (For developed arguments to this effect in connection with Marx's economic analysis, see Little 1986.) The problem here for autonomous social explanations is that for a given class of social phenomena there often are no clear regularities visible at the macro-level at all. In this case we can either give up altogether on the project of explaining the macro-level phenomena, limiting ourselves to providing narratives describing various particular phenomena, or we may turn to an analysis of the underlying mechanisms that produce phenomena of this type. And when we provide an analysis of these mechanisms, we may find that there are regularities at the lower level. In this case, analysis of the microfoundations of the aggregate activity is essential if we are to arrive at a description of the phenomena as law-governed at all.

Here, then, we have a new argument for an individualist stricture on social explanation: Social causation always and unavoidably works through structured individual action, and causal relations among social phenomena can only be established through analysis of the latter because of the common weakness of the causal regularities at the social level. This position draws upon the ontological thesis of methodological individualism and the observation that social regularities are generally much weaker than regularities in other areas of science. And it reinforces the conclusion reached in Chapter 2 that scientific explanation requires that we identify the causal mechanisms that underlie the events and processes we are trying to explain.

Phenomena of underclass politics illustrate the need for microfoundations for social explanations. Classical Marxism postulates that exploitation and class are the central factors that explain processes of underclass politics. Study of various examples of exploitative class societies shows that we do not find the regularity that classical Marxism would predict at the macro-level—that exploited groups eventually support popular movements aimed at assaulting the class system. However when we move to a lower-level description of the phenomena of popular politics—one that analyzes group behavior in terms of the group's specific class arrangements, the variable character of individual political motivation, and the forms of political culture, organization, and leadership available to the group—we find that there are regularities that emerge and divide the phenomena into a number of cases, such as:

- Exploited groups with strong political cultures and ample organizational resources tend to be politically active, tenacious, and effective.
- Exploited groups with weak political cultures and ample organizational resources tend to be only moderately active, vacillatory, and ineffective.
- Exploited groups with strong political cultures and no organizational resources tend to be vigorously active, tenacious, but ineffective.
- Exploited groups with weak political cultures and no organizational resources tend to be inactive, vacillatory, and collectively ineffective.

The search for microfoundations is critical in cases where the regularities existing at the social level are weak and only express tendencies. In this case we must identify the microfoundations of the social phenomena in question to identify the macro-level regularities at all. Attention must be given to some of the concrete mechanisms through which political behavior is shaped, if an empirically adequate theory of popular politics is to be constructed from a Marxian perspective.

If we take the microfoundations approach seriously, it is important to identify individual-level motivational structures and forms of consciousness. We need a specific understanding of the ways in which individuals in various social groups differ in terms of their political ideas, their attitudes (toward family, community, and state), their moral sense, and so on. For some purposes of social explanation, it is sufficient to provide only an abstract and schematic description of these variables (as do rational choice explanations based on a thin conception of rationality, for example), but for other purposes it is necessary to have more concrete information about these variables. Charles Sabel's *Work and Politics* (1982) offers this sort of analysis of working-class attitudes based on consideration of the various social circumstances within which industrialized work takes place (Example 6.3).

Once we accept the point that macroexplanations require microfoundations, we must next ask what types of individual-level processes we should look for. And here there are two broad families of answers: rational choice models and social-psychology motivational models. The first approach attempts to explain a given social process as the aggregate result of large numbers of individuals pursuing individually rational strategies. The second approach attempts to explain the social phenomenon as the complex outcome of a variety of motives, rational and nonrational, that propel individual action.

Example 9.2   The moral basis of resistance

G. Barrington Moore, Jr., attempts to explain variations in political behavior across different exploited groups on the basis of analysis of the sense of justice that these groups embody. He examines a number of cases of social situations in which a group is severely mistreated and in which organized resistance sometimes occurs and sometimes does not. His examples include the labor struggles of German workers in 1848, coal miners in the Ruhr before 1914, and prisoners in German concentration camps. Moore writes, "Evidently social rules and their violation are crucial components in moral anger and a sense of injustice. Essentially it is anger at the injury one feels when another person violates a social rule" (Moore 1978:5). His hypothesis is that human beings absorb a specific "sense of justice" from the cultures in which they find themselves, that this sense of justice structures the way that they perceive actions and events in their social environment, and that the actions that they take in response to these actions and events depends heavily on the particulars of the embodied sense of justice. Groups whose sense of justice is offended by mistreatment are more likely to resist than those who accept the moral legitimacy of their conditions.

Data: historical data on the behavior of a number of exploited or oppressed groups

Explanatory model: hypothesis about the causal importance of a shared sense of justice in explaining patterns of social behavior based on a comparative method

Source: G. Barrington Moore, Jr., *Injustice: The Social Bases of Obedience and Revolt* (1978)

I have given primary emphasis to mechanisms depending on the rational decisionmaking processes of individuals, but much social explanation depends on the idea that norms and values influence individual behavior. Consider, for example, G. Barrington Moore's explanation of patterns of resistance to oppression (Example 9.2). Here Moore is explaining collective behavior in a variety of historical circumstances on the basis of a sense of justice that is to be found in those various social groups. But, as we saw in the discussion of Durkheim's theory of suicide (Example 9.1), this explanation too is fully compatible with the microfoundations requirement because the norms to which the explanation refers are embodied in the individuals who constitute the various social groups. Individuals acquire their sense of justice through specific meaningful interactions with other people; they transmit this sense of justice through their behavior toward other people. A sense of justice, then, is embodied in the individual and is transmitted through well-understood mechanisms at the individual level.

CONCLUSION

The ontological thesis of methodological individualism is uncontroversial but weak: It has few if any implications for the form that social explanations should take. The truth of this portion of methodological individualism may be expressed in the claim that social phenomena supervene on the actions and intentions of individuals. Strictures on meanings and explanations imposed by methodological individualism are unpersuasive, however. There are no convincing general reasons to suppose that social concepts should be reducible to individual concepts or that social explanations should be derivable from laws of individual-level phenomena. However there are several grounds for accepting a stricture on social explanation that has much in common with methodological individualism. These reasons derive from specific features of social phenomena and social regularities. First there are a number of modes of social explanation that can only be supported if they are accompanied by accounts of the individual-level processes that give rise to these explanatory relations: functional explanations and group-interest explanations. And second the empirical regularities found among social phenomena—for example, correlations between types of parliamentary systems and levels of voter participation—are often too weak to allow us to postulate strong causal relationships at this level. For each of these reasons, social scientists need to bear in mind the importance of having some idea of the underlying individual-level mechanisms through which social explanatory relationships obtain.

I therefore defend a weak requirement of individualism that has much in common with the microfoundations program: Social explanations of macrophenomena must be such that it is possible to indicate, at least schematically, the mechanisms at the level of local individual behavior through which the aggregate phenomena emerge. Macroexplanations, that is, require microfoundations at the level of the processes of individual choice and action through which the social patterns and processes evolve. This view may be formulated in these terms: All social processes, causal influences, systemic interactions, etc., are ultimately embodied in the actions of individual actors within a specific social and natural environment. Whenever a social explanation is offered according to which a social factor gives rise to any explanandum, it must be possible in principle to indicate the mechanisms through which individual activity gives rise to this outcome.

For a great many social explanations it is very easy to satisfy this requirement. For example, when Robert Brenner asserts that the system of property ownership in land causally influences the rate of technological change in farming (Example 6.6), the mechanism that he postulates is the rational behavior of farmers, landlords, potential investors, etc., making decisions in the context of the property system. But in considering examples of social explanation, it is always instructive to bear in mind this question: Through what processes at the individual level do the causal relations among social structures and factors described by the author occur?

It is apparent that the microfoundations thesis is related to the doctrine of methodological individualism, but the two are not identical. It is entirely compatible with the microfoundations thesis that a microfoundational account of the determinants of individual action should refer to social relations, structures, etc. The latter are grounded in facts about individuals, but the thesis does not require that the explanation supply the details of such a grounding. Thus the microfoundations thesis is not committed to anything like the individualist thesis about the meaning of social concepts.

NOTES

1. See Kim (1984a, 1984b) for important statements of the theory of supervenience.

2. The arguments of this section closely follow my analysis in *The Scientific Marx* (Little 1986: 127–53).

3. Jerry Fodor provides an important discussion of some of the relations between levels of psychological theory and brain science in "Special Sciences, or the Disunity of Science as a Working Hypothesis" (1980). For an exceptionally clear treatment of reductionism and physicalism see Jeffrey Poland (forthcoming).

SUGGESTIONS FOR FURTHER READING

Alexander, Jeffrey C., Bernhard Giesen, Richard Munch, Neil J. Smelser, eds. 1987. *The Micro-Macro Link.*

Boyd, Richard. 1980. "Materialism Without Reductionism: What Physicalism Does Not Entail."

Elster, Jon. 1985. *Making Sense of Marx.*

Lukes, Steven. 1973. "Methodological Individualism Reconsidered."

Miller, Richard. 1978. "Methodological Individualism and Social Explanation."

Roemer, John. 1982b. "Methodological Individualism and Deductive Marxism."

10
RELATIVISM

A common impression gained from the study of the social sciences is that of diversity across social groups and cultures. Anthropologists describe widely different practices governing family relationships, sociologists report substantial differences in the moral beliefs of different social groups, ethnographers and historians detail strikingly different frameworks of belief about the world in different social settings, and so on through a long list of social characteristics. Some philosophers and social scientists have drawn a general conclusion from the evidence of social diversity. They have held that *cultural relativism* is a deep and abiding feature of human society. Different cultures have distinct ways of managing human relationships, acquiring beliefs about the world, and evaluating human action, and there is no transcultural standard in terms of which to describe and evaluate these different frameworks. This perspective is particularly welcome to interpretive social scientists, for it validates their view that each culture is a unique particular and that social inquiry must begin with the meaningful self-definitions of the culture under study.

This finding brings with it a paradox for the social sciences for if we take as one of the goals of science the discovery of generalizations, then this radical diversity appears as a large obstacle to progress in the social sciences. However, many of the arguments in the preceding chapters provide a basis for narrowing this relativist conclusion. In particular, the explanatory frameworks of rational choice theory and materialism each purport to offer a basis for explaining human behavior via cross-cultural universals (the idea that human societies must adopt social arrangements that function to satisfy material needs and the notion of rational self-interest). And to the extent that these concepts do provide a basis for successful explanations in a variety of cultural settings, the strong claims of cultural relativism are undercut. These arguments are considered in Chapters 2, 6, and 8.

In this chapter I will discuss several versions of cultural relativism: conceptual relativism, belief relativism, and normative relativism. Conceptual relativism (following some strands of recent thought in the philosophy of language and science) holds that different languages embody incommensurable conceptual systems, with the result that different groups or cultures may possess incommensurable ways of categorizing the world. Belief relativism maintains that different cultures possess different standards of belief assessment that may be fundamentally irresolvable, and as a result they possess incommensurable systems of belief; rationality itself is culture-bound. Normative relativism states that different cultures embody radically distinct value systems, so that social science must start anew for every cultural group in attempting to identify the norms and values that underlie everyday life. In each case the core idea is that there is no common theory or standard of evaluation with which to compare or describe concepts, standards of rationality, or norms. In this chapter I will survey and assess the arguments advanced in these three areas and attempt to provide limits on the relativist impulse in each. In general I will argue that relativist claims are generally overstated and that human rationality permits a greater degree of comparison, evaluation, and communication than relativism admits.

The problem of relativism is tied to the search for cross-cultural *universals*—features of conceiving, reasoning, or acting that are found in most or all societies. If such universals exist, then it is tempting to conclude that these derive from human nature, prior to culture and socialization. And arguments in previous chapters developing the rational choice model of social explanation provide an indication of what some of those universals are: concern for individual welfare, the bindingness of some normative constraints, a capacity to arrive at true beliefs about the environment, a capacity to deliberate, and a capacity to regulate action in accordance with a plan. (These are the "core features" of human agency described in Chapter 7.) This chapter, then, begins with the fact of social diversity and attempts to narrow the scope of cultural relativism. It is certainly true that there is immense diversity across cultures, but it will be argued here that there are a number of core features of human society that underlie all cultures—even if they find expression in seemingly different forms.

CONCEPTUAL RELATIVISM

Conceptual relativism asserts that there may be incommensurable differences between "our" concepts and "theirs" and that there are no rational grounds for choosing between these systems. We may formulate this position in these terms:

- Different cultures employ radically different conceptual schemes defining what exists in the world, how things are organized in time and space, what sorts of relations obtain among things, and how some things influence others.
- It is not possible to give rational grounds for concluding that one such scheme is more congruent to reality than another.

The first thesis singles out the most basic assumptions that a people make about the world around them. In our scientific worldview we identify objects with fixed causal properties, located in space and time, and we stipulate that every event has a cause. However the cultural relativist maintains that

---

Example 10.1   Space and time in the Hopi worldview

Benjamin Whorf was a linguist and ethnographer who devoted much of his time during the 1930s to the study of the Hopi language. Through his study he came to the conclusion that Hopi conceptions of space, time, causation, and other fundamental metaphysical categories appeared to be radically different from the counterpart concepts in European languages. The philosopher Kant argued in the eighteenth century that all rational thought depends on the existence of a universal set of concepts in terms of which the agent analyzes the empirical world; physical object, space, time, and causation were among the ideas that Kant believed fundamental and universal. But Whorf argues that the Hopi conceptual scheme was fundamentally different from this Euclidean, Laplacean framework. He writes, "The Hopi language is seen to contain no words, grammatical forms, constructions or expressions that refer directly to what we call 'time,' or to past, present, or future, or to enduring or lasting. . . . At the same time, the Hopi language is capable of accounting for and describing correctly, in a pragmatic or operational sense, all observable phenomena of the universe" (Whorf 1956:57–58). He concludes, therefore, that various cultures may embody conceptual systems so different that they categorize the world in radically dissimilar ways.

Data: ethnographic and linguistic data describing Hopi language
Explanatory model: to understand the Hopi worldview it is necessary to
   reconstruct a radically different set of concepts in terms of which the Hopi
   conceive of the world
Source: Benjamin Whorf, *Language Thought and Reality: Selected Writings of
   Benjamin Lee Whorf* (1956)

---

this is merely one parochial conceptual scheme among many, and the variety of alternatives may be estimated through study of a number of the world's non-Western cultures.

We may begin our discussion of this thesis with a celebrated example—the Whorf hypothesis (Example 10.1). Linguist Benjamin Whorf advanced a theory of Hopi language that represents a particularly strong version of conceptual relativism. Contemporary anthropologist Gary Witherspoon has taken this set of ideas a step further in his consideration of Navajo language and metaphysics (Example 10.2). In Witherspoon's account there are deep differences in the way that Navajo and European cultures divide the world into objects, and it takes deft ethnographic investigation to discover the underlying Navajo conceptual scheme. Both Whorf and Witherspoon, then, hold that non-Western cultures embody different conceptual schemes in terms of which they analyze and categorize everyday reality, and they suggest that it is difficult or impossible to translate these schemes into the Western scientific worldview.

Modern authors discuss conceptual relativism in terms of the idea of incommensurability. In these terms the Whorf hypothesis is that different cultures may have distinct and incommensurable conceptual schemes. The

---

Example 10.2   Navajo syntax and semantics

Gary Witherspoon holds that Navajo speakers presuppose a conceptual scheme organized around a dualism of active and static forms and that Navajo schemes of classification of things (kinship, animals, natural objects) reflect this dualism (Witherspoon 1977:179). The concept of *control* is central: Objects are ranked in a hierarchy according to what types of things can control or influence what other types (Witherspoon 1977:71). He attempts to support these contentions through analysis of the syntax and semantics of Navajo language. "The horse was kicked by the mule" is grammatical and acceptable, whereas "the horse was kicked by the man" is not and provokes hilarity when uttered. Witherspoon's analysis of this asymmetry is that the sentences have been mistranslated by Westerners, and that the sense of the basic construction is "caused itself to be kicked by." Horses and mules are on a par with each other in terms of active powers of control, whereas horses are inferior to men. It is thus a laughable inversion of the control hierarchy to attribute control to the horse over the man (Witherspoon 1977:75–76).

Data: ethnographic study of Navajo language and culture
Explanatory model: the conceptual structure of Navajo language is radically
    unlike European conceptual schemes
Source: Gary Witherspoon, *Language and Art in the Navajo Universe* (1977)

---

general idea is that two conceptual schemes are incommensurable if it is impossible to establish simple definitional equivalence between individual concepts in the two schemes. Suppose that you and I take a walk in the woods and it emerges that my conceptual scheme is more refined than yours: I distinguish between elms, oaks, and beeches, whereas you refer to trees; I distinguish squirrels and rabbits, and you refer to "small forest animals." Further, suppose that I lack the more abstract categories of "tree," "animal," and so forth. These two schemes are distinct but not incommensurable; instead, it is possible to establish simple definitional equivalences between your concepts and mine. Thus your concept of "tree" is equivalent to the union of my concepts of "elm," "oak," and "beech." One way of putting this point is in terms of the ways in which we each break the world down into entities. In this case you and I identify the same entities— particular trees and animals—but place them under more and less comprehensive categories. The two conceptual structures can be aligned so that they overlap precisely; everything that is a "tree" on your scheme is either an oak, elm, or beech on mine and so forth for all other concepts.

What, then, is genuine incommensurability? An important contemporary argument for conceptual incommensurability comes from Thomas Kuhn's analysis of conceptual change in the history of science. Kuhn holds that scientific research is organized around a *paradigm*: a "strong network of commitments—conceptual, theoretical, instrumental, and methodological" (T. Kuhn 1970:42). Kuhn argues for a thesis of incommensurability of concepts across paradigms (T. Kuhn 1970:148–50). A paradigm is a set of models of scientific explanation, exemplary experiments, background assumptions about the world, and the like in the context of which researchers formulate more specific research problems.[1] Paradigms embody comprehensive worldviews, they define the categories in terms of which investigators organize the data available to them, and competing paradigms implicitly constitute systems of concepts and beliefs that cannot be intertranslated. Meanings of theoretical terms, interpretations of empirical data, theoretical assertions, and standards of inference are incommensurable across paradigms. Though a classical physicist and a relativity theory physicist both appear to refer to "mass," in fact this is no more than a case of a homophone; the meanings of this term in the two systems are radically different and mutually incomprehensible. These arguments offer further support for Kuhn's skepticism about a transcendent scientific method for if a theoretical dispute cannot even be couched in a language comprehensible in an unambiguous way to both sides, then clearly there can be no logical resolution of the issue.[2]

Another important argument for incommensurability can be derived from a position advanced by W.V.O. Quine concerning the possibility of translation from one language to another. He argues for the "indeterminacy of translation" (Quine 1960:26–79). According to this view there is no fact of the matter about the correctness of sentence-sentence equivalence when we translate from one language to another; instead, by altering other sentence-sentence pairs suitably, we can provide an overall translation scheme that is consistent with all the speakers' dispositions. "Manuals for translating one language into another can be set up in divergent ways, all compatible with the totality of speech dispositions, yet incompatible with one another. In countless places they will diverge in giving, as their respective translations of a sentence of the one language, sentences of the other language which stand to each other in no plausible sort of equivalence however loose" (Quine 1960:27). According to this position, for any pair of languages there are alternative schemes of translation that are equally consistent with all available evidence but that are not equivalent. The implication of this argument for conceptual relativism goes along these lines: If translation between our language and theirs is indeterminate, then there are equally well-justified hypotheses available to us about their concepts, and there is no way for us to choose among these alternatives. (Hookway 1978 explores the implications of this thesis for anthropology.)

Return now to the example above. Suppose that your concepts and mine are more alien to each other than considered there. I conceive of the world as filled with individual things—cubes of sugar, rabbits, trees—but you conceive of it as consisting of quantities of stuff—sugar-stuff, rabbit-stuff, tree-stuff. That is, you do not possess the concept of an individual thing but rather the concept of different kinds of stuff distributed over the world in clumps. When I say "there is a rabbit," I mean "there is a thing that is a rabbit." When you say "there is a rabbit," however, you mean "there is a bit of rabbit-stuff." (This example is loosely derived from Quine's "gavagai" example in his discussion of the indeterminacy of translation.) Finally, suppose that you speak Alien rather than English; therefore your sentence is "gavagai," which I correlate with "there is a rabbit." In this case you and I have fundamentally different ways of breaking up the world—I into things and you into quantities of stuff—and yet there is no way for me to discover the difference by questioning you.

Here, then, we arrive at the most important idea underlying the notion of incommensurable conceptual schemes: Two cultures may embody radically different frameworks of analysis of the world—what sorts of things there are, how things are individuated from each other, what the structure of space and time is—and yet it may be impossible to discover these differences through ethnographic inquiry.

Upon inspection the arguments for conceptual relativism break down into two types. First, there are several a priori arguments to the effect that it is *possible* that different language communities might employ incommensurable conceptual schemes. Quine's indeterminacy of translation argument and Kuhn's arguments for incommensurability each provide support for this conclusion. Arguments in the second group are empirical; they represent a series of claims to the effect that specific language groups do in fact employ conceptual schemes that are incommensurable with our own. And the force of the two sorts of arguments are quite different: The a priori possibility of radically different conceptual schemes is difficult to refute, but empirical attempts to identify existing schemes incommensurable with our own appear to have failed. This suggests, then, that the thesis of conceptual relativism is logically coherent but not true of existing human cultures.

Consider first the strength of the a priori arguments for the possibility of incommensurable conceptual schemes. Several philosophers have argued that the notion of radical incommensurability is unsupportable because they make the goal of translating across speech communities unintelligible. William Newton-Smith contends, for example, that arguments for conceptual relativism are forced to give up the notion of truth in favor of "truth-for-them" and "truth-for-us." But, he argues, the possibility of translation depends on the availability of truth conditions in terms of which to pair sentences in the two languages. So if we give up the notion of truth, we are equally forced to give up the hope of translating across conceptual schemes (Newton-Smith 1982:110–13). Donald Davidson offers similar criticisms of conceptual relativism in his essay "On the Very Idea of a Conceptual Scheme" (1974). He argues that the idea of incommensurable conceptual schemes collapses of its own weight: If schemes were incommensurable, then all communication would be impossible across schemes. This impossibility is not found to exist; therefore it is not true that human cultures embody incommensurable conceptual schemes.

Likewise, various philosophers of science have cast doubt on Kuhn's arguments about the incommensurability of scientific conceptual schemes. The most convincing line of argument turns on scientific realism—the view that scientific concepts refer to real entities in the world. What makes communication across conceptual schemes in science feasible, in this approach, is the possibility of shared reference to real physical objects and properties. The Newtonian conception of mass treats this quantity as invariant, whereas the relativistic conception of mass is not invariant. For Kuhn this is a deep and unbridgeable conceptual difference. But for a scientific realist, it suffices that the classical physicist and the relativistic physicist both refer to the same physical quantity and share a number of experimental techniques in terms of which they can identify and measure this quantity. Shared reference enables each scientist to translate the other's beliefs and assertions into counterpart claims within his or her own theory and to identify the particular disagreements of belief about the properties of these objects that divide the two theories. (For arguments to this effect, see Newton-Smith 1981:164 ff.) It is thus possible to absorb many of Kuhn's important insights on the character of conceptual change in science without accepting his conclusions about incommensurability. I conclude that it is possible for meaningful communication to occur across paradigm boundaries, that it is possible for empirical methods to narrow the range of disagreement across paradigms, and that the standards internal to a given discipline may be assessed in terms of their rational suitability for the problem of discovering empirical truths.

These arguments against conceptual relativism have a good deal of force, but they cannot be taken as definitive refutations of the possibility of conceptual incommensurability. What they show is that existing philosophical arguments in favor of incommensurability are weaker than they have often appeared.

Whatever the force of these a priori arguments, it is the empirical issue of conceptual relativism that is of greatest concern for us. So let us now return to the Whorf and Witherspoon arguments—empirical arguments to the effect that there are specific cases in which conceptual relativism obtains. Whorf and Witherspoon maintain that they have identified language communities whose most basic conceptual structure is radically dissimilar from ours. Is this a reasonable conclusion to draw from the evidence that they cite? There appear to be persuasive grounds for doubting this. First, there is the problem of cross-cultural interpretation raised by Davidson and Newton-Smith above. If Hopi concepts are incommensurable with European concepts, then it is difficult to see how the ethnographer could ever catch on to them. Communication requires a core set of shared beliefs and concepts; if these are lacking, it is impossible to interpret meanings across language groups. This argument appears to present relativist anthropologists with a dilemma: They can either maintain their relativism and abandon the hope of interpreting the utterances of the other culture, or they can narrow the scope of their relativist claims sufficiently to provide a basis for cross-cultural interpretation. The most natural approach to interpretation across cultural boundaries involves the idea that the ethnographer identifies ordinary objects and their properties and then begins to construct a translation manual for more abstract concepts. But if we hypothesize that the foreign culture conceives of even ordinary objects in radically different ways than we do, then we lack a starting point in this process of interpretation.

Second, there is the related problem of empirical evaluation of a hypothesis about incommensurability. It is one thing to learn that a foreign culture has a concept of a kind of thing that we do not have—for example, unicorns. It is quite another to suppose that the most basic metaphysical categories are different in two cultures for the problem of how we would ever provide empirical support for such a supposition is a perplexing one. Here we can turn Quine's argument about the indeterminacy of translation on its head: Whatever evidence is offered in favor of incommensurability can equally be construed as supporting an alternative translation scheme in which the two language groups share the same concepts about ordinary objects.

Finally, there is an alternative interpretation of the situation of Hopi and Navajo language that avoids conceptual relativism while at the same time preserving the central insights offered by Whorf and Witherspoon. This alternative requires that we distinguish between concepts defining ordinary objects and higher-level beliefs about the properties of those objects. From this perspective, we should postulate that the two cultures share a common world of ordinary objects—trees, animals, hills, buildings, and persons. Each culture, then, possesses a core set of concepts in terms of which speakers individuate things—the concepts of space, time, causal relation, object and property, for example. In addition, each possesses a core set of beliefs about ordinary objects that are shared across the cultural boundary—for example, "objects are heavy," "bread satisfies hunger," or "horses have four legs." Finally, each culture may have a distinctive set of general beliefs about the world that are quite foreign to the other—for example, our beliefs that "the universe is expanding," "matter is interchangeable with energy," or "the earth has a molten core" or their beliefs that "higher-level things must control lower-level things," "trees have spirits," or "history is cyclical." The latter beliefs may be described as "metaphysical"—they reflect particularly deep assumptions and presuppositions that each culture makes about the world and lead to inferences that appear ungrounded to persons from the other culture. Once these assumptions are identified, however, the appearance of conceptual relativism is replaced by a recognition of deep but mutually intelligible disagreements about the way the world works.

I conclude, then, that neither a priori nor empirical arguments establish conceptual relativism; instead, there is good reason to suppose that human cultures share a core set of concepts and beliefs defining the structure of the ordinary world—what sorts of objects there are and what observable properties they have. This core set of concepts and beliefs establishes the possibility of interpretation across cultural boundaries, and it corresponds to the real, observable characteristics of ordinary objects. The existence of an objective shared world with observable properties, then, provides the basis for a core of concepts and beliefs across cultures. And it is clear that this core is surrounded by a network of concepts and assumptions that are *not* shared across cultural boundaries. It is the shared core of ordinary concepts that establishes the possibility of interpretation; it is the diverging assumptions and concepts at more abstract levels that produce the diversity of worldviews in different cultures.

What conclusions may we draw about the thesis of conceptual relativism? This discussion makes several points clear. It is undoubtedly true that different cultures have different sets of concepts in the minimal sense that they single out different types of things and classify them differently. Shore-dwelling peoples may have a much more articulated way of classifying shellfish than inland peoples, for example.[3] Moreover no empirical arguments are available to suggest that different human cultures have radically different conceptions of what a thing is—how objects are identified and individuated. Navajo, Andaman Islander, and Manhattanite alike distinguish between one lamppost and another; that is, they share the metaphysics of objects and properties. It is also possible, though not proven, that some cultures have a different conception of causal relations than the modern scientific worldview: Whereas modern Western science does not permit occult causes or action at a distance, some cultures may permit magical causal relations among events. In such a case "their" conception of the way the world works is importantly different from ours. The more metaphysical arguments advanced by Whorf to the effect that the Hopi lack our conception of space and time, though tantalizing, are unconvincing. It is very difficult to see how appropriate evidence could be offered to justify such a conclusion. And finally, none of the arguments considered above gives convincing ground for believing that the conceptual differences conceded here represent incommensurable differences among cultures. Instead, through further conversation it is possible for persons within a pair of schemes to identify the differences between them. We can compare schemes of classification by considering the entities that each ranges under a given concept, we can compare causal theories by noting the types of entities that are thought to have causal influence on other entities, and so on. I conclude, then, that radical conceptual relativism is a philosophical position without empirical support in the social sciences.

RATIONALITY AND RELATIVISM

The most challenging claim of cultural relativism is that there are no culture-neutral standards of belief rationality. Instead, various cultures embody different standards in terms of which to evaluate "factual" beliefs, and there is no sense in which one such set is superior to another. This problem is raised by the wide diversity of belief systems involving magic, witchcraft, spiritual forces, and the like in various cultures. In their ordinary lives men and women in "primitive" societies interpret crop failures, pieces of good fortune, the rise and fall of leaders, and the vicissitudes of health as the effects of a variety of occult forces. And some philosophers have doubted that there is any culture-neutral way to argue that one way of understanding the world is more rational than another. Thus Peter Winch writes, "We start from the position that standards of rationality in different societies do not always coincide; from the possibility, therefore, that the standards of rationality current in S are different from our own. So we cannot assume that it will make sense to speak of members of S as discovering something which we have also discovered; such discovery presupposes initial conceptual agreement" (Winch 1970:97).

For example, we believe that diseases are caused by viruses and bacteria— microscopic organisms that interfere with the body's normal functioning. Various west African cultures, by contrast, believe that illness is caused by spirits, spells, or malevolent ancestors. Our beliefs are grounded in empirical medical science, theirs in a traditional religious cosmogony. And some anthropologists have maintained that such contrasting systems of belief are only that—contrasting but not superior or inferior to one another in terms of rationality.[4] The relativism of rationality thesis may be put in these terms: Different cultures embody different systems of belief-validation, leading to radically different beliefs about the way the world works, and there is no rational basis for concluding that one such system is superior to alternatives. The opposing position is one that gives special priority to the standards of scientific reasoning: observation, deduction, theory construction and testing, and so forth. It maintains that Western scientific methods are superior to traditional, magical, or religious methods for the purpose of arriving at true beliefs: They are the result of the application of a method of belief evaluation that is more veridical than traditional or magical alternatives. This could be called the "rationalist" position, though it has little to do with the rationalism of Descartes or Spinoza. Rather, it is the view that the practices of empirical science conform approximately to the universal standards of belief formation: They embody rationality.

The most radical position on the cultural relativism of standards of rationality comes from Peter Winch, who holds that belief-forming processes are no more than social practices for which there is no overarching basis of criticism or justification. And the ultimate basis of Winch's position is his denial that there is an objective world to which belief systems may or may not correspond; there is no such thing as "truth." Instead, conceptual systems construct the world to which they apply, and there is no possibility of comparing the truth or falsity of beliefs across conceptual systems (Winch 1970).

Do anthropological data concerning the diversity of belief systems support the idea of the relativity of standards of rationality? Or is it justifiable to maintain that scientific methods are more veridical than traditional or religious methods? Steven Lukes defends the idea that there are universal standards of rationality that apply cross-culturally (Lukes 1970). "I shall argue . . . that beliefs are not only to be evaluated by the criteria that are to be discovered in the context in which they are held; they must also be evaluated by criteria of rationality that simply *are* criteria of rationality" (Lukes 1970:208). His argument turns on the view that there is in fact one world in common between us and the alien culture—or else all communication between us and them will be impossible. We reidentify the same ordinary objects in language and make predictions about their behavior. (Note the parallel between this view and the conclusion of the previous section.) We do not share all the same beliefs about this world, but it constitutes the touchstone that permits communication across cultural boundaries in the first place. This establishes the possibility of truth—not truth-for-us and truth-for-them but truth as correspondence with the way the world is (Lukes 1970:210). Truth, then, is cross-cultural, and the standards of rationality are those that produce true beliefs more reliably than alternatives. Here the argument can be built on the conclusions of the previous section: Once we establish a basis for comparing conceptual schemes in terms of the real entities that fall under concepts, we can move forward to empirical and causal reasoning with some confidence of securing agreement.

What are these standards of rationality? There is no short and comprehensive answer to this question, because the standards are closely intertwined with evolving conceptions of scientific method. However, for our purposes we may identify a small list of principles of inference that appear particularly central. First, there is the principle of deductive closure: If you believe a set of sentences S_i, and P logically follows from S_i, then accept P as well (or else give up belief in some of S_i). This principle invokes all of deductive logic; it imposes a general requirement of logical consistency on scientific reasoning. Second, there is an open-ended number of principles of inductive inference—for example, Mill's methods of causal inference, inference to the best explanation, inference to a generalization based on multiple observations, or inference to a hypothesis based on a test of its deductive consequences.

These inductive principles are substantially weaker than the principles of deductive inference. For one thing they are fallible: It is entirely possible that one might study 1,000 swans and find that each is white, and yet it can still be that there are exceptions to the corresponding generalization. Likewise, it may be that the best explanation of an empirical anomaly available at a given time is E, while it eventually turns out that E^* is the correct explanation, and so on for each of these inductive principles. Each is an exception-laden prescription about how to relate evidence to belief; taken as a whole, though, they represent a strong empirical constraint on belief formation. And, I suggest, these are *justified* principles of inference. They are truth enhancing: If we adopt these principles and engage in empirical observation of the world, our system of beliefs will tend to increase in its correspondence to the world.

Let us consider an extended example. Suppose that "they" believe that a certain disease (malaria) is caused by spells cast by the victim's enemies, whereas "we" believe that it is caused by malarial mosquitos. Our belief can be put in these terms: Whenever malarial mosquitos are present, the incidence of malaria will be greater than zero; when malarial mosquitos are entirely absent, the incidence of malaria will fall to zero. Their belief can be put in these terms: Malaria occurs only as a result of a properly executed spell; if no spells are present, there will be no malarias, and if spells are present, there will be some malarias. Through controlled observation and experiment it should be possible to persuade the open-minded magician of several things: (1) When mosquitos are eradicated in a given region, malaria disappears; (2) when proper spells are cast in mosquito-free villages, malaria does not occur; (3) when no spells are cast in mosquito-ridden villages, malaria continues to occur. We may assume, that is, that low-level factual beliefs are shared across cultures. These low-level factual beliefs together imply the falsehood of the second thesis. This follows from the finding that there are malarias in the absence of spells and spells in the absence of malaria. And these facts are consistent with the truth of the first thesis, though they fall short of establishing its truth (because no finite set of observations can establish the truth of a universal statement). This scenario appears to undercut belief relativism, because it leads to the conclusion that beliefs will converge around causal hypotheses once the relevant background facts have been agreed to.

This conclusion is premature, however, because the inference to the mosquito hypothesis does *not* follow directly from the agreed-upon facts about the incidence of mosquitos, spells, and malaria. Instead, these facts must be conjoined with a set of deductive and inductive principles of inference. Thus factual beliefs by themselves do not force one causal hypothesis or another (mosquitos or spells); rather, the causal hypotheses can only be supported if we presuppose deductive logic and some principles of inductive logic (inference to the best explanation, assumptions about the relation between causation and regular association, and the like). When we apply these principles to facts about the presence and absence of spells, mosquitos, and malaria cases, we can infer that mosquitos cause malaria and spells do not. So the belief relativist can reply that the principles of inference supporting this conclusion are precisely what is at issue: Other cultures do not share "our" principles of scientific causal inference, and as a result they arrive at strikingly different beliefs about the causal structure of the world.

In particular, magic specialists can avoid our conclusion in several ways. It is always possible to deny contradiction by positing new characteristics of the magical process (e.g., the relevant kind of magic associated with mosquitos; when the mosquitos go, the spells lose their efficacy). Such modifications are plainly ad hoc, but the principle of scientific inference that dictates that we avoid ad hoc hypotheses is itself up for grabs in this context. Or magic specialists may refuse to engage in this process of reasoning altogether; they may not admit the legitimacy of this effort to arrive at truth through logic and experimentation. And they may take the offensive and hold that our concept of "malarial mosquitos" is itself logically objectionable for we appear to explain the occurrence of the disease as the effect of a factor that has the disposition to produce malaria (the malarial mosquito). This sounds suspiciously circular to our magic specialists.

We are returned, then, to the problem with which we began: Is it possible to offer a culture-neutral justification of deductive and inductive principles of inference? The position I defend here is that the principles of deductive and inductive inference largely capture the standards of belief rationality and that they are justified in terms of a principle of *veridicality:* Adherence to these principles of inference improves the veridicality of the whole of a system of beliefs. If this position is accepted, then we have a strong ground for rejecting the thesis of belief relativism for, in this account, there is an independent standard with which to compare alternative systems of belief formation—the principle of veridicality.

This defense depends ultimately on two points: the commonality of ordinary factual beliefs across cultures and the role of higher-level beliefs in predicting other ordinary factual states of affairs. If we have true beliefs about unobservable causal processes, we will have a basis for true predictions about future states of affairs. If our causal hypotheses are false, our predictions will tend to be false as well. We can now perform a second-order test of a pair of "inference machines" (systems of deductive and inductive inference). Each inference system produces a set of beliefs about the causal properties of the environment and gives rise to a set of predictions about future and counterfactual states of affairs. If there is a clear difference between the two machines in terms of the truth of the predictions their belief set generates, then the machine with greater veridicality is to be preferred rationally.

Why should we adopt this veridicality criterion of rationality? For two reasons: because of a general preference for truth over falsity and because of the great utility of true beliefs in manipulating the environment. There is a close connection between action and true beliefs; actions premised on false beliefs are unlikely to have the intended effects. Groups and persons who use systematically inferior "inference machines" in their dealings with the environment will be substantially less successful than others: Their canoes will sink, their expeditions will be lost in the wilderness, and they will tend to eat poisonous foods. It is difficult to think of a culture that encounters these sorts of problems, from which I infer that, in their ordinary causal inferences, each culture employs a set of inductive standards much like those mentioned above.

There is one final point to be made in this section. The argument I have advanced for the correctness of the standards of inductive and deductive principles is an argument about the rational grounds of belief. I have contended that something like this inference machine is superior to all other alternatives. Thus rationality is *not* culture-relative. This conclusion does not imply that all cultures share these principles (though the technical and social sophistication of non-Western peoples throughout the world implies that they do). Rather it implies that any cultures that deviate widely from these principles have moved away from rationality and truth.

NORMATIVE RELATIVISM

So far we have considered what might be called *cognitive* relativism: relativism of forms of knowledge and knowledge validation. Let us now look at normative relativism. What is the status of the norms and values that are current in a particular culture? Are there moral universals that do (or should) underlie all normative systems? Or are moral norms essentially similar to aesthetic values—highly variable and lacking in rational foundation?

This topic moves us from belief to action and to a consideration of the role and diversity of systems of norms and values in constraining individual behavior. We have seen at various points in this book that human behavior is influenced by moral and normative considerations. Thus men and women volunteer for military service out of regard for the norm of patriotism, devout Muslims refrain from eating pork out of respect for religious prohibitions, peasants are provoked to militancy through offense to their sense of justice, and parents forgo present consumption for the future well-being of their children. (Recall our discussion in Example 9.2 of Barrington Moore's study of variations in political behavior across different exploited groups based on analysis of the sense of justice that these groups embody.) In each case we have an example of individual conduct that deviates from the straight lines of means-end rationality by accepting moral or normative restraints. Finally, it is commonly observed that these normative commitments are different from one human community to another. Some communities put a high priority on abstract justice, whereas others place a higher value on personal and family relations. Some regard infanticide with abhorrence, and others regard the practice as a legitimate instrument of family planning. These variations in normative commitments give rise to the thesis of *moral relativism*.

Moral relativism is the view that different cultures embody different and incompatible systems of moral values and that there is no rational basis for preferring one system over the other (except from the perspective of a contending value system). Relativists maintain that every society embodies such a set of norms and values and that there is fundamental diversity among value systems of various cultures—the schemes of valuation through which persons evaluate themselves, their friends and enemies, their social arrangements, their artifacts, and so on. Such systems govern local conceptions of justice, manliness, politeness, and beauty. This position may be put in the following way: The systems of norms that regulate human conduct are variable from one culture to another, and there is no rational basis for preferring one system except from the point of view of that system. Consider, for example, the norms that govern family life—what the obligations of a parent to a child are, what the scope of young generation freedom is, what forms of domination are acceptable between male and female, etc. It is well known that family structures vary widely from culture to culture; in some patriarchal societies decisionmaking is concentrated in the senior male, but in others the female has primary authority. In some cultures children are given wide scope for choice, and in others they are expected to follow their parents' wishes.

At least part of this thesis is incontestable. The norms that govern ordinary life—family relations, citizen-state relations, economic relations, and the like—are plainly variable across the world's cultures. This establishes the fact that there are wide bands of variation in social norms. The harder question is whether *all* norms are variable in this way. Some commentators have tried to argue that there are some normative principles that are human universals—either because of common features of the human condition or a common evolutionary history. These theories are forms of *naturalism*—the view that certain facts about the natural situation of human beings determine the content of at least some moral principles. James Scott's theory of the moral economy of the peasant represents a modest version of the first option. Scott holds that the circumstances of peasant production in a variety of cultural settings give rise to an ethic emphasizing the right of all members of society to have a living within current social arrangements (Scott 1976). This ethic may be described as a sense of justice. Scott writes of the subsistence ethic, "Although the desire for subsistence security grew out of the needs of cultivators—out of peasant economics—it was socially experienced as a pattern of moral rights or expectations. . . . The subsistence ethic, then, is rooted in the economic practices and social exchanges of peasant society. As a moral principle, as a right to subsistence, I believe I can show that it forms the standard against which claims to the surplus by landlords and the state are evaluated" (Scott 1976:6–7).

Scott's theory of the subsistence ethic contains two pertinent assumptions: first that there is a common sense of justice experienced among members of a wide range of peasant societies and second that this ethic is caused by common "existential circumstances" of peasants the world over. Peasants are subject to the vagaries of weather and the claims of more powerful agents (landlords, tax officials, etc.), they live close to the subsistence margin, and the subsistence ethic is a natural normative scheme for persons in these circumstances to develop. Obviously the latter conclusion has a functionalist ring to it; it appears to presuppose the idea that normative systems that satisfy important social needs will tend to emerge. As we saw in Chapter 5, this set of assumptions is suspect unless we can stipulate a social mechanism that plausibly leads to this outcome. In this case, though, there is a possible mechanism in the form of the self-interested behavior of peasants: As they formulate norms to deploy in their ordinary lives, they will tend to adopt norms that promote their own security and welfare, and the subsistence ethic does this well.

Suppose that we accept this story about the origins of the subsistence ethic. What does this tell us about normative relativism? In a small way it narrows the scope of relativism by showing that there are normative schemes that characterize a whole class of cultures. What it does not do, however, is give rational ground for the quasi-universal normative scheme. The discovery that peasant societies contain moral systems that condemn landlords who refuse to remit rents in times of crisis does not show that it is really wrong for them to behave in this way; it only shows that many cultures judge it so.

Consider a second possible reply to moral relativism, one that turns on the evolutionary history of the human species rather than the circumstances of human social life. This line is taken by sociobiologists who hope to show that at least some parts of human moral psychology have an evolutionary background. Here the general approach is to draw an analogy between moral behavior and other forms of human behavior that are plainly grounded in evolutionary history—for example, cognitive capacities. The fact that people are able to distinguish among thousands of human faces is an example of a cognitive capacity that plausibly developed within the human cognitive repertoire because of its positive effects on reproductive success. That is, there is a neurophysiological basis for this capacity; it is "natural" that human beings are able to distinguish among thousands of faces.

Sociobiologists attempt to arrive at a similar analysis of ethical competence. Human behavior shows a patterned regularity of deference to certain basic norms—e.g., a moral aversion to committing child abuse. (This behavior might be summarized under the principle "it is wrong to inflict gratuitous pain on children.") Sociobiologists now argue that there may be a genetic basis for this behavioral regularity; they refer to the reproductive advantage conferred on parents who embody this restraint over those who do not. I will not attempt to evaluate the empirical case for such a conclusion (Philip Kitcher subjects this line of argument to devastating criticism [Kitcher 1985:417–23]). But two observations are salient. First, it appears fairly clear that the best we could hope for along these lines is an account of the *capacity* for moral behavior—not a particular set of moral principles or aversions. And second, if it were demonstrable—which it probably is not— that all human beings embody a genetically fixed aversion to child abuse, this would reduce the scope of cultural relativism only slightly for the most obvious feature of human normative behavior is *not* its fixity but rather the reverse.

Thus far we have concentrated on the question of whether there are any normative universals found across cultures. And I have argued that, if there are, they are rare and that this does not tell us anything very deep about human moral principles. In particular, it does not show that the moral universals are valid. Let us turn then to the question of the relativism of moral standards. This is a philosophical position—not primarily a social science issue. It is directly analogous to the problem of the rationality of standards of belief in the preceding section. This form of moral relativism amounts to a claim that there is no such thing as moral truth. Rather there are a variety of moral systems that are incompatible or incommensurable, and there is no rational basis for preferring one to another.

Gilbert Harman offers an interpretation of moral beliefs along these lines. He holds that moral obligations are constituted by an implicit agreement among members of a social group (Harman 1975). This represents a *conventionalist* interpretation: Moral principles are akin to social conventions that regulate individual action through the individual's acceptance of this norm, in the recognition that most or all other members of the social group do so as well. In this account the moral requirement that one should treat other persons with respect derives from the fact that this principle is embodied in the actions of members of a social group; in societies in which this norm is not conventionally respected, there is no such obligation. (J.L. Mackie [1977] makes similar arguments in *Ethics: Inventing Right and Wrong*.) Along this line of thought, moral principles are without foundation but serve an instrumental function in social life; they are at one remove based on social utility.

These views represent various forms of philosophical moral relativism, a position that has acquired a great deal of support from the general climate of antifoundationalism in twentieth-century philosophy. Many philosophers are inclined to agree that there is no ultimate foundation for moral belief; instead systems of values are inherited within a moral culture, and moral theory serves to articulate and rationalize these culturally specific values. Let us consider one philosopher who has attempted to narrow the range of debate over moral principles, however. In his *Theory of Justice* (1971) John Rawls attempts to show that his principles of justice are superior to specific alternatives (utilitarianism and perfectionism), on the ground that rational persons would choose his principles over the alternatives in specified circumstances of choice. Rawls recognizes that this is not an absolute foundation or justification for his theory of justice; there may be other as yet unformulated principles that would be chosen over his, and, more fundamentally, one may reject the idea that the best principles are those that would be chosen by rational persons. Nonetheless Rawls offers a way of marshalling support for a moral theory that gives rational argument a role. It is significant, however, that he weakened the claims that he makes for his justification of this theory in later writings. In "Justice As Fairness: Political Not Metaphysical" (1985), he comes to the conclusion that moral argumentation serves to establish consensus *within* a community's moral culture and that we have no reason for supposing that moral disagreements across cultures are resolvable.

UNIVERSALS

Are there any cross-cultural human universals? Before we can answer this question we must first clarify it a bit. There are several ways in which a characteristic might be regarded as a human universal. We might use this concept to refer to brute universal generalizations about all human beings— for example, "all human beings feel pain." We might identify as universals certain common features of the human situation—for example, "all human beings need food and water." Or we might identify certain common *capacities* as human universals—for example, "human beings can do arithmetic." An important feature of a capacity is that it represents a potential rather than an actual competence; for the capacity to become actualized, some appropriate interaction with the environment is required. Take a particularly clear example: human language acquisition and use. Linguists have now made it clear that human languages depend on a species-wide cognitive capacity to acquire and use language. Thus the capacity to use language is a human universal in the third sense; one feature of the human species is that the typical human being has this capacity. However language use is not an exceptionless universal across the human species, for several reasons. First, there are individual human beings who lack the cognitive capacity to acquire language. Second, there are individuals who have the capacity but are denied the environment within which this capacity is developed; they are isolated from adult speakers during the years of language acquisition. And finally, it would be possible (though I know of no such case) for social arrangements to systematically interfere with language acquisition in a way that results in a whole population that lacks linguistic competence. None of these exceptions shows that language capacity is not a human universal, however; instead, they show only that universals are capacities that require certain environmental cues to be activated and developed. This example illustrates each definition of human universal above, but primary is the "capacity" definition. The strict universal—"all normal adult human beings use language"—is approximately true, and the truth of this universal stems from the fact that all human beings have the capacity to acquire language (a capacity universal) and the fact that all human beings are born into language-using communities (a situational universal).

Let us consider, then, whether there are human universals. Clearly biology establishes one class of such universals. At the most basic level it is a cross-cultural universal that human beings need food and shelter. Likewise, there are cross-cultural patterns of sexual behavior and reproductive behavior that appear to be based in the evolutionary history of the human species (although Michel Foucault argues for the deeply cultural character of sexuality [Foucault 1978]). At a somewhat more subtle level the cognitive sciences have made it plain that major elements of the human cognitive system are genetically determined: The perceptual system, pattern recognition, memory, linguistic competence, tool-using capacities, and other cognitive capacities appear to have a strong basis in neurophysiology and are explained on the basis of the evolutionary history of the human organism. All human beings use natural language, and linguists beginning with Noam Chomsky have attempted to identify linguistic universals that underlie the patent diversity of human languages.

In Chapters 3 and 7 it was argued that there are core features of practical reason that are cross-cultural universals. (This finding underlies the utility of rational choice and materialist frameworks of explanation.) We may speculate that the elements and structure of this human capacity for deliberate choice is likewise a human universal with its own evolutionary history. This capacity depends upon a variety of abilities, cognitive and practical. On the cognitive side we may identify the capacity to formulate beliefs about the world, to hypothesize about causal relations, or to form predictions about future states of the world. And on the practical side there is the capacity to reason about one's goals and purposes, the moral capacity to consider whether a given action is compatible with norms and values to which the agent adheres, and the complex system of passions and emotions that give rise to action in various social circumstances. Human rationality and human emotion are species-specific. These features, however, need to be understood as resources available to human beings that are deployed and used in different ways in different cultures. Here the analogy with language is fruitful: All human beings have the capacity (and the neurophysiology to support the capacity) to acquire a human language. But *what* language they acquire depends entirely on the language community into which they are born. Thus human language displays elements both of universality and cultural specificity. Diversity at the level of phonology, semantics, and syntax does not contradict the presence of a common, universal human capacity to acquire and use one or another human language. Moreover this is not a vacuous universal but rather one that distinguishes the human species from others (perhaps even other intelligent species).

This view suggests that there are important capacities, cognitive and practical, that underpin all human behavior and represent human universals. Are there substantive schemes that are likewise universal across human cultures? In particular are there features of human conceptual schemes, standards of reasoning, and standards of action that are common across cultures? The arguments for conceptual relativism notwithstanding, it is hard to avoid the conclusion that there is a core set of conceptual features that underlie all human cognition. The concepts needed to divide empirical experience into separate objects, the attribution of properties to objects, the location of objects in time and space, and the framework of cause and effect appear unavoidable in human experience. To this we might add the concepts needed to analyze common features of human experience—color, temperature, taste, smell, three-dimensionality of visual experience. This position does not mean that *all* concepts are held in common—a view that is clearly refuted by even cursory study of other cultures. What it does rule out, however, is the radical Whorf hypothesis—that there is diversity even at the most basic level of ontology (the ways in which the world is broken down into things).

When we turn our attention to frameworks of belief, we reach a similar conclusion: There is a core set of standards of empirical and causal reasoning that appear to be present in all cultures. The capacity to learn that fish and birds migrate seasonally and may thus be found in some seasons and not others, the ability to learn the properties of various seeds in order to engage in agriculture, the ability to note the regular movements of the stars and planets, the discovery of the medicinal properties of plants and herbs— all these capacities depend on an ability to observe the environment and arrive at hypotheses and generalizations about empirical regularities. Once again, then, the radical claim of cultural relativity appears overstated (although there is also a wide range of cultural variability in belief systems).

Finally, when we turn to normative relativism, we find that the relativist's position is the strongest but still not wholly convincing. The diversity of human normative systems is wide; at the same time human norms are oriented toward signal features of the human existential situation—the salience of pain, the importance of satisfying human needs, the intensity of parent-child relations. These features are addressed differently in different cultures, but they are all given a place.

Thus it would seem that anthropology has a message for us concerning human variability, but it is not exactly the one advanced by radical cultural relativism. The correct conclusion appears to be this: There is both uniformity and diversity across human cultures at the level of concepts, beliefs, and norms. The diversity shows the creativeness of human capacity for developing cultural instruments and the underdetermination of culture by human need. The uniformity, by contrast, reflects both the biological constants in human life and the common features of the human existential situation. Finally, the fact that human beings are capable of reflective, deliberative thought—philosophy, scientific theory, religious belief—makes it possible that new universals may emerge from the exercise of human reason.

NOTES

1. Kuhn's views have generated a great deal of discussion. Two collections are particularly useful: Lakatos and Musgrave, eds., *Criticism and the Growth of Knowledge* (1970) and Hacking, ed., *Scientific Revolutions* (1981).

2. Newton-Smith (1981), Brown (1983), and Scheffler (1967) offer extensive discussion and criticism of the doctrines of incommensurability. Bernstein (1983) discusses the implications of incommensurability arguments for social science.

3. Twentieth-century U.S. citizens, for example, have five concepts of a "bank," whereas nineteenth-century French citizens were able to make do with just one.

4. Robin Horton makes arguments to this effect in "African Thought and Western Science" (1970).

SUGGESTIONS FOR FURTHER READING

Bernstein, Richard J. 1983. *Beyond Objectivism and Relativism: Science, Hermeneutics, and Praxis.*

Gellner, Ernest. 1985. *Relativism and Social Science.*

Harman, Gilbert. 1975. "Moral Relativism Defended."

Hollis, Martin, and Steven Lukes, eds. 1982. *Rationality and Relativism.*

Jarvie, I. C. 1984. *Rationality and Relativism: In Search of a Philosophy and History of Anthropology.*

Kuhn, Thomas. 1970. *The Structure of Scientific Revolutions.* 2d ed.

Mackie, J. L. 1977. *Ethics: Inventing Right and Wrong.*

Trigg, Roger. 1985. *Understanding Social Science.*

Wilson, Bryan R., ed. 1970. *Rationality.*

Winch, Peter. 1958. *The Idea of a Social Science.*

Wong, David. 1984. *Moral Relativity.*

11
TOWARD METHODOLOGICAL PLURALISM

In this chapter we turn to what is perhaps the most frequently discussed topic in the philosophy of social science: the relationship between the social sciences and the natural sciences. Several of the preceding chapters have shown that social science explanations share important common features with the natural sciences—for example, the centrality of causal explanation, the utility of quantitative reasoning, and the importance of locating higher-level processes within a framework of causal mechanisms at lower levels. We have also encountered a number of features that sharply distinguish the social sciences from the natural—for example, the explanatory role of individual agency in social science, the need to interpret human actions as meaningful, and the weakness of laws and regularities in social science. What, then, is the proper relationship between social science and natural science?

Two polar positions have been taken on this topic in the last century. The first is *naturalism:* the view that the social sciences are methodologically similar to the natural sciences. The other is *antinaturalism:* the view that the social sciences embody one or more features that are radically distinct from the natural sciences. The most common defense of the antinaturalist position depends on the contrast between types of explanation. The natural sciences provide causal explanations, whereas the social sciences provide meaningful interpretations. We will see that neither naturalism nor antinaturalism is wholly persuasive, and against both I will argue for a doctrine of methodological pluralism.

NATURALISM

Many philosophers and some social scientists hold that social science should aim to reproduce the methodological features of natural science. David Thomas puts the point this way: "I am concerned with whether the study of human society can satisfy natural scientific methodology. Throughout I pose the question in the following terms. Can social study conform to a *naturalistic* methodology, that is replicate the methodology of natural science? Is *naturalism*, the doctrine that there can be a natural scientific study of society, correct?" (Thomas 1979:1). And he believes that his analysis shows that naturalism is a legitimate methodological program for social science.

The program of naturalism is ambiguous, moving between two ideas. We may refer to these as weak naturalism (WN) and strong naturalism (SN).

WN It is *possible* to use a methodology based on natural science to investigate social phenomena.

SN It is *necessary* to use a methodology based on natural science to investigate social phenomena.

Weak naturalism holds only that naturalistic social science is possible; strong naturalism holds that if social inquiry is to be scientific at all, it *must* be naturalistic social science. Weak naturalism is thus compatible with the view that some social inquiry is not naturalistic. Plainly, then, strong naturalism is more difficult to defend.

A second preliminary issue arises as well. The content of naturalism varies according to the account we provide of the methodology of natural science. It is obvious enough that the techniques of research, empirical procedures, quantitative methods, and the like differ substantially from one discipline to another—even among the natural sciences. Consequently, if naturalism is to be at all plausible, we must describe the "logic of natural science" at a level of generality that abstracts from these differences. But what are the features of scientific method that might give substance to this conception of unity of science? The most plausible view is a core-periphery analysis of scientific method: There are some features that all scientific enterprises must share, and there are a larger number of features that are held in common among some but not all scientific enterprises. The former constitute the core criteria, and the latter represent something like family resemblance characteristics that weave throughout various scientific enterprises.

The core features of science include at least these criteria: an empirical testability criterion, a logical coherence criterion, and an institutional commitment to intersubjective processes of belief evaluation and criticism. All sciences place a high value on the use of empirical research and observation as a central means of evaluating scientific assertion and hypothesis. All sciences require that systems of belief be logically coherent and developed. And all proceed through a community of inquirers in which the individual's scientific results are subjected to communitywide standards of adequacy.[1]

These criteria plainly do not represent a full description of scientific inquiry; rather they represent a set of minimal standards that any enterprise must satisfy if it is to be judged scientific. (Popper and others offer criteria of these sorts as a "demarcation criterion" upon which to distinguish between science and pseudoscience [Popper 1965].) Beyond these shared features of scientific reasoning is a large set of peripheral features that vary across scientific disciplines. Important peripheral features of science include: the use of quantitative methods and models; commitment to explanation of observed phenomena on the basis of underlying laws, processes, or mechanisms; a conception of theory as a unified system of hypotheses; use of controlled experimentation to evaluate hypotheses; extensive use of predictions based on theoretical reasoning; and commitment to background metaphysical beliefs (for example, no action at a distance, no explanation of individual behavior presupposing pure altruism). These features are peripheral because they are general features shared by many sciences and lacked by many others; there are obvious and important exceptions to these features throughout the range of the sciences. Thus the discipline of thermodynamics throughout much of its history deliberately avoided hypotheses about underlying processes, cultural anthropologists rarely use complex quantitative models, and some areas of social science are not concerned with explanation at all but are content with descriptive accuracy.

If naturalism amounted only to the claim that social science must share the core features of science with the natural sciences, it would be unobjectionable. This would only require that social science give central importance to empirical research and logical rigor and that it possess the right sort of institutional structure. It would appear, however, that advocates of naturalism intend substantially more. Their view, paraphrased in the terms used here, is that the natural sciences share both core features and a significant cluster of peripheral features: substantial use of prediction, explanation based on hypotheses about unobservables, and testing of hypotheses through predictive consequences.

In another place I offer an account of what I refer to as "predictive-theory naturalism" (P-T naturalism). In this account, the cluster features of a natural science methodology over and above the core features of all scientific enterprises include these ideas:

1. Scientific knowledge takes the form of unified deductive theories.
2. Such theories typically describe unobservable mechanisms in order to explain observable conditions.
3. Such theories attempt to describe laws of nature.
4. These theories permit relatively precise predictions.
5. These theories acquire empirical corroboration through their predictive consequences.
6. A central goal of scientific theorizing is to arrive at a unified theory of a domain of phenomena—a single comprehensive theory that permits explanation of all phenomena in the domain.[2]

Here natural science is characterized by theories that have predictive consequences, and scientific theories are empirically evaluated through the predictions to which they give rise. The issue of naturalism is whether social inquiry yields knowledge about the social world with this logical and epistemological structure.

What sorts of considerations recommend naturalism as a philosophy of social science? A central motivation comes from the doctrine of the unity of science, according to which all sciences must share a set of methodological features in common if they are to be sciences at all. A second motivation is related; it stems from the program of physicalism, according to which all phenomena are ultimately grounded in the properties of physical objects. Sciences that appear to be concerned with nonfundamental entities therefore need to be reduced to lower-level sciences. The unity-of-science argument and the case for reductionism will be considered in the next two sections.

Three ideas are particularly important in recommending naturalism beyond these general and programmatic views. First, the strength of the model of theoretical explanation in the natural sciences is a further support for naturalism. The natural sciences have been enormously successful in explaining apparently diverse and disorderly phenomena through formulation of a theory of the underlying mechanisms that produce them. Newton's theory of gravitation provides a parsimonious explanation of tides, planetary orbits, and the law of falling bodies. It is tempting, therefore, to hold that the goal of social science is similar: to formulate a theory of underlying social processes or mechanisms that permits us to systematize a wide range of social phenomena. And some social theories appear to afford this possibility; thus the theory of collective action allows us to explain instances of collective action and free-riding in a variety of social settings.

A second motivation for naturalism derives from the importance of prediction for practical human purposes. The natural sciences provide the basis for numerous forms of human intervention in the environment based on the ability of natural science theories to predict the behavior of natural systems. Thus, for example, engineering rests upon the basic sciences of mechanics, materials, and the like; medicine rests upon the sciences of molecular biology, cellular biology, and biochemistry. By arriving at theories of the underlying causal properties of natural systems, the natural sciences have paved the way for substantial human control of the natural environment. Social phenomena are equally important in the human environment: Wars, recessions, and periods of ethnic violence are all social outcomes that human communities would prefer to avoid if possible. And greater economic productivity, greater equality, greater educational attainment by the disadvantaged, higher levels of social solidarity—these are outcomes that human communities would like to attain. It is tempting, then, to view the social sciences as providing the intellectual basis for social policy: By offering theories of social causation, the social sciences should permit policymakers to predict the effects of current social conditions and to design interventions that bring about desirable outcomes. (Karl Popper [1961] emphasizes this aspect of social science as the basis for "social engineering.")

A final motivation for naturalism stems from the admirable goals of empiricism: the requirement that knowledge claims should be supported by appropriate empirical data and rigorous logical reasoning. The natural sciences have embodied these goals to a substantial degree, and it is appealing to hold that the social sciences would do well to emulate the natural sciences in these methods. This is particularly important in social science because of the proximity between ideology, social philosophy, social mythology, and social science. We all have theories about what causes racism, what stimulates recession, or why wars occur. If the social sciences are to progress beyond these forms of unschooled social belief, social science theories must be subject to rigorous standards of testing and empirical evaluation. And naturalism provides a methodological basis for such standards.

Prediction and theory

Is P-T naturalism a valid basis for social science methodology? Let us consider the central ideas in turn, beginning with the idea that scientific knowledge takes the form of unified deductive theories. Is this a useful model for the organization of social science knowledge? On the whole it is not. There are some examples of social sciences that possess this structure— for example, neoclassical economic theory—and social sciences do employ theories. But only rarely does the theory function in the way postulated by naturalism—as a system of axioms from which social phenomena can be derived. Rather, on the whole, social science explanations depend on what Robert Merton calls "theories of the middle range" (Merton 1967). He writes, "*Theories of the middle range* [are] theories that lie between the minor but necessary working hypotheses that evolve in abundance during day-to-day research and the all-inclusive systematic efforts to develop a theory that will explain all the observed uniformities of social behavior, social organization and social change" (Merton 1967:39). Social scientists more commonly employ theoretical constructs in what Weber characterizes as "ideal-types." According to Weber an ideal-type is a "conceptual pattern [that] brings together certain relationships and events of historical life into a complex, which is conceived as an internally consistent system" (Weber 1949:90). The theoretical construct functions as an organizing device in terms of which the social scientist attempts to analyze and explain concrete social phenomena. The social scientist works back and forth between the abstract theoretical concept and the concrete social phenomena, shedding light on the concrete phenomena by showing how its various elements hang together. But social scientists rarely deduce conclusions about social phenomena based on the abstract logic of the theoretical construct without considering the concrete particularity of the event in question.

Consider one example—efforts by comparative sociologists to analyze collective violence in diverse societies. The concept of a "grain riot" may be useful to characterize bread riots in medieval England and rice riots in Qing China. Each is an instance of collective violence stimulated by immediate food shortages and, perhaps, a popular sense of injustice. This concept enables the social scientist to analyze and discuss events from different cultures. But from beginning to end, the social scientist must bear in mind the facts of historical contingency and cultural diversity; therefore it will be important *not* to force the English and Chinese events into an overly sparse conceptual space of food shortage and collective violence. The concept of a grain riot is a useful tool with which to probe the historical particular, but it does not provide a basis for deducing the necessary course of development of the phenomena that fall under it. So social science knowledge does *not* typically take the form of unified deductive theories; instead it is a theoretically informed effort to analyze historical particulars.

Look next at the idea that theories should describe unobservable mechanisms in order to explain observable phenomena. This feature of naturalism fits more comfortably on many of the examples of social science explanation that we have considered in this book, and it corresponds to the idea that explanation of a phenomenon often involves identifying the cause of the events or pattern in question. And, as we saw in Chapter 2, the most satisfactory causal explanation is one that identifies the mechanism through which cause and effect are connected. We may quibble, though, about whether causal mechanisms are typically unobservable in the social sciences for, unlike the fields and particles of fundamental physics, social causes are generally familiar and observable. Thus, if we hold that Ronald Reagan's election in 1980 was caused by electoral dissatisfaction with the rate of inflation, we have identified as cause an economic variable that is, in the appropriate sense, observable. (By this I mean that there are well-known and justifiable economic measures of this variable.) What is unobservable is not the variable but the causal connection between it and the outcome. Nonetheless many of the examples considered throughout this book do place central emphasis on the problem of identifying underlying causal mechanisms.

Do social explanations rest on laws of nature? We have seen at various points that social explanations do depend on identifying lawlike regularities, but these are not typically laws of nature. Rather they are regularities that are specific to social phenomena—those that derive from the forms of agency found in the persons who constitute social relations and processes of social change. In Chapters 2 and 3 I particularly emphasized the rule-governed character of human action and the regularities that stem from individual rationality as the regularities that underlie social causation. The essential point of statement (3), though, is borne out by many of the examples of social explanation that we have considered: Explanations depend on lawlike regularities. The qualification we are forced to make is a narrow one: Social regularities do not derive from the fixed properties of physical objects but from the circumstances of agency of human actors.

Do social sciences provide a basis for precise predictions? And is it reasonable to hope that they might do so at some point in the future? The answer on both counts is no. Social sciences do admit of predictions, to be sure, but they are rarely precise and rarely reliable. And this fact does not result from the immaturity of the social sciences but from the open-endedness of social causal fields and the indeterminacy of social processes. Suppose that we are interested in predicting the outcome of a hypothetical seizure of power by the New People's Army (NPA) in the Philippines and we analyze a small number of variables: the economic crisis that will be induced by the creation of a radical state, the competition for power that will result within the new ruling class, the policy goals that the NPA has announced in advance of its seizure of power (land reform, abolition of U.S. military bases), and the residual strength of a conservative opposition in the Philippines. Each of these variables can be investigated in considerable detail, and we may arrive at predictions about the sort of influence that each is likely to have on the structure and behavior of the NPA government. But major reservations must be made about the resulting predictions. (1) Predictions about each separate factor are questionable and have a high probability of error. Different analysts may disagree, for example, about how influential stated policy goals are on the actual behavior of policymakers. (2) The problem of aggregating the separate effects of these factors introduces new uncertainties for there may be unanticipated interaction effects among them. For example, economic crisis may exacerbate intragovernment competition more than expected. (3) Finally there are numerous other factors that are potentially significant for the behavior of the new state beyond the four enumerated above: for example, the attitudes and influence of international organizations; the behavior of other major international players—e.g., the Soviet Union, Japan, and China; the possibility of popular discontent arising as a result of new government policies and the pace of reform; crop failure; major storms or earthquakes. Each of these factors introduces a new dimension of uncertainty into the analysis. So predictions about the outcome of the new government are highly questionable and should be regarded as predictions about tendencies rather than actual outcomes. And these limitations do not derive from the immaturity of the relevant social science disciplines; rather they are inherent in the multiple causation present in any complex social phenomenon.

Do social sciences acquire empirical support through testing of their predictive consequences? The preceding comments about prediction should make us skeptical about this claim as well. And in fact study of a range of social sciences shows that empirical evidence often does *not* function in this way in social theory. These theories are not tested as wholes, but instead their various components are evaluated on more or less independent grounds. In the Philippine example above the "theory" that our hypothetical researcher arrives at consists of a number of lesser theories—of economic process, domestic politics, international institutions, leadership motivation, and so on. And the application of each of these theories and hypotheses can be provided with separate empirical evaluation. So the comprehensive theory is not judged in terms of its predictive consequences; it is judged piecemeal through evaluation of its parts.

Finally, let us ask whether unification is a proper goal for the social sciences. Is there such a thing as a "science of society"—a comprehensive theory of the processes and mechanisms that produce all social phenomena and provide a basis for explanation of such diverse things as the structure of the capitalist state, the occurrence of ethnic conflict, and patterns of residential segregation? Is there a sort of "grand unification theory" for social science? In fact, to pose the question is to go a long way toward settling it for this is a misconceived goal, and one that is impossible to attain or approach. Social phenomena are inherently diverse, reflecting both patterned regularities and creative innovations. And even the regularities that are found among social phenomena come from radically diverse sorts of causes—individual rationality, the vagaries of individual psychology, the structural properties of social institutions, the unintended effects of social policies, the interactions between culture and politics, etc. So the goal of arriving at a finished and comprehensive theory of social processes is radically misconceived. Instead, we should think of the social sciences as contributing to an eclectic body of knowledge that sheds light on the various forms of social causation and structured human agency. Such a corpus of knowledge is inherently open-ended and immune to unification under a single comprehensive theory, reflecting the open-endedness of human creativity and capacity for innovation. (Weber actively takes this perspective in " 'Objectivity' in Social Science" [Weber 1949:72–81].)

These considerations suggest that the model of P-T naturalism does not fit the social sciences very closely. But several more general reasons why naturalism has been an attractive doctrine to philosophers of social science are reviewed below.

Unity-of-science considerations

One important reason that naturalism has appealed to some philosophers is the power of the unity-of-science doctrine: All sciences are ultimately part of one large, methodologically uniform enterprise. The unity-of-science doctrine holds that all scientific knowledge ideally conforms to one model of logical organization (the model of the unified deductive theory) and one method of inquiry and justification (hypothesis formation and theory testing through experiment). The doctrine of naturalism states that all social scientific knowledge—if scientifically adequate at all—should share fundamental logical and methodological features with the natural sciences. However, examination of a range of social explanations reveals that they share various elements, but there is no single model of scientific reasoning that covers all cases. The examples considered in this study thus cast doubt on the traditional view that science is a "seamless web" of connected methods and theoretical structures. Rather, I will conclude that the cases considered here support a pluralistic conception of social science.[3]

Above I provided a core-periphery analysis of scientific method. This analysis permits us to formulate two versions of the unity-of-science doctrine. The weak version (WUS) holds only that there are minimal standards that must be satisfied before any enterprise can be considered scientific; the strong version (SUS) holds that all sciences share these minimal features and an assortment of others.

WUS All sciences share the core features of science.

SUS All sciences share the core features and a significant cluster of the peripheral features.

The weak doctrine is probably true but somewhat vacuous, whereas the strong doctrine is probably false.

Study of the many examples of social explanation surveyed in this book suggests that the weak unity-of-science doctrine finds support but that any stronger theory of the unity of science is disconfirmed. Each example discussed in preceding chapters shows a fundamental commitment to the core standards of scientific research: empirical control, logical rigor, and intersubjective evaluation of scientific findings. In each case we find researchers who have defined a domain of empirical phenomena and attempted to provide a systematic and empirically grounded explanation of these phenomena. And many embody an explanatory paradigm that closely resembles the pattern of causal explanation in the natural sciences. Moreover, the course of these debates underlines the institutional aspect of social science research. In each case an investigator advances his or her hypothesis, interpretation, or theory to a community of scholars, and sharp critical evaluation ensues. These debates are carried out through professional journals, newsletters, and books as well as conferences, scholarly meetings, and private correspondence. It is plain that these forms of intersubjective peer evaluation substantially determine the success or failure of a given hypothesis in the discipline. Thus it seems reasonable to conclude, first, that the practitioners themselves are guided by the core criteria of scientific objectivity identified above and, second, that the institutions of the social sciences enforce these criteria on social-scientific research as effectively as the corresponding institutions do in the natural sciences. So in terms of a core commitment to empirically controlled, intersubjectively evaluated investigation, the social sciences surveyed here satisfy the weak unity-of-science doctrine.

If we ask whether any stronger version of the doctrine is borne out here, however, the answer appears to be no. Whether we consider methods of research, techniques of factual inquiry, standards of theoretical adequacy, or empirical testing procedures, we find substantial variation in different cases and disciplines. Each of these debates represents a high level of rigor internally. But the regulative context of the debates—the standards of explanatory adequacy, the background assumptions about what sorts of questions must be raised and about research methods and empirical procedures—are very much the product of the particular histories of the various disciplines. The paradigms of research at work in European economic history, political science research into peasant behavior, and symbolic interpretation of millenarian rebellion are widely diverse. This diversity does not imply that interaction between these disciplines and enterprises is impossible or fruitless; the contrary is true. But it does imply that it is useless to look for a general methodology of social science that all these investigations employ and that can function as a lingua franca among them. Unity-of-science considerations, then, do not provide strong support for naturalism as a theory of social science methodology.

Reductionism and the social sciences

A second general reason for favoring naturalism is the attractiveness of reductionism as a model of explanation for higher-level sciences. Some philosophers hope that the social sciences will eventually be reducible to various natural sciences. John Stuart Mill, for example, held that the social sciences depend ultimately on the science of "ethology"—the science of human character (Mill 1950:338). Jerry Fodor puts the reductionist program in this way: "All true theories in the special sciences should reduce to physical theories 'in the long run' " (Fodor 1980:120). Along this line of thought, the various sciences are arranged in well-defined hierarchies from higher-level to lower-level sciences. And higher-level sciences should be reducible to lower-level sciences in two respects: It should be possible to demonstrate the equivalence of entities in the two theories, and it should be possible to derive the laws of the higher-level science from the laws of the lower-level one.

The reductionist approach in the philosophy of social science recommends that we attempt to perform a similar reduction from certain central social sciences—e.g., economics or sociology—to the disciplines of individual psychology—personality psychology, social psychology, and so forth. Suppose, for example, that it is a law within a sociology of prisons that when conditions become more crowded, the incidence of prisoner violence increases dramatically. The reductionist approach would suggest that we try to derive this regularity from more basic laws of individual psychology. Consider reductionism as applied to social science as consisting of the following requirements:

- All social entities must be definable in terms of facts about individuals and individual psychology.
- All social laws must be derivable from regularities of individual psychology.

In Chapter 9 we found that reductionism is far too strong a requirement on higher-level sciences and that there are good reasons for supposing that there may be autonomous social concepts and laws that are not reducible to individual-level concepts and laws. There may be autonomous (i.e., nonreducible) explanations and theories in the social sciences that do not derive from regularities at the level of individual psychology. And this in turn discredits reductionism as a ground for naturalism.

Conclusions on naturalism

I conclude, therefore, that the reductionist thesis is *not* a valid methodology constraint on social explanation and theory. The emphasis on the idea of knowledge as a unified deductive system and the assumption that science is primarily concerned with prediction fare badly when applied to typical social explanations. Social explanations make use of a variety of theoretical premises, but rarely are they designed to reduce a large domain of social phenomena to a small set of theoretical axioms. The predictions that are associated with social science theories are weak predictions, easily overcome by competing social factors. Finally, typical social science research involves a much larger core of relatively straightforward empirical investigation, independent from abstract social theory, than is suggested by the framework of predictive-theory naturalism.

What survives of naturalism, then, is a thesis about causal explanation and a requirement of rigorous empirical reasoning. If we chose to reformulate naturalism in light of these observations, the doctrine could be couched in terms of a principle of "reform naturalism":

- All social sciences should attempt to provide causal explanations of social phenomena;
- These explanations should be grounded on analysis of the circumstances of agency of participants;
- Social theories should be supported with rigorous use of empirical evidence in order to rule out alternative explanations.

This account comes closer to describing many of the examples considered here (and a wide range of actual social science practice). Its flaw is its comprehensiveness for, as we have seen at various points, there are areas of social science that do *not* take the form of causal explanations. In particular, there is a valid domain of interpretive social science that is based on the interpretation of concrete meaningful social action and practice. As a final emendation, consider "weak reform naturalism": Many examples of good social science explanation conform to the standards of reform naturalism. Thus the arguments in this section do not support the main forms of *anti*naturalism for if weak reform naturalism is true, then strong antinaturalism is false. Instead I suggest an interpretation of social science that is eclectic, both in theory and in method, and I cast doubt on the idea that it should be possible to provide a general account of social science methodology that fits all inquiries equally well. Therefore, weak reform naturalism represents one important current in good contemporary social science; a suitably revised, weak antinaturalism does so as well. I will return to these issues in the final section.

ANTINATURALISM

Let us turn now to the opposing position—the view that the social sciences are radically different from the natural sciences, in method and in substance. This position is referred to as "antinaturalism"; it may also be termed a "hermeneutic" or "interpretive" theory of social science. This strand of the philosophy of social science maintains, first, that the social sciences share a set of common and essential characteristics and, second, that these characteristics radically distinguish the social sciences from the natural sciences. The characteristics most commonly attributed to the social sciences along these lines are related. It is held that the social sciences share a method of inquiry—the interpretive method described in Chapter 3—and a distinctive subject matter—meaningful human action rather than causally determined events.

One major critic of naturalism is Charles Taylor. He writes of naturalism in the following terms: "There is a constant temptation to take natural science theory as a model for social theory: that is, to see theory as offering an account of underlying processes and mechanisms of society, and as providing the basis of a more effective planning of social life. But for all the superficial analogies, social theory can never really occupy this role. It is part of a significantly different activity" (C. Taylor 1985:92). There is a crucial disanalogy between social theory and physical theory, according to Taylor: Given that social phenomena are partially constituted by the self-understanding of the participants, a social theory can alter the social arrangements or facts that it describes (C. Taylor 1985a:98). "Unlike with natural science, the theory is not about an independent object, but one that is partly constituted by self-understanding" (C. Taylor 1985a:98).

What, then, is the antinaturalistic alternative? I will present antinaturalism as consisting in these claims:

- Social phenomena—behavior, social practices, and social institutions— are inherently meaningful; they are constituted by the meanings that participants attach to them;
- Social phenomena can only be explained through a hermeneutic unpacking of the meanings that constitute them;
- Interpretations of social phenomena can only be evaluated in terms of their internal coherence and their fit with the behavior and avowals of the participants;
- Causal explanation has no legitimate role in social science;
- Inductive regularities and predictions have no legitimate role in social science.

Let us briefly consider the first part of the antinaturalist framework— the assumption that all social sciences share essential characteristics. We have now considered dozens of examples of explanations drawn from the social sciences, so we have some feel for the diversity of social science research. Is it plausible that there is a set of characteristics common to all these examples and the research traditions from which they derive? One trivial affirmative is available: They all involve social phenomena, the interactive behavior of human beings in social relations. However, this common feature does not take us very far. And if we take the next step argued by antinaturalistic social scientists—that all social sciences involve the interpretation of meaningful human action—then we find that the thesis is implausible. Consider some of the explanations that are offered by social scientists:

- Navajo speakers find the sentence "the horse was kicked by the man" amusing because they believe that horses cannot "control" men.
- Classical slavery collapsed because the system was not able to replace slaves fast enough.
- Capitalism experiences crises of underconsumption because employers have an incentive to keep wages low.
- Burmese peasants revolted in the Saya San rebellion because they felt unjustly treated by the state.
- Poor city dwellers have longer life expectancy than poor rural people because the former have access to free health care.
- The practice of prolonged lactation is found in hunter-gatherer society as a means of depressing fertility.

These examples are drawn from a range of social sciences. Some—for example, the first and the fourth—conform to the interpretive dictum; they do involve the interpretation of social behavior as meaningful. Others do not fit this requirement; the fifth case, for example, involves identifying a structural difference between urban and rural life, and the second involves identifying a structural constraint on the Roman slave system. The third example is intermediate. It depends on consideration of the incentives presented to the typical capitalist and in this respect involves interpretation of meaningful action, but the account is highly abstract and culture-neutral and gives rise to a standard causal explanation. Thus there is a spectrum of explanatory paradigms at work here, ranging from interpretation of meaningful action to analysis of a pattern of social causation. In every case meaningful human action comes into the story at some point, but this is simply the trivial consequence of the fact that we are dealing with social phenomena, which by definition involve individual action. I would conclude, then, that the strong thesis—that all social sciences have the same logical character—is invalid.

Moreover, some branches of the antinaturalistic school run the risk of violating the core features of science. Consider the particularly sharp rejection of naturalism found in the methodological writings of Clifford Geertz. Geertz emphatically rejects the notion that the social sciences should model themselves on the paradigms of the natural sciences—the discovery of causal relations, covering-law explanations, and objective descriptions of objective phenomena. Instead, he urges social scientists to develop their affinities to other enterprises—literary criticism, dramaturgy, and other areas of symbolic interpretation. And he urges social scientists to abandon what he regards as a spurious quest for objectivity and truth. (These views are presented in a number of places in Geertz's work; particularly relevant is "Blurred Genres" [Geertz 1983].)

However, this is a radical departure, not only from naturalism but from the core conception of science described above. It suggests a model of social inquiry that would make social research more akin to literary interpretation— fluid, ambiguous, and radically underdetermined by empirical constraints—

than to more orthodox conceptions of science. Geertz's position (in his more extreme methodological moods, in any case) appears to be a change of subject; he is no longer talking about social *science* but rather an interpretive discipline within which standards of empirical evaluation are taken substantially less seriously. (Paul Shankman [1984] explores this criticism of Geertz in "The Thick and the Thin: On the Interpretive Theoretical Program of Clifford Geertz.")[4]

These arguments take us part of the way to refuting antinaturalism—but only part of the way. It is the all-inclusiveness of the doctrine that is its downfall. We may consider "weak antinaturalism," which maintains only that *some* social sciences depend on a method that is radically different from the natural sciences; this is the interpretive method. (This parallels the similar gambit that we pursued in connection with "weak reform naturalism.") But is weak antinaturalism a legitimate position on social science methodology? Are there forms of social science research that are primarily interpretive rather than causal?

We have seen enough examples of interpretive social science throughout this work to agree that a provisional yes is warranted to this question. Geertz's interpretation of the Balinese cockfight, Witherspoon's analysis of Navajo metaphysics, Michael Adas's treatment of millenarian religions, or Robin Horton's study of African magical beliefs are all strong candidates for interpretive social science. In each case we have a better understanding of a cultural milieu and a better basis for interpreting the actions and words of the persons who live in those cultures, and these are genuine contributions to social science. Moreover, Geertz and Taylor are probably right in saying that, for these questions, no other method will do. In particular, a causal, structural, or reductionist approach will not illuminate the central questions. When we are concerned about the meaning of human behavior and practices, unavoidably we must advance hypotheses based on the level of meanings, not causes or structures.

The most pressing concern raised by antinaturalism is tied to the role of empirical evidence in evaluating scientific belief. What distinguishes science from common sense is the availability of appropriate standards of empirical adequacy for the former. If interpretive sociology lacks such standards, then it would be reasonable to conclude that interpretive sociology is not social science. Is there any reason to think that is true?

Positivistically minded philosophers have tended to doubt that interpretive social science *can* be empirically supported. However, their skepticism turns on philosophical views that are themselves dubious—in particular, a sort of latent behaviorism. Consider the following argument: Empirical data must be logically independent from the hypotheses for which it is presented as evidence. And, ideally, it should be wholly observational. The "data" available for a hermeneutic interpretation is doubly tainted. It requires that we attribute meanings to participant behavior that is in turn used to evaluate hypotheses about participant meaning (thus violating the requirement of logical independence). Furthermore meanings themselves are not observable, so data reporting meaningful behavior is defective. Purely behavioral descriptions would be acceptable, but these are notoriously incapable of pinning down meanings. Therefore there is no empirical basis for assessing hypotheses about participant meanings, and interpretive sociology cannot be given empirical support.

This argument, however, is unacceptable. It is now well established in the philosophy of science that data is often or always theory-laden. Even in physics there is no purely observational vocabulary in terms of which to couch empirical data; instead observations bring with them substantial parts of physical theory. And the requirement that social data should be based on purely behavioral description is discredited by the collapse of behaviorism as a viable approach to the problems of thought, consciousness, cognition, language use, and the like in theoretical psychology. Therefore there is no obstacle to interpretation theory providing empirical support for hermeneutic hypotheses on the basis of observations that themselves presuppose that we understand at least some of the meanings of participants' behavior. The "hermeneutic circle" (the fact that observation and interpretation of meanings are inseparable) is no more damaging for the empirical credentials of interpretive sociology than the corresponding circularity of theory and theory-laden observations is for natural science.

This argument establishes the fact that there is no logical obstacle to an empirically well-grounded interpretive sociology. To know whether interpretive sociology in fact succeeds in producing an empirically grounded discipline, however, we must examine the practice of interpretive social scientists. And here the results are mixed. Some (like Geertz in some moods) are so distrustful of "positivism" that they flout the requirements of empirical adequacy. But this is not unavoidable, and there are in fact many strong examples of ethnographic and hermeneutic studies that are highly rigorous and strongly committed to providing evidence for their conclusions. Thus Witherspoon's analysis of the Navajo conceptual scheme is strongly supported by evidence ingeniously gathered through study of Navajo grammar (Witherspoon 1977); Victor Turner's analysis of the significance of religious pilgrimages is carefully supported by data from a variety of cultures (Turner 1974:166–228); and Geertz's own treatment of the symbolic and material cultures of Bali in Negara is grounded on careful, rigorous assessment of available evidence (Geertz 1980). These examples show that it is possible for interpretive sociology to be supported by appropriate empirical methods, which is all that we need to conclude that weak antinaturalism is a legitimate approach to some problems of social research.

Thus weak antinaturalism is sustained by consideration of many of the examples treated in this book: The interpretive, hermeneutic method is a legitimate basis for social science investigation. It must be emphasized, however, that it is equally important for interpretive social science to rest upon appropriate empirical methods, as is the case in other areas of science. Moreover, this approach is just one of several legitimate methods, and methods organized around empirical regularities, causal mechanisms, and rational choice explanations are equally legitimate in turn.

METHODOLOGICAL PLURALISM

These arguments show that neither strong naturalism nor strong anti-naturalism provides a credible basis for understanding the social sciences. Against naturalism we have found that the model of scientific knowledge as a unified deductive theory does not adequately fit the range of social science examples considered here. These cases do not typically take the form of unified deductive theories giving rise to predictive consequences. Further, the cases show that theoretical models may be used to different effect and for different purposes in different areas of social science. There are also significant differences in empirical practices in different areas of social science. The plurality of methods and approaches in the social sciences thus defies simple summary. The social sciences contain a variety of methods and problems, and these are not neatly captured by the traditional categories of interpretation theory, naturalism, hermeneutics, or materialism. Finally, the practitioners themselves do not appear to be guided by a model of scientific knowledge derived from the natural sciences. Few of the scientists whose work is described here appear to be interested in the issue of naturalism or the relation between the methods of the social and natural sciences.

Does this provide support, then, for a doctrine of *anti*naturalism—a view that the social sciences are in principle distinct from the natural sciences? It does not; rather it suggests that social scientists can and should define their problems of research, methods of investigation, models of explanation, and the like independently from the models available in the natural sciences. This suggests that the constructions of social science will sometimes closely parallel theory construction in the natural sciences and sometimes will make use of models, methods, empirical procedures, etc., that have little close analogy to natural science methods. Both naturalism and antinaturalism err in orienting the practice of social science to a few models drawn from the natural sciences—either positively or negatively.

Neither naturalism nor antinaturalism wins the field, then, and the shortcoming of each is the same. Each framework makes overly demanding assumptions about the essential features of science, either natural or social. The antinaturalists err in claiming that all social science involves the interpretation of meaningful phenomena; the naturalist framework assumes implausibly narrow strictures on explanation and mechanism. Against each claim I argue for the position of methodological pluralism. Methodological pluralism views the sciences more as a fabric of related enterprises than as a single unitary activity defined by the "scientific method." In this way it agrees with antinaturalism; certain strands of science may be more dissimilar to each other than others. Pluralism parts with antinaturalism, however, in denying that there is some small set of features in terms of which all social sciences are more similar to each other than they are to any natural sciences (the meaningfulness of social action and the irrelevance of causal analysis). Instead, the fabric is seen to be densely interwoven: Some areas of social science—for example, econometrics—are more similar to areas of natural science—for example, population biology—than they are to other areas of social science, and some areas of natural science are closer to social sciences than to typical natural sciences. (Weather forecasting, for example, is as distant from classical mechanics as it is from public opinion sampling, it would seem.) And we will best understand the logic of the social sciences if we pay close attention to the details of research in a variety of areas and remain sensitive to the important strands of diversity that exist in methods of inquiry, forms of empirical reasoning, and models of explanation.

NOTES

1. W. H. Newton-Smith offers substantial description of the epistemic importance of the institutional structure of science in *The Rationality of Science* (1981). Robert Merton's *The Sociology of Science* (1973) provides a classic collection of empirical studies of the institutional structure of science.

2. These theses are reproduced from Little (1986:14). It should be noted that they represent an idealization of scientific knowledge that fails even in application to many examples of natural science.

3. Alan Ryan provides a clear discussion of the unity-of-science doctrine in application to social science in his introduction to *The Philosophy of Social Explanation* (Ryan, ed. 1973).

4. These criticisms, it should be noted, pertain to Geertz's explicitly methodological contributions, not his field work. In the latter—for example, *Agricultural Involution* (1963) and *Negara* (1980)—Geertz shows an admirable attention to empirical detail and rigorous, nonspeculative analysis. In fact he presents an example of a fairly common phenomenon in science—the practitioner whose methodological writings describe a model of scientific thinking that is not found in his own work and that is substantially less convincing than the implicit standards of reasoning embodied in that work.

SUGGESTIONS FOR FURTHER READING

Braybrooke, David. 1987. *Philosophy of Social Science.*
Geertz, Clifford. 1983. *Local Knowledge.*
Hempel, Carl. 1942. "The Function of General Laws in History."
Putnam, Hilary. 1978. *Meaning and the Moral Sciences.*
Roth, David. 1987. *Meanings and Methods: A Case for Methodological Pluralism in the Social Sciences.*
Rudner, Richard. 1966. *Philosophy of Social Science.*
Stinchcombe, Arthur L. 1978. *Theoretical Methods in Social History.*
Taylor, Charles. 1985a. *Philosophy and the Human Sciences: Philosophical Papers 2.*
Thomas, David. 1979. *Naturalism and Social Science.*
Van Parijs, Philippe. 1981. *Evolutionary Explanation in the Social Sciences.*
Weber, Max. 1949. *The Methodology of the Social Sciences.*
Winch, Peter. 1958. *The Idea of a Social Science.*

BIBLIOGRAPHY

Achinstein, Peter. 1983. *The Nature of Explanation*. Oxford: Oxford University Press.

Adas, Michael. 1979. *Prophets of Rebellion: Millenarian Protest Movements Against the European Colonial Order*. Chapel Hill: University of North Carolina Press.

Adelman, Irma, and Cynthia Taft Morris. 1967. *Society, Politics, and Economic Development: A Quantitative Approach*. Baltimore: Johns Hopkins University Press.

_____. 1973. *Economic Growth and Social Equity in Developing Countries*. Stanford, Calif.: Stanford University Press.

Adorno, Theodor W., et al. 1969. *The Positivist Dispute in German Sociology*. New York: Harper & Row.

Alexander, Jeffrey C., Bernhard Giesen, Richard Munch, Neil J. Smelser, eds. 1987. *The Micro-Macro Link*. Berkeley: University of California Press.

Althusser, Louis, and Etienne Balibar. 1970. *Reading Capital*. London: New Left Books.

Arrigo, Linda Gail. 1986. "Landownership Concentration in China: The Buck Survey Revisited." *Modern China* 12:259–360.

Aston, T. H., and C.H.E. Philpin, eds. 1985. *The Brenner Debate: Agrarian Class Structure and Economic Development in Pre-Industrial Europe*. Cambridge: Cambridge University Press.

Axelrod, Robert. 1984. *The Evolution of Cooperation*. New York: Basic Books.

Ball, Terence, and James Farr, eds. 1984. *After Marx*. Cambridge: Cambridge University Press.

Bates, Robert H., ed. 1988. *Toward a Political Economy of Development: A Rational Choice Perspective*. Berkeley: University of California Press.

Becker, Gary. 1976. *The Economic Approach to Human Behavior*. Chicago: University of Chicago Press.

Berger, Peter L., and Thomas Luckmann. 1966. *The Social Construction of Reality*. Garden City, N.Y.: Doubleday.

Bernstein, Richard J. 1983. *Beyond Objectivism and Relativism: Science, Hermeneutics, and Praxis*. Philadelphia: University of Pennsylvania Press.

Blalock, H. M., Jr., ed. 1971. *Causal Models in the Social Sciences*. Chicago: Aldine-Atherton.

Bloch, Marc. 1966. *French Rural History*. Berkeley: University of California Press.

Block, Ned. 1980. *Readings in Philosophy of Psychology* vol. 1. Cambridge: Harvard University Press.

Bohrnstedt, George W., and David Knoke. 1988. *Statistics for Social Data Analysis*. 2d ed. Itasca, Ill.: F. E. Peacock.

Bonner, John. 1986. *Introduction to the Theory of Social Choice*. Baltimore: Johns Hopkins University Press.

239

Boserup, Ester. 1981. *Population and Technological Change: A Study of Long-term Trends.* Chicago: University of Chicago Press.

Bourdieu, Pierre. 1977. *Outline of a Theory of Practice.* Cambridge: Cambridge University Press.

Boyd, Richard. 1980. "Materialism without Reductionism: What Physicalism Does Not Entail" in *Readings in Philosophy of Psychology* vol. 1. *See* Block 1980.

———. 1984. "The Current Status of Scientific Realism" in *Scientific Realism. See* Leplin 1984.

Braverman, Harry. 1974. *Labor and Monopoly Capital.* New York: Monthly Review.

Braybrooke, David. 1987. *Philosophy of Social Science.* Englewood Cliffs, N.J.: Prentice-Hall.

Brenner, Robert. 1976. "Agrarian Class Structure and Economic Development in Pre-Industrial Europe." *Past and Present* 70:30–75.

———. 1982. "The Agrarian Roots of European Capitalism." *Past and Present* 97:16–113.

Brodbeck, May, ed. 1968. *Readings in the Philosophy of the Social Science.* New York: Macmillan.

Brown, Harold. 1979. *Perception, Commitment, and Theory.* Chicago: University of Chicago Press.

———. 1983. "Incommensurability." *Inquiry* 26:1.

———. 1987. *Observation and Objectivity.* Oxford: Oxford University Press.

Buchanan, Allen. 1979. "Revolutionary Motivation and Rationality." *Philosophy and Public Affairs* 9:1.

Chomsky, Noam. 1965. *Aspects of the Theory of Syntax.* Cambridge, Mass.: MIT Press.

Cohen, G. A. 1978. *Karl Marx's Theory of History: A Defence.* Princeton: Princeton University Press.

———. 1982. "Functional Explanation, Consequence Explanation, and Marxism." *Inquiry* 25:27–56.

Dalton, George. 1969. "Theoretical Issues in Economic Anthropology." *Current Anthropology* 10:63–102.

———. 1971. *Economic Anthropology and Development.* New York: Basic Books.

Dalton, George, ed. 1967. *Tribal and Peasant Economies.* Garden City, N.Y.: Doubleday.

Davidson, Donald. 1963/80. "Actions, Reasons, and Causes" in *Essays on Actions and Events. See* Davidson 1980.

———. 1974. "On the Very Idea of a Conceptual Scheme." *Proceedings and Addresses of the American Philosophical Association* 47:5–20.

———. 1980. *Essays on Actions and Events.* Oxford: Oxford University Press.

Dawkins, Richard. 1976. *The Selfish Gene.* Oxford: Oxford University Press.

Douglas, Mary. 1958/67. "Raffia Cloth Distribution in the Lele Economy" in *Tribal and Peasant Economies. See* Dalton 1967.

Durkheim, Emile. 1897/1951. *Suicide: A Study in Sociology.* New York: Free Press.

———. 1938. *Rules of Sociological Method.* New York: Free Press.

Elster, Jon. 1979. *Ulysses and the Sirens.* Cambridge: Cambridge University Press.

———. 1982. "Marxism, Functionalism, and Game Theory." *Theory and Society* 11:453–82.

———. 1983. *Explaining Technical Change.* Cambridge: Cambridge University Press.

———. 1985. *Making Sense of Marx.* Cambridge: Cambridge University Press.

———. 1986. "Three Challenges to Class" in *Analytical Marxism. See* Roemer 1986.

Elster, Jon, ed. 1986. *Rational Choice.* New York: New York University Press.

Esherick, Joseph W. 1981. "Number Games: A Note on Land Distribution in Pre-revolutionary China." *Modern China* 7:387–411.

Evans-Pritchard, E. E. 1940. *The Nuer: A Description of the Modes of Livelihood and Political Institutions of a Nilotic People*. Oxford: Oxford University Press.

Fei, Hsiao Tung. 1987. "Peasantry as a Way of Living" in *Peasants and Peasant Societies*. *See* Shanin 1987.

Fernbach, David, ed. 1974a. *The Revolutions of 1848: Political Writings* vol. 1. New York: Vintage.

——. 1974b. *Surveys from Exile: Political Writings* vol. 2. New York: Vintage.

Ferro, Marc. 1973. *The Great War 1914–1918*. Boston: Routledge & Kegan Paul.

Flanagan, Owen. *Varieties of Moral Personality: Ethics and Psychological Realism*. Cambridge: Harvard University Press, forthcoming.

Flew, Antony. 1985. *Thinking About Social Thinking*. London: Blackwell.

Fodor, Jerry. 1980. "Special Sciences, or the Disunity of Science as a Working Hypothesis" in *Readings in Philosophy of Psychology* vol. 1. *See* Block 1980.

Foster, John. 1974. *Class Struggle and the Industrial Revolution*.

Foucault, Michel. 1978. *A History of Sexuality*. New York: Pantheon.

Frohlich, Norman, Joe Oppenheimer, and Oran R. Young. 1971. *Political Leadership and Collective Goods*. Princeton: Princeton University Press.

Garfinkel, Alan. 1981. *Forms of Explanation: Rethinking the Questions of Social Theory*. New Haven: Yale University Press.

Geertz, Clifford. 1963. *Agricultural Involution: The Process of Ecological Change in Indonesia*. Berkeley: University of California Press.

——. 1968. *Islam Observed*. New Haven: Yale University Press.

——. 1971a. *The Interpretation of Cultures*. New York: Basic Books.

——. 1971b. "Religion as a Cultural System" in *The Interpretation of Cultures*. *See* Geertz 1971a.

——. 1971c. "Thick Description: Toward an Interpretive Theory of Culture" in *The Interpretation of Cultures*. *See* Geertz 1971a.

——. 1971d. "Ritual and Social Change: A Javanese Example" in *The Interpretation of Cultures*. *See* Geertz 1971a.

——. 1971e. "Deep Play: Notes on the Balinese Cockfight" in *The Interpretation of Cultures*. *See* Geertz 1971a.

——. 1980. *Negara: The Theatre State in Nineteenth-Century Bali*. Princeton: Princeton University Press.

——. 1983. *Local Knowledge*. New York: Basic Books.

——. 1984. "Culture and Social Change: The Indonesian Case." *Man* 19:513–32.

Gellner, Ernest. 1985. *Relativism and Social Science*. Cambridge: Cambridge University Press.

Giddens, Anthony. 1979. *Central Problems in Social Theory: Action, Structure and Contradiction in Social Analysis*. Berkeley: University of California Press.

Gillis, Malcolm, Dwight H. Perkins, Michael Roemer, Donald R. Snodgrass. 1987. *Economics of Development*. 2nd ed. New York: W. W. Norton and Company.

Glymour, Clark. 1980. *Theory and Evidence*. Princeton: Princeton University Press.

Gramsci, Antonio. 1971. *Selections from the Prison Notebooks of Antonio Gramsci*. Edited and translated by Q. Hoare and G. Nowell-Smith. New York: International Publishers.

Griffin, James. 1985. "Some Problems of Fairness." *Ethics* 96:100–118.

Gurr, Ted Robert. 1968. "Urban Disorder: Perspectives from the Comparative Study of Civil Strife." *American Behavioral Scientist* 11:50–55.

Gutman, Herbert. 1976. *Work, Culture, and Society in Industrializing America: Essays in American Working-class and Social History*. New York: Knopf.

Hacking, Ian, ed. 1981. *Scientific Revolutions*. Oxford: Oxford University Press.

Hahn, Frank, and Martin Hollis, eds. 1979. *Philosophy and Economic Theory*. Oxford: Oxford University Press.

Hanley, Susan B. 1985. "Family and Fertility in Four Tokugawa Villages" in *Family and Population in East Asian History*. See Hanley and Wolf 1985.

Hanley, Susan B., and Arthur P. Wolf, eds. 1985. *Family and Population in East Asian History*. Stanford, Calif.: Stanford University Press.

Hardin, Russell. 1982. *Collective Action*. Baltimore: Johns Hopkins University Press.

Harman, Gilbert. 1975. "Moral Relativism Defended." *Philosophical Review* 84:3–22.

Harré, Rom. 1970. *Principles of Scientific Thinking*. Chicago: University of Chicago Press.

Harré, Rom, and E. H. Madden. 1975. *A Theory of Natural Necessity*. Oxford: Basil Blackwell.

Harris, Marvin. 1978. *Cannibals and Kings: The Origins of Cultures*. New York: Vintage.

_____. 1980. *Cultural Materialism: The Struggle for a Science of Culture*. New York: Vintage.

Harsanyi, John C. 1976. *Essays on Ethics, Social Behavior, and Scientific Explanation*. Dordrecht, Holland: D. Reidel.

_____. 1985. "Does Reason Tell Us What Moral Code to Follow and, Indeed, to Follow Any Moral Code at All?" *Ethics* 96:42–55.

Hayami, Jujiro and Vernon, Ruttan. 1985. *Agricultural Development: An International Perspective*. Baltimore: Johns Hopkins University Press.

Hempel, Carl. 1942/65. "The Function of General Laws in History" in *Aspects of Scientific Explanation*. See Hempel 1965.

_____. 1965. *Aspects of Scientific Explanation*. New York: Free Press.

_____. 1966. *Philosophy of Natural Science*. Englewood Cliffs, N.J.: Prentice-Hall.

Herrnstein, Richard J. 1973. *I.Q. in the Meritocracy*. Boston: Little, Brown.

Hindess, Barry, and Paul Q. Hirst. 1975. *Pre-capitalist Modes of Production*. London: Routledge & Kegan Paul.

Hollis, Martin, and Steven Lukes, eds. 1982. *Rationality and Relativism*. Cambridge, Mass.: MIT Press.

Hookway, Christopher. 1978. "Indeterminacy and Interpretation" in *Action and Interpretation Studies in the Philosophy of the Social Sciences*. See Hookway and Pettit 1978.

Hookway, Christopher, and Philip Pettit, eds. 1978. *Action and Interpretation: Studies in the Philosophy of the Social Sciences*. Cambridge: Cambridge University Press.

Horton, Robin. 1970. "African Thought and Western Science" in *Rationality*. See Wilson 1970.

Hsieh, Winston. 1978. "Peasant Insurrection and the Marketing Hierarchy in the Canton Delta, 1911–12" in *Studies in Chinese Society*. See Wolf 1978.

Huang, Philip C. C. 1985. *The Peasant Economy and Social Change in North China*. Stanford, Calif.: Stanford University Press.

Hull, David. 1974. *Philosophy of Biological Science*. Englewood Cliffs, N.J.: Prentice-Hall.

Jarvie, I. C. 1984. *Rationality and Relativism: In Search of a Philosophy and History of Anthropology*. London: Routledge & Kegan Paul.

Jensen, Arthur Robert. 1973. *Educability and Group Differences*. New York: Harper & Row.

Kahneman, D., P. Slovic, and A. Tversky. 1982. *Judgment Under Uncertainty: Heuristics and Biases*. Cambridge: Cambridge University Press.

Keat, Russell, and John Urry. 1975. *Social Theory as Science*. London: Routledge & Kegan Paul.

Keohane, Robert O. 1984. *After Hegemony: Cooperation and Discord in the World Political Economy*. Princeton: Princeton University Press.

Kim, Jaegwon. 1984a. "Supervenience and Supervenient Causation." *Southern Journal of Philosophy* 22:45–56, supplement.

──────. 1984b. "Concepts of Supervenience." *Philosophy and Phenomenological Research* 14:153–76.

Kitcher, Philip. 1985. *Vaulting Ambition*. Cambridge, Mass.: MIT Press.

Kohli, Atul. 1987. *The State and Poverty in India: The Politics of Reform*. Cambridge: Cambridge University Press.

Kuhn, Philip A. 1980. *Rebellion and Its Enemies in Late Imperial China: Militarization and Social Structure, 1796–1864*. Cambridge: Harvard University Press (paperback ed.).

Kuhn, Thomas. 1970. *The Structure of Scientific Revolutions*. 2d. ed. Chicago: University of Chicago Press.

Lakatos, Imre, and Alan Musgrave, eds. 1970. *Criticism and the Growth of Knowledge*. Cambridge: Cambridge University Press.

Laudan, Larry. 1977. *Progress and Its Problems*. Berkeley: University of California Press.

Lee, Ronald. 1986. "Population Homeostasis and English Demographic History" in *Population and Economy*. See Rotberg and Rabb 1986.

Leplin, Jarrett, ed. 1984. *Scientific Realism*. Berkeley: University of California Press.

Levi, Isaac. 1967. *Gambling with Truth: An Essay on Induction and the Aims of Science*. Cambridge, Mass.: MIT Press.

Lévi-Strauss, Claude. 1963. *Structural Anthropology*. New York: Basic Books.

──────. 1969. *The Elementary Structures of Kinship*. Boston: Beacon Press.

──────. 1969. *Convention*. Cambridge: Harvard University Press.

Lewis, David K. 1983. "New Work for a Theory of Universals." *Australasian Journal of Philosophy* 61:109–43.

Little, Daniel. 1986. *The Scientific Marx*. Minneapolis: University of Minnesota Press.

──────. 1988. "Collective Action and the Traditional Village." *Journal of Agricultural Ethics* 1:41–58.

──────. 1989. *Understanding Peasant China: Case Studies in the Philosophy of Social Science*. New Haven: Yale University Press.

Luce, R. D., and Howard Raiffa. 1958. *Games and Decisions*. New York: Wiley.

Lukes, Steven. 1970. "Some Problems About Rationality" in *Rationality*. See Wilson 1970.

──────. 1973. "Methodological Individualism Reconsidered" in *The Philosophy of Social Explanation*. See Ryan 1973.

──────. 1982. "Relativism in Its Place" in *Rationality and Relativism*. See Hollis and Lukes 1982.

MacIntyre, Alasdair. 1973. "Is a Science of Comparative Politics Possible?" in *Rationality*. See Ryan 1973.

──────. 1984. *After Virtue*. 2d ed. Notre Dame, Ind.: University of Notre Dame Press.

MacKay, Alfred. 1980. *Arrow's Theorem: The Paradox of Social Choice*. New Haven: Yale University Press.

Mackie, J. L. 1965. "Causes and Conditions." *American Philosophical Quarterly* 17:4.

──────. 1974. *Cement of the Universe*. London: Oxford University Press.

──────. 1977. *Ethics: Inventing Right and Wrong*. Harmondsworth: Penguin.

Malinowski, Bronislaw. 1922/61. *Argonauts of the Western Pacific*. New York: E. P. Dutton, 1961.

Margolis, Howard. 1982. *Selfishness, Rationality, and Altruism: A Theory of Social Choice*. Chicago: University of Chicago Press.

Marx, Karl. 1850/1974. *The Class Struggles in France* in *Surveys from Exile*. See Fernbach 1974b.

_____. 1852/1974. *The Eighteenth Brumaire of Louis Bonaparte* in *Surveys from Exile*. See Fernbach 1974b.

_____. 1867/1977. *Capital* vol. 1. New York: Vintage.

_____. 1846/1970. *The German Ideology*. New York: International Publishers.

Marx, Karl, and Frederick Engels. 1848/1974. *The Communist Manifesto* in *The Revolutions of 1848*. See Fernbach 1974a.

Mason, Edward S., Mahn Je Kim, Dwight Perkins, Kwang Suk Kim, and David C. Cole. 1980. *The Economic and Social Modernization of the Republic of Korea*. Cambridge: Council on East Asian Studies, Harvard University.

McMurtry, John. 1977. *The Structure of Marx's World-view*. Princeton: Princeton University Press.

Merton, Robert K. 1963. *Social Theory and Social Structure*. New York: Free Press.

_____. 1967. *On Theoretical Sociology*. New York: Free Press.

_____. 1973. *The Sociology of Science: Theoretical and Empirical Investigations*. Chicago: University of Chicago Press.

Migdal, Joel. 1974. *Peasants, Politics and Revolution*. Princeton: Princeton University Press.

Miliband, Ralph. 1969. *The State in Capitalist Society*. New York: Basic Books.

_____. 1977. *Marxism and Politics*. Oxford: Oxford University Press.

Mill, John Stuart. 1950. *Philosophy of Scientific Method*. New York: Hafner.

Miller, Richard W. 1978. "Methodological Individualism and Social Explanation." *Philosophy of Science* 45:387–414.

_____. 1987. *Fact and Method*. Princeton: Princeton University Press.

Moore, Barrington, Jr. 1978. *Injustice: The Social Bases of Obedience and Revolt*. White Plains, N.Y.: M. E. Sharpe.

Morris, Morris David. 1979. *Measuring the Condition of the World's Poor: The Physical Quality of Life Index*. New York: Pergamon Press.

Mueller, Dennis C. 1976. "Public Choice: A Survey." *Journal of Economic Literature* 14:395–433.

Myers, Ramon H. 1970. *The Chinese Peasant Economy*. Cambridge: Harvard University Press.

Nagel, Ernest. 1961. *The Structure of Science*. New York: Harcourt, Brace & World.

Nagel, Thomas. 1970. *The Possibility of Altruism*. Oxford: Oxford University Press.

Naquin, Susan. 1976. *Millenarian Rebellion in China: The Eight Trigrams Uprising of 1813*. New Haven: Yale University Press.

Nash, Manning. 1965. *The Golden Road to Modernity: Village Life in Contemporary Burma*. New York: Wiley.

_____. 1966. *Primitive and Peasant Economic Systems*. San Francisco: Chandler.

Newton-Smith, W. H. 1981. *The Rationality of Science*. Boston: Routledge & Kegan Paul.

_____. 1982. "Relativism and the Possibility of Interpretation" in *Rationality and Relativism*. See Hollis and Lukes 1982.

North, Douglass C., and Robert Paul Thomas. 1973. *The Rise of the Western World: A New Economic History*. Cambridge: Cambridge University Press.

O'Brien, P. K., and C. Keyder. 1978. *Economic Growth in Britain and France, 1780–1914*. London: George Allen & Unwin.

Olson, Mancur. 1965. *The Logic of Collective Action: Public Goods and the Theory of Groups*. Cambridge: Harvard University Press.

Outhwaite, William. 1975. *Understanding Social Life: The Method Called Verstehen*. London: George Allen & Unwin.

Oye, Kenneth A., ed. 1986. *Cooperation Under Anarchy*. Princeton: Princeton University Press.

Pampel, Fred C., and John B. Williamson. 1989. *Age, Class, Politics, and the Welfare State*. Cambridge: Cambridge University Press.

Pasternak, Burton. 1978. "The Sociology of Irrigation: Two Taiwanese Villages" in *Studies in Chinese Society*. See Wolf, ed. 1978.

Perry, Elizabeth J. 1980. *Rebels and Revolutionaries in North China 1845–1945*. Stanford, Calif.: Stanford University Press.

Poland, Jeffrey. *Physicalism: The Philosophical Foundations*. Oxford: Oxford University Press, forthcoming.

Polanyi, Karl. 1957. *The Great Transformation*. Boston: Beacon Press.

Popkin, Samuel L. 1979. *The Rational Peasant*. Berkeley: University of California Press.

———. 1981. "Public Choice and Rural Development—Free Riders, Lemons, and Institutional Design" in *Public Choice and Rural Development*. See Russell and Nicholson 1981.

Popper, Karl. 1947. *The Open Society and Its Enemies* vol. 2. London: Routledge & Kegan Paul.

———. 1961. *The Poverty of Historicism*. London: Routledge & Kegan Paul.

———. 1965. *Conjectures and Refutations: The Growth of Scientific Knowledge*. New York: Basic Books.

Poulantzas, Nicos. 1973. *Political Power and Social Class*. London: New Left Books.

Przeworski, Adam. 1985a. *Capitalism and Social Democracy*. Cambridge: Cambridge University Press.

———. 1985b. "Marxism and Rational Choice." *Politics and Society* 14:379–409.

Putnam, Hilary. 1978. *Meaning and the Moral Sciences*. London: Routledge & Kegan Paul.

Quine, Willard Van Orman. 1960. *Word and Object*. Cambridge, Mass.: MIT Press.

Radcliffe-Brown, A. R. 1922/64. *The Andaman Islanders*. New York: Free Press.

Ragin, Charles C. 1987. *The Comparative Method: Moving Beyond Qualitative and Quantitative Strategies*. Berkeley: University of California Press.

Rapoport, Anatol. 1966. *Two-Person Game Theory*. Ann Arbor: University of Michigan Press.

Rapoport, Anatol, and A. M. Chammah. 1965. *Prisoners' Dilemma: A Study in Conflict and Cooperation*. Ann Arbor: University of Michigan Press.

Rawls, John. 1971. *A Theory of Justice*. Cambridge: Harvard University Press.

———. 1985. "Justice as Fairness: Political Not Metaphysical." *Philosophy and Public Affairs* 14:223–51.

Regan, Donald. 1980. *Utilitarianism and Co-operation*. Oxford: Oxford University Press.

Roemer, John. 1981. *Analytical Foundations of Marxism*. New York: Cambridge University Press.

———. 1982a. *A General Theory of Exploitation and Class*. Cambridge: Harvard University Press.

———. 1982b. "Methodological Individualism and Deductive Marxism." *Theory and Society* 11:513–20.

_____. 1988. *Free to Lose: An Introduction to Marxist Economic Philosophy*. Cambridge: Harvard University Press.

Roemer, John, ed. 1986. *Analytical Marxism*. Cambridge: Cambridge University Press.

Rosenberg, Alexander. 1988. *Philosophy of Social Science*. Boulder, Colo.: Westview Press.

Rotberg, Robert I., and Theodore K. Rabb, eds. 1986. *Population and Economy Population and History from the Traditional to the Modern World*. Cambridge: Cambridge University Press.

_____. 1989. *The Origin and Prevention of Major Wars*. Cambridge: Cambridge University Press.

Roth, David. 1987. *Meanings and Methods: A Case for Methodological Pluralism in the Social Sciences*. Ithaca, N.Y.: Cornell University Press.

Ruben, David-Hillel. 1985. *The Metaphysics of the Social World*. London: Routledge & Kegan Paul.

Rudner, Richard. 1966. *Philosophy of Social Science*. Englewood Cliffs, N.J.: Prentice-Hall.

Russell, Clifford S., and Norman K. Nicholson, eds. 1981. *Public Choice and Rural Development*. Washington, D.C.: Resources for the Future.

Ryan, Alan, ed. 1973. *The Philosophy of Social Explanation*. Oxford: Oxford University Press.

Sabel, Charles F. 1982. *Work and Politics*. Cambridge: Cambridge University Press.

Sabel, Charles F., and Jonathan Zeitlin. 1985. "Historical Alternatives to Mass Production: Politics, Markets and Technology in 19th Century Industrialization." *Past and Present* 108:133–76.

Sahlins, Marshall. 1972. *Stone Age Economics*. New York: Aldine Publishing.

_____. 1976. *Culture and Practical Reason*. Chicago: University of Chicago Press.

Salmon, Wesley C. 1984. *Scientific Explanation and the Causal Structure of the World*. Princeton: Princeton University Press.

Sandler, Todd, and John T. Tschirhart. 1980. "The Economic Theory of Clubs: An Evaluative Survey." *Journal of Economic Literature* 18:1481–521.

Scheffler, Israel. 1967. *Science and Subjectivity*. Indianapolis: Bobbs-Merrill.

Schelling, Thomas C. 1978. *Micromotives and Macrobehavior*. New York: Norton.

Schofield, Roger S. 1986. "Through a Glass Darkly: *The Population History of England* as an Experiment in History" in *Population and Economy Population and History from the Traditional to the Modern World*. See Rotberg and Rabb 1986.

Schoultz, Lars. 1987. *National Security and United States Policy Toward Latin America*. Princeton: Princeton University Press.

Schultz, Theodore W. 1964. *Transforming Traditional Agriculture*. New Haven: Yale University Press.

Scott, James C. 1976. *The Moral Economy of the Peasant*. New Haven: Yale University Press.

Sen, Amartya K. 1970. *Collective Choice and Social Welfare*. San Francisco: Holden-Day.

_____. 1973/86. "Behaviour and the Concept of Preference." *Economica* 40:241–59. Also in *Rational Choice*. See Elster 1986.

_____. 1979. "Rational Fools" in *Philosophy and Economic Theory*. See Hahn and Hollis 1979.

_____. 1981. *Poverty and Famines: An Essay on Entitlements and Deprivation*. Oxford: Oxford University Press.

_____. 1982. *Choice, Welfare and Measurement*. Cambridge, Mass.: MIT Press.

_____. 1987. *On Ethics and Economics*. New York: Basil Blackwell.

Shanin, Teodor. 1985. *Russia as a "Developing Society."* New Haven: Yale University Press.

Shanin, Teodor, ed. 1987. *Peasants and Peasant Societies.* 2d ed. Oxford: Blackwell.

Shankman, Paul. 1984. "The Thick and the Thin: On the Interpretive Theoretical Program of Clifford Geertz." *Current Anthropology* 25:261–79.

Shubik, Martin. 1982. *Game Theory in the Social Sciences: Concepts and Solutions.* Cambridge, Mass.: MIT Press.

Simon, Herbert A. 1969/81. *The Sciences of the Artificial.* 2d ed. Cambridge, Mass.: MIT Press.

———. 1971. "Spurious Correlation: A Causal Interpretation" in *Causal Models in the Social Sciences.* See Blalock 1971.

———. 1979. "From Substantive to Procedural Rationality" in *Philosophy and Economic Theory.* See Hahn and Hollis 1979.

———. 1983. *Reason in Human Affairs.* Stanford, Calif.: Stanford University Press.

Skinner, G. William. 1964/65. "Marketing and Social Structure in Rural China." 3 parts. *Journal of Asian Studies* 24:1, 24:2, 24:3.

———. 1977. "Cities and the Hierarchy of Local Systems" in *The City in Late Imperial China.* See Skinner, ed. 1977.

Skinner, G. William, ed. 1977. *The City in Late Imperial China.* Stanford, Calif.: Stanford University Press.

Skocpol, Theda. 1979. *States and Social Revolutions: A Comparative Analysis of France, Russia, and China.* Cambridge: Cambridge University Press.

Skyrms, Brian. 1980. *Causal Necessity: A Pragmatic Investigation of the Necessity of Laws.* New Haven: Yale University Press.

Soboul, Albert. 1975. *The French Revolution 1787–1799: From the Storming of the Bastille to Napoleon.* New York: Vintage.

Sperber, Dan. 1985. *On Anthropological Knowledge: Three Essays.* Cambridge: Cambridge University Press.

Ste. Croix, G.E.M. de. 1981. *The Class Struggle in the Ancient Greek World from the Archaic Age to the Arab Conquests.* Ithaca, N.Y.: Cornell University Press.

Stich, Stephen. 1983. *From Folk Psychology to Cognitive Science: The Case Against Belief.* Cambridge, Mass.: MIT Press.

Stinchcombe, Arthur L. 1978. *Theoretical Methods in Social History.* New York: Academic Press.

Suppes, Patrick. 1984. *Probabilistic Metaphysics.* Oxford: Basil Blackwell.

Szymanski, Albert. 1978. *The Capitalist State and the Politics of Class.* Cambridge, Mass.: Winthrop.

Taylor, Charles. 1985a. *Philosophy and the Human Sciences: Philosophical Papers 2.* Cambridge: Cambridge University Press.

———. 1985b. "Interpretation and the Sciences of Man" in *Philosophy and the Human Sciences.* See C. Taylor 1985a.

———. 1985c. "Neutrality in Political Science" in *Philosophy and the Human Sciences.* See C. Taylor 1985a.

Taylor, Michael. 1976. *Anarchy and Cooperation.* London: Wiley.

———. 1982. *Community, Anarchy and Liberty.* Cambridge: Cambridge University Press.

———. 1986. "Elster's Marx." *Inquiry* 29:3–10.

———. 1987. *The Possibility of Cooperation.* Cambridge: Cambridge University Press.

———. 1988. "Rationality and Revolutionary Collective Action" in *Rationality and Revolution.* See M. Taylor, ed. 1988.

Taylor, Michael, ed. 1988. *Rationality and Revolution.* Cambridge: Cambridge University Press.

Thomas, David. 1979. *Naturalism and Social Science.* Cambridge: Cambridge University Press.

Thompson, E. P. 1963. *The Making of the English Working Class.* New York: Vintage.

_____. 1978. *The Poverty of Theory and Other Essays.* New York: Monthly Review.

Tilly, Charles. 1964. *The Vendée.* Cambridge: Harvard University Press.

_____. 1984. *Big Structures, Large Processes, Huge Comparisons.* New York: Russell Sage Foundation.

Tilly, Charles, Louise Tilly, and Richard Tilly. 1975. *The Rebellious Century 1830–1930.* Cambridge: Harvard University Press.

Tong, James. 1988. "Rational Outlaws: Rebels and Bandits in the Ming Dynasty, 1368–1644" in *Rationality and Revolution. See* M. Taylor, ed. 1988.

Trigg, Roger. 1985. *Understanding Social Science.* London: Blackwell.

Tufte, Edward. 1974. *Data Analysis for Politics and Policy.* Englewood Cliffs, N.J.: Prentice-Hall.

Turner, Victor. 1974. *Dramas, Fields, and Metaphors: Symbolic Action in Human Society.* Ithaca, N.Y.: Cornell University Press.

Van Parijs, Philippe. 1981. *Evolutionary Explanation in the Social Sciences.* Totowa, N.J.: Rowman & Littlefield.

Vlastos, Stephen. 1986. *Peasant Protests and Uprisings in Tokugawa Japan.* Berkeley: University of California Press.

Von Wright, Georg Henrik. 1971. *Explanation and Understanding.* Ithaca, N.Y.: Cornell University Press.

Ware, Robert and Kai Nielsen, eds. 1989. *Analyzing Marxism. Canadian Journal of Philosophy.* Supplementary vol. 15.

Watkins, J.W.N. 1957. "Historical Explanation in the Social Sciences." *British Journal for the Philosophy of Science* 8:104–17.

_____. 1968. "Methodological Individualism and Social Tendencies" in *Readings in the Philosophy of the Social Sciences. See* Brodbeck 1968.

Weber, Max. 1949. *The Methodology of the Social Sciences.* Edited and translated by E. Shils and H. A. Finch. Glencoe, Ill.: Free Press.

_____. 1958. *The Protestant Ethic and the Spirit of Capitalism.* New York: Scribner's.

_____. 1978. *Economy and Society* vol. 1. Berkeley: University of California Press.

Weintraub, E. 1979. *Microfoundations.* Cambridge: Cambridge University Press.

White, Lynn. 1962. *Medieval Technology and Social Change.* Oxford: Oxford University Press.

Whorf, Benjamin. 1956. *Language, Thought, and Reality: Selected Writings of Benjamin Lee Whorf.* Edited by John B. Carrol. Cambridge, Mass.: MIT Press.

Williams, George C. 1966. *Adaptation and Natural Selection: A Critique of Some Current Evolutionary Thought.* Princeton: Princeton University Press.

Williamson, Samuel R., Jr. 1989. "The Origins of World War I" in *The Origin and Prevention of Major Wars. See* Rotberg and Raab 1989.

Wilson, Bryan R., ed. 1970. *Rationality.* Oxford: Blackwell.

Winch, Peter. 1958. *The Idea of a Social Science.* London: Routledge & Kegan Paul.

_____. 1970. "Understanding a Primitive Society" in *Rationality. See* Wilson 1970.

Witherspoon, Gary. 1977. *Language and Art in the Navajo Universe.* Ann Arbor: University of Michigan Press.

Wolf, Arthur P. 1978. "Gods, Ghosts, and Ancestors" in *Studies in Chinese Society. See* Wolf, ed. 1978.

Wolf, Arthur P., ed. 1978. *Studies in Chinese Society*. Stanford, Calif.: Stanford University Press.

Wolf, Eric. 1966. *Peasants*. Englewood Cliffs, N.J.: Prentice-Hall.

Wong, David. 1984. *Moral Relativity*. Berkeley: University of California Press.

Wright, Erik Olin. 1978. *Class, Crisis and the State*. London: Verso.

Wrigley, E. Anthony, and Roger S. Schofield. 1981. *The Population History of England, 1541–1871: A Reconstruction*. Cambridge: Harvard University Press.

ABOUT THE BOOK
AND AUTHOR

Professor Little presents an introduction to the philosophy of social science with an emphasis on the central forms of explanation in social science: rational-intentional, causal, functional, structural, materialist, and interpretive. The book is very strong on recent developments, particularly in its treatment of rational choice theory, microfoundations for social explanation, the idea of supervenience, functionalism, and current discussions of relativism.

Of special interest is Professor Little's insight that, like the philosophy of natural science, the philosophy of social science can profit from examining actual scientific examples. Throughout the book, philosophical theory is integrated with recent empirical work on both agrarian and industrial society drawn from political science, sociology, geography, anthropology, and economics.

Clearly written and well structured, this text provides the logical and conceptual tools necessary for dealing with the debates at the cutting edge of contemporary philosophy of social science. It will prove indispensable for philosophers, social scientists, and their students.

Daniel Little, associate professor of philosophy at Colgate University and visiting scholar at the Center for International Affairs, Harvard University, is the author of *The Scientific Marx; Understanding Peasant China: Case Studies in the Philosophy of Social Science;* and many journal articles on the philosophy of social science and on analytic Marxism.

INDEX